BARBRA
THE SECOND DECADE

ARTIST: CHRIS NICKENS

BARBRA
THE SECOND DECADE

Karen Swenson

A CITADEL PRESS BOOK
PUBLISHED BY CAROL PUBLISHING GROUP

To Myra LaBine
1954 - 1976

First Carol Publishing Group Edition 1990

Copyright © 1986 by Karen Swenson

A Citadel Press Book
Published by Carol Publishing Group

Editorial Offices
600 Madison Avenue
New York, NY 10022

Sales & Distribution Offices
120 Enterprise Avenue
Secaucus, NJ 07094

In Canada: Musson Book Company
A division of General Publishing Co. Limited
Don Mills, Ontario

Designed by Paul Chevannes

Manufactured in the United States of America

10 9 8 7 6 5 4 3 2

Library of Congress Cataloging-in-Publication Data

Swenson, Karen.
    Barbra, the second decade.

    1. Streisand, Barbra. 2. Singers--United States--
Biography. I. Title. II. Title: Barbra, the 2nd
decade.
ML420.S915S93 1986   784.5'0092'4 [B]   86-26442
ISBN 0-8065-0981-3

Surveying Atlanta Stadium, 1966. ▷

CONTENTS

Introduction 9

One More Look at *The Way We Were* 21

Recording, 1974-1986 35

The Way We Were, 36
ButterFly, 38
Funny Lady, 40
Lazy Afternoon, 41
Classical Barbara, 42
A Star Is Born, 44
Streisand Superman, 49
Songbird, 53
Eyes of Laura Mars, 53
Barbra Streisand's Greatest Hits/Volume 2, 56
The Main Event, 59
Wet, 60
Guilty, 65
Memories, 67
Yentl, 69
Emotion, 74
The Broadway Album, 79

The Future 91

In Concert/On Television 93

Funny Girl to Funny Lady, 94

The Tonight Show, 96
Concert—Tempe, Arizona, 97
Barbra: With One More Look at You, 98
1977 Academy Awards, 99
The Stars Salute Israel at 30, 99
1980 Grammy Awards, 100
ACLU Tribute to the Bergmans, 102
I Love Liberty, 104
"Memory," 105
A Film Is Born, 108
"Left in the Dark," 109
"Emotion," 110
"Somewhere," 113
Putting It Together: The Making
of the Broadway Album, 115

The Movies, 1974-1986 127

For Pete's Sake, 128
Funny Lady, 141
A Star Is Born, 162
The Main Event, 188
All Night Long, 205
Yentl, 234
The Future, 255

ACKNOWLEDGMENTS

It is impossible to grasp the magnitude with which entertainment personalities can affect our lives. For those who have not themselves become participants, let me say that a star obsession can be a thankless one. But I was lucky. My interest in Barbra Streisand propelled me into a future surrounded by an extraordinary group of people; it was much more than teenage ambitions could project. And for that I would like to acknowledge, above all, Barbra. Her intelligence, strength, passion, wit, integrity *and* artistry have been inspirational to me. I hope that I have been, in her words, "true to the spirit."

Of course, no book like this is possible without the support of family and friends, and I am eternally grateful to all of them. A special nod to Jim Spada, Chris Nickens and Vernon Patterson for their belief in me; Guy Vespoint, Allison Waldman and John Graham for helping to make this book more than it might have been; Michel Parenteau, Greg Rice, Bruce Mandes, Mike Hawks and Bob Scott for their earnest—and tireless—assistance; and a host of Streisand admirers and collectors who selflessly made their collections available to me: Richard Giammanco, Wynn Pascoe, Jeff Yeakley, Jim Kimbrell, Lynne Pounder, David Salyer and Dennis Berno. These people cared.

Thanks and appreciation also to Lee Solters and Jain Glass of Solters/Roskin/Friedman, as well as Peter Afterman, Jay Presson Allen, John Arrias, Kenny Ascher, Gary Bell, Artie Butler, Mike Campbell, Harry Caplan, Peter Daniels (courtesy of the Westwood Marquis), Nick DeCaro, Joe DiAmbrosio, Marty Erlichman, Bob Esty, Stu Fleming, Milos Forman, Ian Freebairn-Smith, Marilyn Fried, Paul Grein, Don Hahn, Stephen Holden, Patrick Kehoe, Sally Kirkland, Rusty Lemorande, Peter Matz, Paula Moccia, Barbara Oishi, Marty Paich, Nehemiah Persoff, Jon Peters, Sid Ramin, Phil Ramone, Jack Roe, Peter Reilly, Bruce Roberts, Armin Steiner, Larry Storch, Lee Sweetland…Columbia Records…all of whom graciously gave of their time in order to share background materials and/or reminiscences.

When interviews fail, research helps and, once again, I am indebted to the cooperative staff of the Margaret Herrick Library at the Academy of Motion Picture Arts and Sciences (thank you Carol and Lisa), in addition to the New York Public Library at Lincoln Center, the UCLA and USC Research Libraries, the Louis B. Mayer Library at the American Film Institute, and to Kevin Burns for *I Remember Barbra*.

Because no one can be at work and at the library or on an interview at the same time, I am grateful to Marlene, Nancy, Teri, Loch, Lisbeth and especially Lanny ("Can you at least make it in by 10:00?") for their patience, generosity and understanding.

Thanks and gratitude, too, to my editor, Allan Wilson.

Finally, you can't beat the unqualified love and support of the Swenson clan. Dad, Mom, Barbara, Diane, Len…I love you, too.

With Jane Fonda at NOW dinner, June, 1984.

INTRODUCTION

Maintaining a successful show business career is not easy. In this age of the super media, Andy Warhol's prophecy that anyone can be a star for fifteen minutes has been fulfilled time and time again throughout the '60s, '70s and '80s. Million-seller albums and motion pictures which exceed the $100 million mark have become the rule rather than the exception. But such "milestones" rarely seem to mean anything five or ten years later.

Imagine then chronicling a career which included such highlights as a host of singles soaring into the Top 10 in England, France, Germany, Italy, Holland, Australia, the Philippines, Japan and many other countries as well as in the United States; a string of motion pictures grossing over $500 million internationally; a second Academy Award; three more Grammys; and an armful of Golden Globes, culminated by the "debut" of an actress/singer/producer/writer/director nonpareil.

And imagine that each of these peaks was attained in the Second Decade of that entertainer's career.

It is a seemingly impossible feat. For anyone but Barbra Streisand. By anyone's standards, her career has been remarkable; after all is said and done, *who* is there to compare her to? In music, with the possible exception of an Aretha Franklin or even Bob Dylan, none of the other "contemporary living legends" who established themselves in the '60s are still around (or actively producing viable work). In film, the situation is even more perplexing: there are many "superstars"—Fonda, Redford, Eastwood, Streep—but no other figures around whom the swelling public interest in their lives and careers has accorded them legendary status.

So much has been written about Streisand's early childhood and the first decade of her career: the father who died when she was but 15 months old...growing up in Brooklyn and the traditions and mores that restricted an adolescent's imagination, the result of which was the evolution of a fierce individualism and independent spirit...testing that spirit as a young adult out on her own in the wilds of Manhattan...that "first break" when she won a talent contest at a seedy club in Greenwich Village...the Bon Soir...*I Can Get It for You Wholesale* ...an impressive recording contract...*Funny Girl* ...a series of TV spectaculars...and, finally, Hollywood.

The first decade was a Cinderella story and Barbra—née Barbara Joan—Streisand had many glass slippers in her possession. The question when you're on top, however, is how to keep each Prince (and his kingdom) happy when the challenge had been snagging him in the first place. Miraculously, Barbra managed to pull if off by building onto her mountain, this time with measured plateaus that *appeared* to be peaks—until she moved on to the next step. The challenge now has been for audiences to keep up with her. The plan is deceptively simple, and ingenious.

"Life is a series of journeys," Barbra said in 1984, "... circles that meet and start (over) again."

And, so, as we celebrate Barbra Streisand's 25th anniversary in show business, it behooves us all to take a look back at the evolution of this multi-faceted career. What follows is strictly a narrative of her life as it relates to the second decade of that career. It begins as the first decade ended—with the magic and romance of *The Way We Were*.

 ISU   MAXINE EDDLESON   JACK MARTIN   ADELE ALONSO   JAY

W ALBERT GRENNINE   BARBARA STREISAND   JOHN AUSTIN   MAUREE

A page from Barbara's 8th grade yearbook.

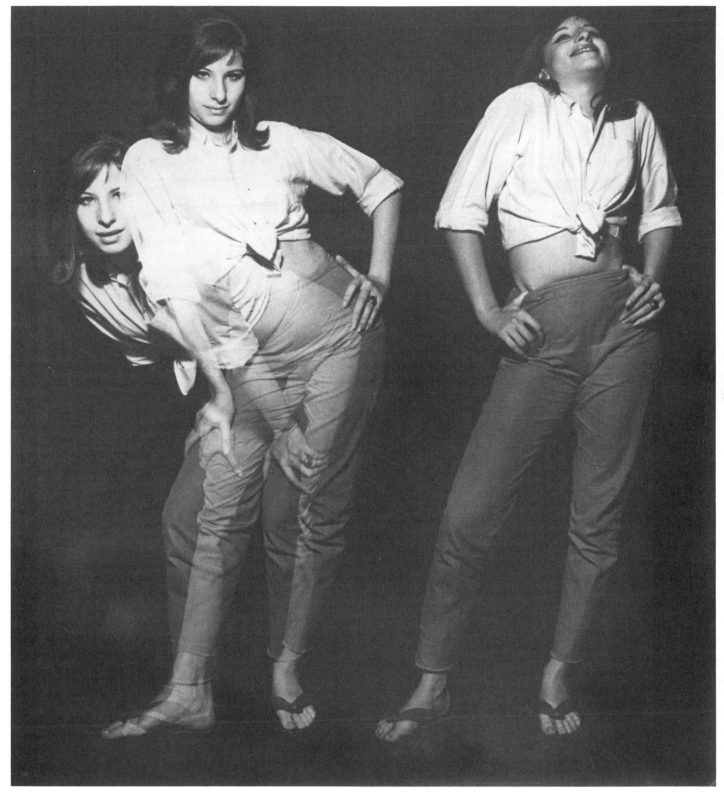

Experimenting with her look, circa 1961.

"Miss Marmelstein," her show-stopping num[ber] from I Can Get It for You Wholesale.

With Sidney Chaplin in Funny Girl, *1964.*

Showing off one of two Grammys (for Best Female Vocalist and Best Album) in 1964 for The Barbra Streisand Album.

With CBS Records president Goddard Lieberson. "One thing I do have to thank him for," she told a Columbia publicist, "he lets me do whatever I want to do."

Already a giant in the industry, Barbra towers over a miniature of the Hello, Dolly! set, 1968.

Barbra on Film.

Barbra in the '70s with a new attitude and a new comedy: The Owl and the Pussycat.

Filming the opening sequence for On a Clear Day, *1969. Director Vincente Minnelli is at the far right. (Photo courtesy of the Richard Giammanco Collection)*

The girl (and the costume) the whole world talking about following the 1969 Oscars, with Stark.

A romantic moment with Ryan O'Neal during the filming of What's Up, Doc?, 1971.

A light moment on the set of Up the Sandbox, 1972.

Lou Adler thought his client, Carole King, should close the "4 for McGovern" concert in Los Angeles. Organizer Warren Beatty (discussing the show with Barbra) wasn't so sure. (Photo courtesy of the Bob Scott Collection)

Daisy Gamble.

Melinda Winifred Wayne Moorpark Tentrees.

ON A CLEAR DAY YOU CAN SEE FOREVER, 1970

HELLO, DOLLY!, 1969

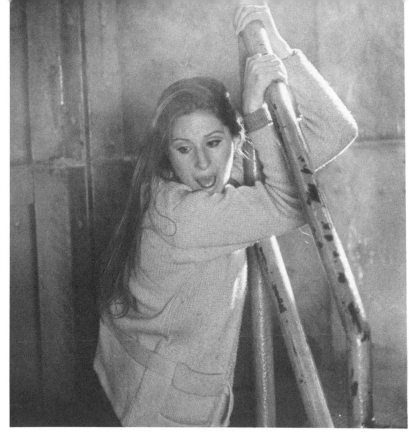

WHAT'S UP, DOC?, 1972

△ UP THE SANDBOX, 1972 ▽

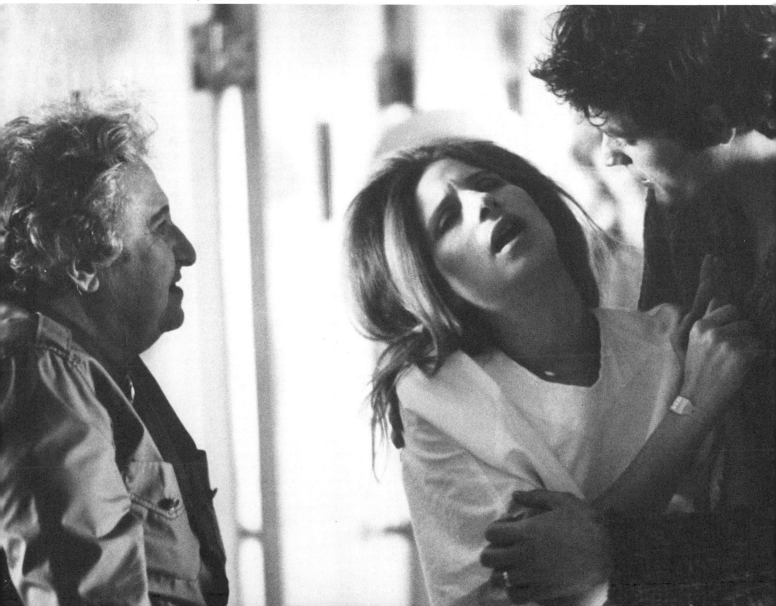

Old Hollywood meets the New. Barbra poses backstage at the 1970 Academy Awards with John Wayne.   (Photo courtesy of the Bob Scott Collection)

This glamorous vision of Katie Morosky didn't make it into the movie, but she did appear on the cover of Barbra's The Way We Were solo LP. (Photo courtesy of the Vernon Patterson collection)

One More Look at
THE WAY WE WERE

*"Predominantly Streisand, little for Redford.
Good production, sluggish direction. Should
open big, but weak legs seen."*

Variety's review for *The Way We Were* missed it by a long shot. The film's "weak legs" walked circles around the competition. *The Way We Were* was *the* smash hit of the 1973/74 holiday season. It singlehandedly resuscitated a studio which had been in serious financial straits. It inspired a nostalgic look at "the way we never really were" across the nation. No less important, it established its reluctant male star as a romantic idol—and, after years of flirting with such success, a superstar.

What seems even more amazing is how the film's quality and appeal have increased in the estimation of former cynics. An erstwhile two-star, soppy tearjerker would, within a few short years, become an acclaimed four-star classic; the ideal contemporary model for a movie romance. Premature predictions of doom and gloom—from *Time* magazines's depiction of "[an] ill-written, wretchedly performed and tediously directed film" to Pauline Kael's complaint about "a whining title-tune ballad [which] embarrasses the picture in advance"—could not begin to measure what the movie would inevitably mean to young adults coming of age during the 1970s. It has become our *Casablanca*. "It is hard not to be carried away by the film's lush romanticism,"

Howard Kissel wrote in *Women's Wear Daily*. "The *Way We Were* is the sort of film that makes you wish Hollywood were thriving again."

The comparison to *Casablanca*, an all-time movie favorite, is not without justification. Both productions were troubled from the outset. As with Robert Redford and *The Way We Were*, *Casablanca* would propel Humphrey Bogart onto the uppermost rung of movie stardom—as a romantic leading man—but not before multiple screenwriters were consulted in an effort to give his character more depth. There was much in fighting on the *Casablanca* set between the producer, director and writers; Warner Bros. wasn't sure they weren't throwing their money away on a "grade-B turkey." When the film was released, the audience response was solid but the reviews were mixed. No matter. It was a quintessential romance and the Best Picture of 1943.

Nearly thirty years later, producer Ray Stark commissioned Authur Laurents to write a story for Barbra Streisand. Laurents delivered a fifty-page treatment—a poignant tale of a star-crossed love set against the sweeping political landscape of America in the late '30s through the early '50s. Sydney Pollack, the director of *They Shoot Horses Don't*

Robert Redford: "Barbra, with all this talk about her being difficult, was easy. She's so alive."

A brief moment in the sun in Malibu.

An innocent toast in Ballston Spa.

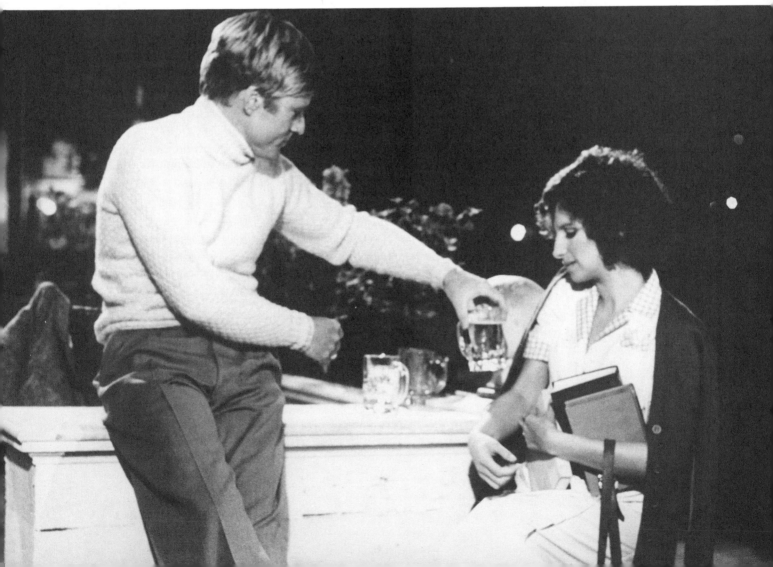

They?, was set to direct. Pollack's first reaction was that his friend Robert Redford had to play the role of Hubbell Gardiner. To his surprise, he discovered that Redford had already passed on the project when it was submitted to him in treatment form. But neither the director nor Barbra could give up on him; both felt that Redford was the only one who could bring any kind of realism to this All-American version of Sir Lancelot. After Laurents completed a first draft of the screenplay, Pollack again showed it to his friend, but Redford still didn't understand what he saw in the project. "He didn't want to do *The Way We Were* in any way, shape or form," the director revealed to author James Spada. "He didn't like the script, he didn't like the character, he didn't like the concept of the film, he didn't think the politics and love story would mix. There was nothing about it he liked and, in fact, he kept saying to me, 'Pollack, you're crazy! What are you doing this for?' That's the longest running battle I've ever had with him."

Pollack still believed he had a shot. From Lola Redford he learned that the conflict extended into their home life. "I wish he would make up his mind already. He's driving me crazy," she told him. "He sits up at night and says, "What should I do? I don't like it. Pollack is really turned on by it. I trust him. Maybe he sees something I don't see..." Pollack persisted in his campaign. "It had to be those two (together). They were so prototypical of what the story was about. I couldn't see doing it with anyone else," he said. "I must say my greatest ally was Barbra, who felt the same way. I needed the strength that Redford brings on the screen and Barbra understood that."

The picture's producer wasn't convinced that only Robert Redford could fulfill that part of the equation. According to Marty Erlichman, "Ray Stark called Barbra and said, 'If we're going to get Redford, you're going to have to give up a lot of scenes.'" But Barbra wasn't worried about screen time. "He's a valuable asset to the film," she replied. "I'd rather have fewer scenes than not have him in the picture."

On June 10, Pollack received an ultimatum from Stark. Bored with what he considered to be a game on Redford's part, Stark had given the director an hour to get a commitment from Redford regarding *The Way We Were*; otherwise he was offering the role of Hubbell Gardiner to Ryan O'Neal. End of discussion. At 11:30 p.m. that Thursday evening the producer got a call back from Pollack: Redford said yes.

"The reason I took it was that I wanted to work with Barbra and I felt it was a wonderful premise for a love story," he told Spada. The original script was written with more of a feel for the woman's role, he noted. "The question was, could you bring a balance into things?" Alvin Sargent and David Rayfield were called in for script surgery—a move that would cause considerable resentment on Laurents' part—with instructions not to tamper with the story but to enrich it by giving both protagonists a viewpoint. According to Laurents, no less than twelve writers were brought in, including Francis Ford Coppola and Dalton Trumbo, before he was called to put everything back together again.

Pollack: "I spent enough time with Barbra prior to shooting to let her know where my head was...to listen to what her fears were...and to discuss what this picture was about, where we might have trouble, what was moving to me and what was moving to her. I think it's safe to say she trusted me." The director told Donald Zec and Anthony Fowles that he never felt threatened by Barbra "because I was so impressed with the way she was thinking about the part. When I hear an actress talking to me with an understanding of a role that's so close to my own understanding, that makes me feel confident that we're not going to have a problem. And we didn't. The least of my problems was Barbra, funny enough."

Principal photography began on September 18, 1972, in Schenectady, New York, where Union College had been redressed to resemble an Ivy League campus circa 1937. Seven hundred and fifty college students submitted to period haircuts and styles in order to sign on as movie extras. To many, the odd but intriguing chemistry between Streisand and Redford that would excite movie-goers a year later, was immediately apparent in Schenectady, and no less revealing than in their opposing acting styles. "Bob is a very instinctive actor," Pollack has expressed on several occasions. "He doesn't like to talk about a role a lot, and he doesn't like to rehearse a lot. However, he doesn't mind a number of takes as long as you give him something different to do; if you don't, he'll change the performance from take to take anyway. Barbra, on the other hand, is very thorough and obsessive. She likes to talk about her role."

The director's job was to balance the two performances so that he gave Barbra enough time to warm up, but not too much before Redford cooled off. It was a difficult task made a little easier because both actors were very taken by each other's work and therefore sympathetic to their *mutual* problem. "There was no friction," Pollack emphasized, "because it all got aired out. He would say, 'I understand, I understand. I'm just not used to doing this.' And she would say, 'I understand totally, and I don't want to do it too much. But I don't know where I am if I don't talk it out first.'...Barbra wanted to go "straight" with this movie and not rely on what we

A foreign single sleeve for The Way We Were, *1974.*   *The Japanese pressing of* The Way We Were *(b/w "People").*

Photos of Barbra and Jon Peters decorated the
ButterFly *jacket, as well as some of the picture sleeves
abroad. This one is for "Guava Jelly."*

normally expect of her—the timing, the gestures, the facial expressions. She didn't want to use any tricks. She and Redford fed each other. It's really a combination of two rare talents with charisma and acting ability as well."

Sally Kirkland, who worked with the duo later in the shoot, felt that "There was almost a mystery about Streisand and Redford in the way they were together. It was almost like they held onto that mystery in order to keep the romantic sexual tension between them in the film."

At a 1978 seminar sponsored by the American Film Institute in Los Angeles, the director would illuminate how *his* rapport with his leading lady helped to coax some of this potential to the surface. "In the first week of shooting, we came to a scene in a writing class where the professor reads a story written by the Redford character. The girl Barbra plays is heartbroken because she wants more than anything for her story to be picked. She runs out of class, down a path to a wastebasket and tears her story to shreds. The camera rises to her face, and she's supposed to be

crying. The assistant director [Howard Koch, Jr.] came to me and said, 'I think she's a little uptight about this scene.' When we began rehearsing the shot, what I saw was an actress getting more and more upset in anticipation of a scene. She's supposed to cry and thinks she can't. Now, that's like a stew that's cooking; you just let it stew for a bit, then if she can relax, the tears will come.

"Barbra went back to her starting position behind a big tree to get ready for a take. I said to Koch, 'OK, you wait here. I'm not going to say "roll it," and I'm not going to say, "action." When I give you a wave, turn on the camera.' Now, I can't explain this exactly, but I walked up behind her and I put my arms around her. I just held her gently for about 20 seconds, and she started sobbing. I waved my hand…and pushed her off. She did the scene beautifully, in one take. And for the rest of the picture I didn't have to say or do much in similar scenes because once she knew she could do it, she did it [by herself]."

Sometimes, Pollack dismissed the crew for an

hour while the trio discussed the staging of a scene. James Woods, who played Frankie McVeigh, recalled a moment when this camaraderie worked to his own advantage in terms of screen time. "I had a five-line part, and there was a scene where Streisand and Redford are in the library and she's looking at him and yearning for him. I said to the director, 'I should be in this scene. I'm her boyfriend.' He said, 'Get out of here.' So I went up to Barbra and said, 'Let me ask you a question. If you were sitting in the library and you were looking at Redford—that would be interesting. *But* if your boyfriend was sitting opposite you and you had to wait until he was looking down at his book to sort of steal a look at Redford...that would be twice as exciting, wouldn't it?' She said, 'You bet!' And if you notice, I did make it into the scene."

As might be expected, residents of Schenectady and the neighboring Ballston Spa have contrasting stories of Barbra Streisand in their hometowns. One talks about the retiring superstar who preferred staying with her son in a rented home in the older, more secure part of Schenectady; the rest of the cast and crew stayed at a Holiday Inn near the college. Another recalls the time Barbra was riding her bicycle across the campus and was invited by some students to join their touch football game—which she did. Far more telling was the treatment of the production by the local Teamsters. Near the end of filming, 15 members of the cast and crew were invited to a lavish home-cooked meal courtesy of one family of Teamsters. The next day, Rastar received time cards from each family member indicating several hours overtime for the dinner. They were paid.

The Way We Were journeyed to Manhattan the first week in October for a hectic week on location in front of the Plaza Hotel, St. Patrick's Cathedral, the New York Public Library at 42nd Street, Grand Central Station, Carnegie Hall and in Central Park. Sally Kirkland was hired to play Pony Dunbar, Katie's Communist-sympathizing friend. The reason she was hired, she was told, was because "you're the kind of person Barbra would like, and that's important. We want to capture that on film." The reason she accepted (when she was playing important leads Off-Broadway) was because "I absolutely adored Barbra Streisand."

But Kirkland's connection with Barbra extends beyond a surface appreciation of her talent. First of all, both are native New Yorkers who sought creative and intellectual stimulation in Greenwich Village. As a birthday surprise, a friend took Sally to see a young performer at the Bon Soir; she was knocked out by her stage presence and "a voice that could break hearts."

Tea time with the Prince: During a rare West Coast visit, Britain's Prince Charles surprised everyone by asking to meet Barbra. She was busy at work on the Funny Lady *soundtrack*, so they met in the recording studio. After a private tête-à-tête, the prince promised to play Barbra's records at home. "Wonderful," she replied. "I've never played the Palace."

Kirkland kept track of Streisand's progress, tuning in to see her on "The Tonight Show" or "PM East." "I thought that she was hysterically funny, and risky," she says. "She would always say outrageous things and take chances like I had never seen anyone take. As a "kooky" personality, she presented herself in such a charming, loving, ballsy way. She had the *guts* to be a comedienne just being a person. Sometimes when people see performers like Cyndi Lauper or Madonna they don't realize that Barbra started that, in a way. She had all this incredible character built on her. And she has continued to allow herself to be what I call a life actor. In other words, her life is the act."

Barbra became something of a role model for the eccentric side of Kirkland's personality, a choice that was reinforced in a most bizarre manner. "Interestingly enough, when Barbra first met Elliott Gould, she lived over a seafood restaurant called Oscar's on Third Avenue. Well, the guy who moved into that apartment after her was my boyfriend…so I lived in that apartment with him for years. It was a railroad flat—a skinny L-shaped kind of room, and the floor was uneven," she recalls. "I thought, for New York, it was a really nice apartment because everything was wood."

The two actresses met face to face on West 75th Street. The initial scene Kirkland was hired for didn't make it into the final cut, but at the time the filmmakers thought it was important. "The scenario was that we hadn't seen each other in a long time, and she comes running down the street, grabs me in her arms, hugs me, kisses me and blurts out some incredible, happy news about Hubbell. I was very nervous because it was my first Hollywood film. I remember I had these earrings on and at the moment she hugged me, one of them fell off. Then I got flustered and she tried to improvise it into the scene, but I think she burst out laughing. And it was one of those shots where Sydney Pollack and his cameramen were way up on this crane and there were all of these extras. It had to have cost a lot of money to reshoot. Anyway, afterwards she said, 'I like you!' and I'll never forget it because here I made this incredible *faux pas* and she just laughed. I think it reminded her of the kind of thing she would have done a few years earlier…and it endeared her to me because she was vulnerable enough to pick up on my vulnerability."

By October 11, the cast and crew were back in Los Angeles, and Columbia was glad to have them where they could watchdog the production (already a few hundred thousand dollars over budget). The constant worrying over finances, added to previously-voiced concerns about the script, made most of the production team feel like they were doing time

in prison. Barbra had even more to worry about. That Fall she went up to San Francisco with several friends, including Freddie Fields and Sue Mengers, for a sneak preview of *Up the Sandbox*. "In the past I haven't fought hard enough for what I believe should be done in my pictures," she would say. "When I haven't followed my instincts its' been a mistake. I didn't particularly like making *What's Up, Doc?*. I didn't feel it was much of a growth experience. Yet I appreciate the fact that it made people laugh. I just hope they'll laugh during *Up the Sandbox*, too, though it will be a different kind of laughter."

In the famed Bay City, the preview audience laughed—but it was nervous, awkward laughter. They had expected *Doc* and got something closer to *Diary of a Mad Housewife*. The response was upsetting to Barbra, who had a big emotional investment in *Sandbox*. Back in Los Angeles, Arthur Laurents suggested to her that there was too much psychoanalytic jargon in the script. "She over-reacted," he said, "but she could still balk at the advice and then take it. She actively worked on the re-editing of the movie to make it better, less preachy."

Jump cut. Barbra the actress/producer still had to complete *The Way We Were*. Sally Kirkland was brought to Hollywood to film a short scene with her and Barbra as wartime switchboard operators. "And again it was 'Sally, how are you? What have you been doing?' She couldn't have been more warm," Kirkland adds. "She just stopped everything she was doing and behaved like a girlfriend. It was very sweet. All of these people complain about her rudeness or temper and I never got any of that in *The Way We Were*. What I got from Barbra was that she was curious about me, really looked, really listened and really wanted to know everything about me. She absorbs people; she takes them in. And she has one of the most insatiable curiosities I've ever seen in anyone."

Another recurring aspect of the work was the late-night telephone calls, mostly directed at Sydney Pollack. But Pollack didn't seem to mind. "She called out of compulsive worry," he said, "the way I'm a compulsive worrier. And I loved her for it. As a matter of fact, when she gave me a gift at the end of the picture, she wrote on it: 'For all those eleven o'clock phone calls.' She knew."

The Way We Were wrapped on December 3, 1972. On the 21st, Barbra's latest motion picture opened in New York. "*Up the Sandbox* is a joy," Howard Thompson enthused in *The New York Times*. "Yes, think of it. An hour after seeing the new one, which is ripe, yeasty fun, it's hard not to think of this extraordinary young woman, perfectly wedded to the camera with her instant Modigliani face and timing." "Forget the euphemisms: *Up the Sandbox* is an untidy melange of overproduced and heavy-handed fantasy....Miss Streisand's name will spark some opening week interest in the $3,000,000 National General Pictures release," forecast *Daily Variety*, "but its holding power is dubious." Unfortunately, in terms of audience response, the latter opinion turned out to be closer to the truth (despite a concerted promotional effort on Barbra's part). "I remember taking a friend to the theater in Westwood (L.A.) and there were four people there," Barbra told Larry Grobel. "It sure made me feel bad."

Discussing a song for Lazy Afternoon *with producer/composer/arranger Rupert Holmes. Holmes found working with Barbra to be a tough act to follow. "She's been my advocate and also, without doubt, the most gifted exponent of my writing that I'll ever have. I'm probably even more of a Streisand fan now than I was then, and I was a fan then." (Photo credit: Sam Emerson)*

"Call it a Jewish *Love Story* or a WASP dilemma: Set in the '40s, it's about a girl passionately committed to the political left who considers herself an ugly duckling. Politics was the only area in which she could find an identity. She is drawn to an All-American boy, a kind of Prince Charming, who apparently has everything she could never have and has always been considered wonderful. He is attracted to her because she represents a commitment and a passion, something he doesn't have in his life."
—Robert Redford

On May 3, 1973, just as Barbra was about to begin work on her classical album, the principal cast of *The Way We Were* was recalled to shoot an additional sequence on a Bel-Air estate. Columbia Pictures' faith in their major release for the Fall of 1973 was fading fast. "The initial responses [to *The Way We Were*] in rough-cut [form] were not good," Sydney Pollack confirmed to Zec and Fowles. "And then in September, we went to San Francisco for a preview and I did something I'd never done before.

We scheduled two previews, one on a Friday night and one on Saturday. At the first, the film was going very well. Until we hit a spot in the third act where we just lost the audience completely. I went up to the projection booth with [editor] Margaret Booth, taking a razor blade with me…and made a cut of about eleven minutes. It was a whole sequence where [Katie] was being named as a Communist, which precipitated the break up. The problem was that the break up was inherent in the picture right from the beginning…so it wasn't necessary to [stop everything] for this new development. When we previewed it the next night the audience absolutely loved the picture. All of a sudden everybody was ecstatic at it and morale [at Columbia] turned around."

One could argue that the film's potential would have been even greater "if it had more meat on its bones," but it certainly wasn't for lack of trying. Throughout the production, Pollack tried to make politics "more organic" to the film, weighing the political dimensions versus the personal ones. One thought he had was to make the Redford character an informer. "The danger, he said, "was that the background would become so interesting to those of us making the film that people watching it would say, 'Oh, yes, this is all very interesting. But let's get back to "Is he going to kiss her?" or "Are they going to fall in love?" or "Are they going to get together?"' That's what the film is about. I think it dealt very well with politics, but it's hardly the definitive film about McCarthyism. It was never intended to be….What I basically like about the film is what attracted me in the first place. When I read it, I cried, and I managed to get that on the screen."

Arthur Laurents, who described his story as *Beauty and the Beast…*the man happens to be Beauty but he feels like the Beast," felt that a fully realized performance from Barbra was the magic key. "She could have made the film glow in the dark," he said. Because of his great belief in her, he was somewhat surprised that she didn't fight more for her own point of view during production. "I asked her why she didn't fight harder and she said she felt she could take a stand on certain things, but not everything." Perhaps that resignation added to the growth of her character onscreen. "As Streisand's pictures multiply, it becomes apparent that she is not about to master an actress's craft," Pauline Kael would write of her performance in *Up the Sandbox*, "but, rather, is discovering a craft of her own, out of the timing and emotionality that make her a phenomenon as a singer. You admire her not for her acting—or singing—but for herself, which is what you feel she gives you in both.…She is a great undeveloped actress…if there is such a thing as total empathy, she has it."

On October 16, New York and Los Angeles had a chance to see that both Streisand and Redford had empathy—together. Much has been said about his subsequent transformation into a Hollywood sex symbol, not enough has been said about Streisand's acceptance in a similar vein. *The Way We Were* established Barbra as the perfect screen heroine of the '70s: a liberated woman who was eager to be on equal footing with men, but reluctant to give up the romantic traditions of the past. "Here we see Barbra Streisand at her most convincing. For if she is made to seem somewhat foolish as the political activist, she is absolutely marvelous as the modern woman poised between pride and desire," Catherine Hiller wrote in her *New York Times* article, "The Sleeping Beauty was a Man." For many, the pair's first night together—with a drunken Hubbell making love to Katie as if on automatic pilot—was an all-too-familiar slice of contemporary relationships and a refreshing twist on the usual "meet cute" scenarios of such love stories. Streisand's Katie Morosky was both aggressive and passive. She pushed Hubbell, but downplayed her own talents; ironically, she respected his talent more than he did (perhaps he really did want an easygoing girl from Beekman Place). It is her rediscovery of her real self near the end—when she and Hubbell recognize the way they *are* and stop traumatizing themselves with fantasies about the way they might have been—that makes their final meeting so poignant. The great love is still there, only now they see the futility of pining for something that cannot be. And it's the timelessness of these emotions that keeps the film from dating.

In addition, *The Way We Were* was the first of Barbra's films to reverse the sexual clichés. She could be the pursuer, the decision-maker, the stronger partner—but always as a woman operating in the masculine world, not as a "butch" *Mildred Pierce* stereotype. In analyzing the film with James Spada, Redford surmised that "[Barbra's] femininity brings out the masculinity in a man, and her masculinity brings out a man's femininity, vulnerability, romanticism…whatever you want to call it." Through films like *Up the Sandbox* and *The Way We Were*, Barbra began to effectively develop this duality in her nature onscreen. Pauline Kael noted in the *The New Yorker*, "The tricky thing about the role of Katie Morosky is that Streisand must emphasize just that element in her own persona which repelled some people initially. Her fast sass is defensive and agressive in the same breath. But its part of her gradual conquest of the movie public that this won't put people off now."

Negative reviews notwithstanding—and there were enough to suggest some critics took great pains to avoid being drawn in by the love story—a large percentage of critics waxed poetic about *The Way We Were*. *Christian Science Monitor*: "What really makes the film such a gripper is two-fold. First, the really lustrous performances of its two superstars, Streisand and Redford. They are perfect foils for each other in romantic comedy [the] way that Katherine Hepburn and Cary Grant were. It is her funny, pummeling energy and style versus his effortless charm, cool and beauty." *Films Illustrated*: "The movie is one of the best, most glamorous portrayals of aching, impractical, unspeakable infatuation (on her part) that has ever been put on film....They don't live *for* love, they live in *spite* of it, and that's good drama." *Playboy:* "If we must have tearjerkers bigger than life itself, *The Way We Were* is probably as good as they get—so eat your heart out. When did you last see a love story in which the honeymoon ended with a passionate political debate?"

Inspecting the cover art for Classical Barbra *during a break from* A Star Is Born *music rehearsals, 1976.*

The Way We Were garnered six nominations from the Academy of Motion Picture Arts and Sciences, including Best Actress, Cinematography, Art Direction, Costume Design, Original Dramatic Score and Song. (Redford was nominated that year for *The Sting*.) Barbra had given the standout female performance of the year, but with Joanne Woodward's Best Actress citation (for *Summer Wishes, Winter Dreams*) from the New York Films Critics and the Golden Globe going to Marsha Mason (for *Cinderella Liberty*), there were no odds-on favorites for the Academy Award. Each actress had enough support to split the Academy vote and on April 2, 1974, Glenda Jackson took home the award for her light comedy performance in *A Touch of Class*. The loss devastated Barbra, who was waiting backstage after rushing to the ceremonies from the set of *Funny Lady*. This time, she felt more than deserving of the acknowledgment— "Unlike the year I was up for *Funny Girl*, and there were five strong performances, this time I felt it was the best performance of the year"—and such validation was not to be forthcom-

Barbra: "Soon after Rupert and I met, he played a song he had written expressly for me about the father that all of us have wanted and needed at some time or another.... I asked him why he had written this particular lyric and he explained that he thought it might reflect some of my own feelings." She would consider "My Father's Song" a very personal gift.

ing. (She did, however, win Italy's equivalent of the Oscar, the David DiDonatello Award, as Best Foreign Actress. It was the second time she'd been accorded that honor.)

What would it have taken for Streisand to receive such attention? Arthur Laurents theorized she made a big mistake by hiding her face and not wringing every tear out of her climactic telephone appeal to her lover/friend. "It was a set piece for her, from the very first draft of the screenplay. She did not grab the chance and it was her loss," he told author Rene Jordan. Pollack disagreed: "I can tell you for a fact that that was done in one take and she was really crying," he told Zec and Fowles. "There was no attempt to hide the fact that she was crying...and her eyes were plenty red." Conspiracy theories ran rampant among fans. Subsequent snubs for *Funny Lady* and *A Star Is Born* only added fuel to the fire.

But it would not be until *Yentl,* ten years later, that many acknowledged the reality of a certain resentment within the motion picture industry against Streisand. During 1974 they thought she should content herself with the picture's success.

Indeed, box-office for *The Way We Were* was strong throughout Thanksgiving and Christmas. Only three and a half months into its release it was ranked number 4 among the films of 1973. (On Barbra's movie list it would fall just shy of *What's Up, Doc?* and *Funny Girl.*) Its box-office reputation looms even larger in people's memories, no doubt aided by the smash single and albums to follow. "I had to beg her to sing ['The Way We Were']," 1974's triple Oscar-winner Marvin Hamlisch laughed. "Everybody in the picture had to vote before she'd sing it. We all out-voted her."

31

Another break provides a chance to practice "Evergreen" on the guitar.

THE SECOND DECADE
...and After

"I HAVE *never known a great star whose "secret" wasn't simply that he worked harder than anyone else. Barbra is all that doubled, tripled and squared.... Any agent or mother or entrepreneur who believes he has another Barbra Streisand tucked away on a pedestal in the corner, waiting to be unveiled, had better either switch cigarettes or change professions. There is just not going to be another Barbra Streisand, now or ever. What she is, happens once...."*

—Alan Jay Lerner

A Lazy Afternoon *recording session, 1975.*
(Photo credit: Sam Emerson)

RECORDING
1974-1986

She doesn't read music. She rarely listens to the radio—or even records. When she does she prefers classical music. Vocally, her own range is slightly less than two octaves…and yet what she is able to project within that limited range has established Barbra Streisand as "arguably, the greatest voice of this century," says one music industry analyst. "The finest female voice pop music has heard," according to another.

Streisand commands respect from most musicians because she is considered the ultimate professional. She herself is unimpressed by reputations; quality impresses her more. "She is in a class by herself," Walter Yetnikoff, president of CBS Records, reported to *Billboard* in 1983. "Aside from the financial rewards, she adds class and distinction [to the label]." Columbia Records senior vice-president and general manager Al Teller concurred. "She's a tremendous calling card," he said. "If I had to sit down and list the criteria of a true superstar—a term often abused—one of the absolute essential requirements…[would be] the ability to reach a broad demographic [audience], from children to mature adults. Barbra Streisand's durability and appeal as a record seller is remarkable."

During the '70s there emerged a new breed of Streisand fan: lacking the opportunity to appreciate her impact as a performance artist, the new generation was drawn instead by her recorded work. On film, tape and, perhaps most significantly, on vinyl. Astute selection of material and uncanny timing put Barbra right at the forefront of popular music. At the same time it helped to solidify one of the largest core audiences of any contemporary performer. "You could put Barbra in front of a rock band or a symphony orchestra," said former Columbia Records president Bruce Lundvall, "she would still be Barbra Streisand. Not compromising, not uncomfortable; the audience would not think she was out of her territory. And that's the basis of a great talent: a great singing voice and interpretive skill."

But in that mass acceptance there was also an element of irony for Barbra. "When I was younger and my records always sold in the big cities [but] didn't sell in the little cities," she reflected in a 1979 interview for Australian television, "part of me felt bad about that because I wanted my work to be understood by lots of people. But part of me was happy that I *wasn't* understood by the masses."

Commercial artists are assumed to have compromised their artistic integrity. Barbra Streisand wanted the freedom to investigate less popular avenues of her art as well as maintain her position as a dominant force in music (and films). How she dealt with these issues is the story of the Second Decade.

Barbra Streisand/The Way We Were (PC 32801)

Produced by Tommy LiPuma, Marty Paich and Wally Gold
Arranged by Nick DeCaro, Marty Paich, Peter Matz and Claus Ogerman
Engineered and mixed by Al Schmitt

The Way We Were Original Soundtrack recording (KS 32830)

Produced by Fred Salem
Arranged by Marvin Hamlisch
Engineered by Dan Wallin

In 1972 Alan and Marilyn Bergman collaborated with composer Billy Goldenberg on a theme song for *Up the Sandbox*. The song, "If I Close My Eyes," was intended for use under the final credits. Subsequent to its recording, however, the producers elected to stick with the basic simplicity of the music (played on a toy piano) without vocals. For *The Way We Were* everyone agreed on evocative vocal from Barbra would be a tremendous asset to the picture. Marvin Hamlisch, who was Barbra's rehearsal pianist during the New York run of *Funny Girl*, was signed to write the score and the Bergmans encored as lyricists on the title tune.

The fact that the songwriters completed their work while the film was in the initial stages of being edited, two and a half months before Barbra was due to record the theme, yielded an unexpected bonus. Having the luxury of time, the couple was inspired to write lyrics for an additional song, also to be called "The Way We Were," and they convinced Hamlisch to join them. "Everyone liked the song that we now know as 'The Way We Were'... but we felt that there was another way to write it," Alan Bergman explained to a songwriter's workshop in Los Angeles several years later. "There are many different ways to write a theme about the way we were. To function in the movie, it had to be a current that took you back in time. So we wrote another song with an entirely different melody and lyrics."

The ambitious scheme almost backfired on them. Barbra recorded both songs with a basic piano track, and then each was played against the opening credit sequence. As a matter of personal choice, Streisand, Pollack and the Bergmans all preferred the second ballad— "It was more intricate, more compli-

cated," said Marilyn Bergman—but the consensus was that the first was more effective in accomplishing its objective. "The second didn't work *at all* with the images on the screen," Alan Bergman continued. "But the original song worked beautifully....So that was our answer, plain and simple." (The second song became known as "The Way We Weren't.")

Preview audiences for *The Way We Were* showed great interest in the movie's theme. "The fans really seemed to pick up on it," Paich, who was asked to produce and arrange the single, recollects. "I know that when we recorded it there was a tremendous sense of urgency about it. We had to do it *right now*. I did a new chart with a hotter rhythm section, because the lush orchestral arrangement wasn't formatted for Top 40 radio, and within a week we had gone into the studio, mastered the song and sent it back to New York."

Despite the preliminary excitement, "The Way We Were" had to prove it had a life of its own before radio programmers added it to their regular playlists. In 1964 and 1965 Barbra was the only female soloist to earn a gold album, but less than ten years later the competition was fiercer than ever. Released on September 26, 1973, "The Way We Were" took nearly a month before it even hit the charts and began making a slow, 14-week climb up to the hallowed number 1 spot. It was Barbra's first chart-topping single and the biggest record of her career to date (her first gold), as well as the top pop single of 1974. "What really matters is that [Streisand] can still stop a show with one song," Robert Adels wrote in *Record World*. "Right now, that song is the ballad "The Way We Were"...and the show is our own industry in which she is still a regally red-hot property and the prototype for all pop female vocalists who aspire to anything near greatness."

Barbra's *Way We Were* solo LP and soundtrack were released in January 1974 within a week of each other. Both albums contained different renditions of the ballad (with the soundtrack gaining the edge as far as the quality of Barbra's vocals is concerned), but since the solo album featured a substantial amount of new material, it sped into the Top 10 while the original soundtrack peaked at number 20. In March, the solo LP topped the charts for three weeks. A year later, Rastar Productions, producers of the Columbia motion picture, would file suit against Columbia Records, charging unfair competition and breach of contract. The complaint focused on the record company's use of the title *The Way We Were* without Rastar's permission, a move they maintained was calculated "to deceive and mislead" record buyers into believing they were buying the soundtrack album. The suit, settled out of court, led to the cumbersome retitling of the solo album. It is now officially known (though certainly not by fans) as *Barbra Streisand Featuring "The Way We Were" and "All in Love Is Fair."* The soundtrack is still known as the soundtrack.

Reviews:

"Streisand has a lot more going for her on this album than that silver voice and golden sensitivity; she has arrangers who know how to frame that

With Kris Kristofferson. Writing about Barbra in Rock-a-Bye, Baby, *Aida Pavletich suggested that Streisand "offers a large, easily attacked target because she overextends herself; chutzpah, she doesn't know her place. There are few aspects of performing she will not attempt, and, more mud in the face of her detractors, succeed in....She has made it evident that there is no need to apologize for aspirations, a factor even her fiercest critics must respect."*

beauty....'Pieces of Dreams' is for me one of the perfect Streisand offerings. The melody recalls overwhelmingly wistful moments....It is a superb, timeless recording. The important thing about this album is that Streisand is back doing things that absolutely no one else can do; and if you don't know what this is, or have reason to doubt that her subtle powers exist, listen to how she says, 'It's over' the second time on 'How About Me?' That's what quiet holocausts are all about."

—Poughkeepsie Journal

FINAL NOTE: In 1974, "The Way We Were" was honored as Best Original Song by the Hollywood Foreign Press Association and the Academy of Motion Picture Arts and Sciences; the motion picture score won an additional Oscar for Marvin Hamlisch, Hamlisch won two Grammys in 1975 for Song of the Year and Best Original Motion Picture Score. None of Barbra's vocals were nominated.

ButterFly (PC 33005)

Produced by Jon Peters
Arranged by Tom Scott and Lee Holdridge
Engineered by Hank Cicalo and Michael Lietz

The stories surrounding Jon Peters' introduction to Barbra continue to be embellished to this day. They met in the late Spring of 1973, prior to production on *For Pete's Sake*. The relationship itself didn't evolve until after the film had been completed. That Peters, a hairdresser-turned-self-made-millionaire, was to become someone who'd henceforth play a pivotal role in Barbra's career was evidenced most profoundly in the near spontaneous barrage of criticism that enveloped him as his relationship with her became the focus of local gossip. Personal opinions aside—and one might note that few people knew this new man in Barbra's life well enough to have much of an opinion—what seemed to unsettle Hollywood most was that it had become entangled in its own mythology. Movie stars are American royalty, and they are expected to live up to that station. A hustling hairdresser operating on the fringe of celebrity was a decided step down, especially for Barbra Streisand. Had she lost her senses? Could someone whose career judgment had always been on target be seriously listening to Peters' nonsense ideas about what she should be doing? Critics and supporters needed to look no farther than *ButterFly* for proof positive of their opposing arguments.

But Barbra was anything but a hands-off national monument to Jon. Even more to the point, *he* was *her* first vital connection with the outside world in years. He re-awakened the inquisitive young student who was unafraid to ask (or try) anything...the person "who had no time for fear."

Involving people who are important to her in her career has always been a logical part of the process to Barbra, and Peters was no exception. In the midst of production on *Funny Lady* attention turned to how to follow up the highly successful *Way We Were* albums. Barbra originally chose a group of show tunes which "no one was particularly thrilled about," she divulged to the *Chicago Tribune's* Aaron Gold. Admittedly, her latest, undeniably successful work had been a regression from the inroads she'd made with producer Richard Perry. There was concern that her new pop audience would feel neglected if she continued along this path. While some thought that wouldn't be a problem, Jon was unafraid to voice a contrary opinion. And he took it one step further by suggesting that it was a mistake not to develop the pop audience by exhibiting "the new Barbra," the girlish side of this child/woman who

could be as in tune with the times as the hippest background singer. As the producer of her new LP, his job would be to guide her toward the appropriate material.

By June of 1974 they were ready to go into the studio to prepare some of their choices. During the first rehearsals, Barbra, hampered by a slight cold, worked on Carole King's "You Light Up My Life"; "On Broadway," a major hit in the '60s for The Drifters (soon to be re-made by George Benson); an R&B song called "Turn Me On (It's a Funky-type Thing)"; "Everything Must Change," a staple in Sarah Vaughan's repertoire which touchingly speaks of music that "makes me cry" and butterflies that are free to fly away; "I Won't Last a Day Without You" by Paul Williams and Roger Nichols; and "Crying Time," the Buck Owens classic which, for apparent legal reasons, didn't make it as a duet onto the *Musical Instruments* soundtrack. "I hear something in my head and I'm not quite connecting with it," Barbra told one of her collaborators as she toiled on one number. Most of these cuts were ultimately scrapped in favor of a new list of songs. Tom Scott, an L.A. session musician well-known in the industry for his work with Joni Mitchell, was called in to arrange and conduct.

Although Hollywood observers are rarely interested in what goes on in a recording studio, *ButterFly* was especially newsworthy. *Los Angeles Times* columnist Joyce Haber was alerted about possible problems and contacted engineer Al Schmitt, who had reportedly quit the project after three short days. "They've recorded seven or eight songs for this LP. Columbia played them and they were unhappy with what they heard," he told her. "Barbra always gives me goosebumps; she has this incredible sound. This album has a flat, one-dimensional sound." Barbra, taking exception to the implication that she had put herself in the hands of an inept producer, called Haber back. "This is possibly the best singing I've ever done....For the first time in my life...my work has become fun for me, and it used to be a drag. My attitude has changed towards people. I'm less afraid. That's Jon," she insisted. "It kills me to have him put down more than to have me put down."

ButterFly was released in October, 1974, with little promotional fanfare, and no advance single. Favorable trade reviews were to be expected, as was the preponderance of negative input from rock-oriented critics ("an all-time recording low...the closest thing to a total mistake Streisand has ever done"), but even Barbra and Jon must have been caught by surprise by *The New York Times*. "Beyond the fashionable cracks at Peters' profession—and there have been many these past months—his role as

Backstage at the 1978 Grammys, Barbra poses with the first of her two awards for "Evergreen."

producer certainly has enhanced this album. *ButterFly* is one of Streisand's finest albums in years," Shaun Considine wrote. "It is a revelation of what this performer can do when she leaves her legend outside the studio doors....Love becomes the lady."

Placed in its proper context, one can see that with *ButterFly* Barbra started to find a tone and an approach to pop music which allowed her to function with a minimum of affectation and artifice. Her vocals are amazingly relaxed. Even on the heavily-criticized "Life on Mars" (which the composer, David Bowie, called "bloody awful") her attraction to the material is apparent. Lyrically, because, like "Mother" from *Barbra Joan*, it had autobiographical overtones; musically, because, again like "Mother," it allowed her to start softly and build a crescendo to a high emotional level. On cuts such as "Love in the Afternoon," "Guava Jelly" and "Let the Good Times Roll" there is a boldness, an earthy sexiness that brings a fresh dimension to her work.

Though not the blockbuster that *The Way We Were* was, *ButterFly* flew to a respectable number 13 on *Billboard's* LP list and reached gold certification by January. Seemingly as an afterthought, Columbia released two singles: "Guava Jelly"/"Love in the Afternoon" ("From balladry to sweet jammin', she's stupendously spreadable," *Record World* exclaimed in its write-up of the December 10 release) and "Jubilation"/"Let the Good Times Roll" (April 15). Neither charted.

Reviews:

"*ButterFly* is, in some ways, her most daring album. That's not the same as saying it is her most successful....Streisand touches a wide variety of musical bases—from reggae to David Bowie to gospel-soul to country. Her voice is as lovely as it has been in years, often open and warm. But her interpretations are still narrow and unconvincing....The problem, I'm afraid, is that Streisand has no clear feel for interpreting contemporary pop music. She obviously enjoys the various musical styles represented on the album, but she has given us no new way to look at them or no emotion to feel over them."

—Los Angeles Times

Funny Lady (Arista Records - AL 9004)

Soundtrack album coordinator: Peter Matz
Arranged and conducted by Peter Matz
Engineered by Kevin Cleary and John Neal

"The thing that amazed me the most about her was that at 8:00 in the morning, after having Chinese food or something and her eyes just opening up, she'd come into the studio and start singing like this incredible bird. I mean, it was just incredible."

—James Caan

Prior to Rastar's complaint against Columbia Records, it was announced that the soundtrack album for *Funny Lady* would be released by Arista Records. The new record company was a partnership between Clive Davis and Columbia Pictures. The score—including complete versions of each number in the "Crazy Quilt" sequence, plus an elongated, almost operatic musical intro to "Let's Hear It for Me"—was recorded at MGM Studios in Culver City during March and April of 1974. The project reunited Barbra with the songwriting team of Kander and Ebb ("My Coloring Book," "I Don't Care Much"). Peter Matz, who had since moved on to become the music director for Carol Burnett's weekly TV series, was called in to orchestrate and conduct, as well as supervise the music in general and compose the film's underscore.

Without a doubt the centerpiece of the new material was "How Lucky Can You Get," a drop-dead standard which poignantly reflected Fanny Brice's emotional state at a time in her life when she was "on top of the world professionally and in the basement emotionally." Juxtaposed with the Kander and Ebb songs were a number of "nuggets" from the '30s including "If I Love Again," "More Than You Know" and "Am I Blue."

Content and in love while she worked on *Funny Lady*, Barbra felt she'd become much more realistic about her work. "I see it in its proper perspective," she said. "Because I don't care as much, my work is better, more relaxed, more spontaneous. Oh, I *care*. For example, if I'm working on an orchestration that is very specific and detailed, then I want it to be right. But once it *is* right I can go on and sing it on the first take. I don't listen as critically as I used to, which is more like life—not attention paid to every word....Before, I'd do 25 takes to get one perfect. Now, I sort of go along with it because there's a kind of flow...a natural rhythm."

The *Funny Lady* soundtrack was released a week before the film's March 1975 premiere—amidst the cacophony of David Bowie, Al Green, Roberta Flack and *Tommy* (the motion picture adaptation of the classic rock opera from The Who). All were vying to replace favorites such as Led Zeppelin and Olivia Newton-John on the charts. Despite the absence of a single in the Hot 100 ("How Lucky Can You Get" was released April 22), *Funny Lady* had enough gumption to make it to number 6 on the *Billboard* chart; it was Barbra's 17th gold certification, her fourth in two years. A quadrophonic version of the LP—with substantiallly different vocals and mixes on most songs—was released later in the year.

Reviews:

"Barbra Streisand's magical interpretive powers translate the score of five new works plus nine well-known evergreens into a musical vehicle which listeners of all ages can appreciate. Fred Ebb and John Kander's new tunes lack the vocal punch that the older works have, but Barbra's beautifully smooth, silken voice glides over some tingling melodies, notably on "Isn't This Better," a fine new ballad. There's punch and gusto and humor in the material and the charts reflect the grandiose productions ("Great Day") around which much of the story revolves."

—*Billboard*

FINAL NOTE: "How Lucky Can You Get" and the musical score were both nominated in their respective categories for an Academy Award as well as a Golden Globe.

Lazy Afternoon (PC 33815)

Produced by Jeffrey Lesser and Rupert Holmes
Arranged and conducted by Rupert Holmes
Engineered by Jeffrey Lesser

Early in 1974, Barbra's office phoned composer Rupert Holmes in New York "and asked if I'd prepare two of my tunes for her because she was interested in performing them....I thought it was somebody at the bowling alley playing a joke," he later admitted. "A few hours later I was called again and asked if I would come to Los Angeles." Fearing that he was completely out of his depth, Holmes almost said no. But, when the composer arrived in the Golden State the next day, he discovered Barbra was absolutely sincere in her belief in his work. She wanted him to develop some material for *A Star Is Born*.

Within a couple of weeks, Holmes came to Barbra with a song he had written for her. "My Father's Song" was an intensely personal statement

Listening to a playback with producer Gary Klein.

that touched her deeply. Originally intended for the film, it found a more immediate placement on vinyl when script problems opened the door for an additional collaboration between Streisand and Holmes: in the recording studio.

On April 11, 1975, the pair entered Capitol's recording facility in Hollywood with Rupert's producing partner, Jeffrey Lesser, to cut "My Father's Song," plus two more of Barbra's favorite Holmes compositions. The session commenced with the bittersweet story of "Letters That Cross in the Mail." For "Widescreen," Holmes had rewritten the final verse in order to project some of Barbra's own feelings.

A few weeks later, they booked the Record Plant to cut Stevie Wonder's "You and I," a dance version of the Four Tops' "Shake Me, Wake Me," a song written for *A Star Is Born* entitled "Everything" (like "The Way We Weren't," a different song but the same concept as what ended up in the film), the orchestrated "A Child Is Born," and a song director Francis Coppola had suggested to Barbra, "Lazy Afternoon." The final session, which took place at RCA, started with "Moanin' Low," a song Barbra had teased audiences with thirteen years earlier on "The Garry Moore Show;" and "Better," a tune by *A Chorus Line*'s lyricist Edward Kleban. Then the producers sent the band home, keeping just the string and rhythm sections for Paul Williams and Roger Nichols' "I Never Had It So Good" and "By the Way."

The latter song was a collaborative effort between Streisand and Holmes. It came about during the process when the two were at the piano discussing keys for various arrangements. Barbra remembers being bored and starting to pick out a melody on the upper keyboard, with Holmes soon faking chords along with her. The composer told Jay Padroff in 1982 that *he* was "chomping" chords on the piano, "and she said, 'Oooh, that's nice,' and she started humming a little melody against it. It was interesting because I realized that if she ever wanted to, Barbra could be a brilliant songwriter on a recurrent basis.... She knew that all she had to do to write the song was to know what she felt she should sing next. Barbra has incredibly good taste in melody lines. It wasn't so much writing as hearing herself sing a song that had never been written." After they put their work on tape, they began discussing lyrics. Holmes delivered a completed lead sheet the following day.

The actual recording of *Lazy Afternoon* took three days. The mixing took that many months. It was a painstaking process, the complexities of which could revolve around a detail as "minor" as whether or not the lyric of "A Child Is Born" should say "what world..." or "what *worlds* will be formed by

her fingers?" or perhaps overdubbing a few lines on "By the Way." ("Singers—they don't understand what a writer goes through," Barbra wrote.) Holmes' only regret? That in sequencing the songs he didn't put "Shake Me, Wake Me" (the second single) as the final cut on Side One instead of preceding "I Never Had It So Good." "Just as you've solidified this gorgeous mood, "Shake Me, Wake Me" comes in. It's jarring. And while it's fun to clear the air, it wouldn't have been bad if that was the end of the side."

"My Father's Song" backed with "By the Way" was released on August 19, 1975. *Record World* would call it Barbra's "most spine-tingling single since "The Way We Were"..." *Cashbox* predicted "Barbra's interpretation is bound to earn her kudos and a high pop chart position." Incredibly, it earned her *no* position in the Hot 100; "My Father's Song" sailed exclusively on the Easy Listening charts (number 11). The album arrived in record stores in October. Day-to-day reports on the perils of Barbra and Jon and pre-production on their "$6 million home movie" kept the album visible. It reached number 12 on *Billboard's* Top LP's chart and was certified gold by the RIAA the following April. More than a decade later, it remains one of the few albums Barbra can bear listening to without hearing all the flaws. "She genuinely, genuinely loved [making] that record," *The New York Times'* Stephen Holden attests.

Reviews:

"Her most satisfying album in years. One may, in fact, have to go back to before Streisand's *Stoney End* pop-rock flirtation to find her so comfortable and secure in her vocals....In restoring her to the pop mainstream Holmes ironically has given Streisand her most authentic connection yet with contemporary pop influences. *Lazy Afternoon* may not have the supreme highs of some of Streisand's most heralded early works, but it is a consistent and engaging album that suggests she is back on the right musical path."

—*Los Angeles Times*

Classical Barbra (CBS Masterworks - M 33452)

Produced by Claus Ogerman
The Columbia Symphony Orchestra under the direction of Claus Ogerman
Engineered by Mickey Crofford, Lee Hirschberg, Eddie Brackett and Frank Laico

With production on *A Star Is Born* due to commence in February of 1976, Barbra decided it was time to release her much talked-about classical

LP. Neither Columbia nor Barbra had been very successful at keeping it under wraps. Teasers about *Follow the Lieder* (the album's working title) had been popping up in the press since production began in Los Angeles three years earlier. But the concept of performing art songs was something she had been considering much longer. Vocal coach Lee Sweetland recalls Barbra discussing the possibility of doing an album of arias in 1967. "She has a wonderful lyric soprano. It's not big enough for the Met, but that, too, might have been possible if she had wanted to put in the years of intensive training. But then why should she," he adds, "when she's already established herself as one of the finest pop singers we've ever had?" Ultimately, Sweetland says, Barbra thought her audience would be confused by such an offering, "and maybe she was right. But it's too bad."

During the massive activity of 1973, Barbra asked Claus Ogerman to produce, arrange and conduct an album of her singing a collection of classical songs in different languages. "I feel all music has its roots in classical music," she expressed. They chose a selection of quiet, mostly contemplative songs by Debussy, Faure, Schumann and Handel. Columbia was, admittedly, wary of public response to the LP, fearing "a possible attack by classical music aficionados and ultimate confusion by her pop fans." "Record companies haven't changed," Marty

Erlichman says. "The classical album was something they could live with, but certainly nothing they would foster." They did, however, assign the project to their prestigious Masterworks division.

Already a student of French and Italian, Barbra was to learn German and Latin phonetically (under Ogerman's tutelage). Lacking any formal training, she also committed herself to learning how to phrase lieder—and the songs themselves—by listening to other recorded works. It was her most difficult singing project, she explained to Stephen Holden in 1985, "because classical singing is such a disciplined art form."

Although Barbra was tempted to print "This is a work in progress" on the back jacket, both Marty and Jon felt strongly that there was no need for her to do anything that might be construed as an apology for her work. After months of anticipation, Columbia finally set a February 1976 release date—too late to capitalize on the Christmas rush, but still a visible period due to the usual lack of superstar product. The album was now called *Classical Barbra*, a title that certainly reflected Barbra's serious aspirations more accurately than the coy *Follow the Lieder*. "Barbra did this with 100 percent purity, and I don't want it to be bastardized," Marty related to *People* magazine. The attractive packaging featured photos by Francesco Scavullo and a gushing back cover endorsement from Leonard Bernstein.

Was *Classical Barbra* a sad case of "misguided talent" or were both artist and record company to be

The lone art of recording.

"congratulated for this innovative venture"? Would the public buy it...or didn't it matter? (Doesn't it always?)

Reviews:

"*The Classical Slant:* Streisand's crooning vocalism is certainly attractive, but unrevealing when it comes to subtleties of expression that in more skilled hands might illuminate the poetic intent of music and text.

"*The Pop Slant:* Those who knock Streisand miss the point of her new LP. She dares to be different....All the deplorable affectations—the exaggerated, unnatural phrasing and unreal enunciation of the most celebrated classical vocalists are absent in the 10 Streisand tracks....*Classical Barbra* is a revelatory LP. It shows a warm and emotional side of a woman that was previously unsuspected....Only Streisand in this dreadful era of musical mediocrity could pull it off."

—*Billboard*

FINAL NOTE: "It doesn't matter what people think of it," Barbra stated in 1979, "what matters is the work itself. And, actually, [the album] pleased a lot of people." Preliminary reports had 150,000 records being sold the first two weeks of release. The LP entered the *Billboard* chart at number 99 and jumped 32 places in one week. By the end of March it had ascended to number 46...and then stalled. But *Classical Barbra* did spend four months in the Top 10 on the classical chart. No one seriously expected a Top 10 pop album; neither did they consider that Barbra would be nominated for a Grammy under the Best Vocal Soloist Performance—Classical. It was Barbra's first nod from NARAS in four years.

"I do not, however, want to leave the impression that Streisand should give up on the classics," the late Glenn Gould wrote in *High Fidelity*. "Indeed, I'm convinced that she has a great 'classical' album in her. She simply needs to rethink the question of repertoire and to dispense with the yoke of respectability which burdens the present production." Gould would have been amused to hear some of the rumors *Classical Barbra* wrought. One of the most intriguing was that Barbra would debut at La Scala in *La Vera Storia*, a new opera by avant-garde composer Luciano Berio. The latest has her recording a duet from Mozart's *Don Giovanni* with tenor Placido Domingo.

A Star Is Born (JS 34403)

Produced by Barbra Streisand and Phil Ramone
Orchestrations by Roger Kellaway, Kenny Ascher, Tom Scott, Jim Pankow, Ian Freebairn-Smith and Pat Williams
Engineered by Phil Ramone, Tom Vicari and Dan Wallin

When it became known that Barbra planned to remake *A Star Is Born* and update its setting to the world of music, a curious public anxiously wondered if she would be able to tackle the inevitable comparisons to the Judy Garland musical as well as the "alien" world of rock 'n' roll. By now everyone knows that the music from *A Star Is Born* isn't rock. But the soundtrack did require an *approximation* of it for John Norman Howard that wouldn't go against the grain of Kris Kristofferson's Nashville orientation, just as Esther Hoffman would have to be a believable contemporary performer who would not alienate Streisand's following.

As it turned out, the musical image Barbra had in mind for her character was more in the Joni Mitchell/Carole King vein; both women were respected exemplars of the singer/songwriter era.

Artistically, Barbra has always tended to downplay her formidable musical gifts in favor of emphasizing her acting talents. *A Star Is Born* would find her re-dedicating herself to a major commitment and involvement in her musical career. While writers were being interviewed, she began her own research, which included taking piano and guitar lessons. It was a new experience for her, and a pivotal one. During one fortuitous session she asked her guitar teacher, Lori Barth, to play some of her own compositions.

"I was so *impressed* with the fact that she wrote these songs, and I felt really terrible, you know? I remember getting very emotional and very insecure and very upset about it because I thought, 'God, I only sing. I only sing these songs that other people write.' Overwhelmed with emotion, she ran into the bathroom and started to cry. Then Jon came in. "It was really this lovely moment," she described in *Playboy*, "he was comforting me and saying, 'You can do it. You can do anything you set your mind to. Try to write a song.'"

It wasn't the only time Barbra may have felt inadequate being "just the singer" who interprets other people's work, but it was the first time she was moved into action. One day during a lesson, the melody of "Evergreen" started flowing naturally out of her. "I just started to fool around with chords [and] instead of a star is born, a song was born. But it really was true. It just came out of absolute impatience, you know?" According to Barth, the song's structure, which was polished during subsequent sessions, was based on basic guitar chords Barbra

The love theme from A Star Is Born *was also recorded in French, Italian and Spanish.*

was learning. Even the hand-picked rolling chords were part of her original rendition. That's how she first played it for producer Phil Ramone and arranger Ian Freebairn-Smith. "I remember her coming from [her] guitar lessons and playing me a melody sung over a very classical kind of left hand," Ramone says. "The melodic structure of the song struck me as so unusual....Emotionally, it came right from her heart."

Like "Ma Premiere Chanson" and "By the Way," "Evergreen" was born out of distraction, but it shares many compositional qualities with them as well as subsequent forays into songwriting such as "Answer Me" and "Here We Are At Last." The thread that weaves this fabric together is Barbra's appreciation of the simplicity of a clear melodic line, certain word changes, a possible modulation in the key or change in tempo and minimal repetition. Significantly, these are the same things she looked for in the music she shaped as a younger singer. "What Barbra was doing in her nightclub act was really no less than composing," Peter Matz affirms. "From her

song selection to interpretation, she was creating musical lines."

"If you've spent any time with Barbra, you will hear her sing and create melodies as she's humming in the car," adds Ramone. "The fact that she may not write it down or bother to commit to a writing career, for somebody who has spent so much time acting and performing or whatever, is almost inconsequential....I've worked with quite a few singer songwriters and watching Barbra, who has always been a great interpreter of other people's work, turn within herself and write a song like 'Evergreen' was quite a moment to have been part of."

At the time Rupert Holmes became a key contributor to the music of *A Star Is Born,* he had "nothing more than Barbra's belief in me and some nice reviews" backing him up. Starry-eyed in Hollywood, he threw himself completely into the work, hoping to create songs that would reflect the characters and not Rupert Holmes. "I took very seriously the fact that in the movie Barbra's character was a songwriter and was writing her own songs," he

Taking the "diva" off of her pedestal: Barbra clowns around for the Streisand Superman *promotional art, 1977.*

related to Jay Padroff. "Sometimes I wrote four songs all for the same purpose in the script." (Included on that list were titles such as "Love Out of Time" and "Lullaby for Myself.") Where a newcomer like Holmes surely got confused was in the daily additions to the script—not simply line changes but drastic changes fleshing out the concept and characters. "It was chaos," he told the *Los Angeles Times,*"...I couldn't keep track of the story."

Still, it was a once-in-a-lifetime experience not without its humor. "I remember Jon and Barbra and I were driving along, going across a canyon in L.A., and Jon got all excited about the idea of [doing] this deco production number, and he pulled the car over to the side of the road [where] there's this drop of about 400 feet...and hopped out of the car and said, 'Look, this is how it could go.' He started choreographing this scene while the car is sitting about four feet away from the cliff. And Barbra is sitting in the front seat, and the parking brake isn't on, and I'm in the back [thinking] to myself, 'If this car goes over the cliff, I'll only make the fourth paragraph: "Also

in the car was Reuben Helms." They'll get my name wrong.'"

Sensitive to pressure from outside sources, Holmes tried to prove Barbra's trust in him was justified; inevitably, he realized he was in over his head and he slowly, regrettably, began pulling away from the project. Before he left, Barbra, anticipating the shift, called Paul Williams in to supervise the music. "I got a call to write a song for *A Star Is Born,*" he told *Billboard.* "I had a meeting with Barbra and Jon and we went over the script and I suggested a song at the beginning, and they didn't like it. Then I suggested another one a little further into the script, and they didn't like that. The third suggestion, they liked. Barbra said, 'You're not intimidated by this, are you?' I said, 'No.' She said, 'And you're not afraid to have bad ideas along with the good ones. I like that.'"

Other respected writers, arrangers and musicians would be consulted as the start date loomed before them, but above and beyond the extent of their contributions, the single, most important factor to

46

shape the musical score would be Barbra's decision to record the music live. When she came to Hollywood for *Funny Girl,* it never occurred to her that music recorded on even the most insulated soundstage would be judged inferior to what could be captured in a recording studio. She had assumed she'd be singing live, much as the concert sequences of her TV specials were recorded live. Lip syncing, of course, required great compromises of Streisand the actress to Streisand the singer. Having recorded most of her numbers weeks earlier, she was expected to perform within the limits of that previous performance, regardless of insights she had gained since then.

For the most part, Barbra respected the archaic musical tradition of lip syncing and envisioned a day when she could express herself within the same moment as an actress and a singer. As the executive producer of *A Star Is Born* she had just such an opportunity. To help accomplish this with the greatest of precision, she called in Phil Ramone, a producer/engineer of renown who had pioneered the area of live recording and with whom she'd worked on her Central Park and *Funny Lady* concert specials.

Unwilling to be pushed into filming until she was fully ready, Barbra bought some extra time by scheduling extensive rehearsals—for music only—in November '75 at Warner Bros. "We rehearsed for a month on a soundstage there before we recorded anything," recalls Ian Freebairn-Smith. "That's why everything came out so well, I think." The purpose of the sessions, he says, was to get the feel of the material as performance songs and make everyone comfortable with how each tune was going to be presented. "I must say that the things that Barbra suggested about tempos, phrasings, feelings and even some background lines were always so musical that I didn't have any trouble at all," he says. "If they hadn't been, I would have said something." Working with just a rhythm section (guitar, bass, drums), they'd "run the tunes down, change the key when it didn't feel right or maybe change something in the arrangement or sketch in some counter melodies. Then we'd come back the next day and do it all over again. I've never had the luxury of doing that before."

As the deadline approached Ramone suggested to Barbra that she take another look at some of the songs she had put in the "B" file. One of those songs was Rupert Holme's "Everything," a composition which hadn't been completed lyrically. Ramone called Holmes in London to inquire if he'd mind having Paul Williams take a look at it. "It's not an easy process to have to say to somebody, 'Listen, you now have a co-writer with you,' but he was quite

amenable; quite happy and thrilled that a song of his had survived and that Barbra had the time to review it."

"It was a funny collaboration," Holmes admitted. "I hate to always give Paul a hard time about it, but a couple of lines that were written have been attributed to me, and they're not my lines. Paul wrote: 'I'd cure the cold and the traffic jam/If there were floods, I'd give a dam.' I've had a lot of people come down on me about that line and I did not write [it]." Yet if dramatic content means anything, and the attitude was that these songs were written by the *characters,* not Williams or Holmes, an argument can be made for "Everything" establishing Esther Hoffman as a commercially viable songwriter with a distance to go before the full flowering of her talents.

One line which Holmes didn't write but which intrigued him nonetheless was, "I'd like to have the perfect twin/One who'd go out as I came in." "I have a sneaking suspicion that Barbra might have written that," he said. "Barbra loves dramatic duality...[having] a scene or song written which is completely the opposite of what the person is feeling. [And] she is capable of writing a very good line and never taking credit."

Ninety percent of what finally ended up in the film and on vinyl was either recorded on the road or in live studio situations (such as Barbra and Kris's "Evergreen" duet, which was recorded and filmed at A&M). A small fraction was overdubbed after the completion of principal photography in April. While Barbra supervised the editing of the film out of a facility she and Jon had installed in one of their Malibu guest houses, Ramone commuted between The Burbank Studios (where he was mixing the record), Todd-AO in Hollywood (where he did the premix on the songs in the film), and occasionally Malibu.

At the end of July, the 1976 CBS Records convention concluded with a personal appearance by Barbra and a 20-minute preview of the movie. If the conventioneers had any doubt about the upcoming *Star Is Born* soundtrack, they would find that Jon Peters didn't, and to prove it he brought in the Scotti Bros. to help coordinate the promotional effort for the album and film. Columbia had planned on releasing the LP in October; Peters convinced them to push that date back to November.

"Love Theme from *A Star Is Born* (Evergreen)," was shipped to radio stations on the 16th, backed by a huge advertising and promotion campaign. Jon and the Scotti Bros. had hoped to create a hit before the picture opened, but the single wasn't to hit the charts for four weeks. Nevertheless, the record trades were predicting great success. "Expect this one to be a

A homespun pose with Sadie II, the poodle Jon bought to replace Barbra's first dog. (Photo courtesy of the Richard Giammanco collection)

monster," *Cashbox* said, "should be on the charts for quite a long spell." *Billboard* likened the song's appeal to "The Way We Were": "If the rest of the *Star Is Born* score and movie are this good, Barbra and Jon Peters will be able to buy the state of California."

The soundtrack, with its inflated list price ($1.00 more than the '76 standard), followed "Evergreen" by two weeks and took off quickly. Despite some scathing reviews, in five short weeks retail record stores tallied 1,200,000 albums sold; it was Barbra's first platinum LP. (The RIAA began platinum certification earlier in the year.) On February 12, 1977, it jumped over the Eagles' *Hotel California* and Stevie Wonder's *Songs in the Key of Life* to claim the number 1 spot. "Evergreen" followed suit on March 5. It was to be Barbra's second gold single, her first international hit since "The Way We Were" (she also recorded the song in French, Italian and Spanish). The song spent 25 weeks on the charts; *A Star is Born* 51.

Streisand recordings have rarely been big on album-oriented radio, but due to the immense popularity of "Evergreen"—and of the film itself—the LP dominated sales reports for a long time. *Saturday Night Fever* notwithstanding, *A Star Is Born* was *the* breakthrough pop/rock soundtrack in an era when rock musicals were considered a lost cause. It would take another "monster" album, Fleetwood Mac's *Rumours,* to surpass it on the charts. *A Star Is Born* remained on the Top 100 for the rest of 1977. Most importantly, the soundtrack re-established Barbra in the industry and public mind as a singles *and* album seller. It signalled to even the most casual bystander that the transition was complete, and Streisand's position as an acceptable pop performer was no longer in question. She was indeed the top pop singles female artist of 1977.

Reviews:

"It really does have the feel of an original score in the sense of bringing together a wide variety of musical styles. Most of the music is Barbra doing her inimitable big-voiced, note-sliding shtick on tremulous ballads or strong production tunes. She also does a creditable fem-group rock novelty. Kristofferson, at least the way he's mixed here, doesn't sound quite at ease in the macho rock numbers his fading-superstar character performs onstage but he reveals an interesting smoother, lighter range in the love duets that would be well worth exploring further."

—*Billboard*

FINAL NOTE: Perhaps critics weren't being truthful in articulating their real resentment—that rock in the '70s no longer seemed to represent the needs of youth to rebel against what their parents considered acceptable. Barbra Streisand was acceptable, and rock had become the establishment. In an interview with James Spada, Richard Perry made some astute observations regarding *A Star Is Born:* "As it turns out, the material was not rock 'n' roll. It was somewhere in between. It was a little bit of contemporary pop and the other songs were a mixture of other musical elements. Whatever it was it certainly caught the public eye. It was the first time that the industry started to realize the potential popularity of soundtracks. I mean, when one stops and thinks five and a half million albums—those sales transcend even Barbra. America was clamoring for a soundtrack to a musical picture that they liked. At that time, it seemed phenomenal, but yet the potential was really so much greater (as witnessed with *Saturday Night Fever).* What seemed phenomenal maybe wasn't all that extraordinary compared to what it could have done, you know? Imagine if there were two or three 'Evergreens' in there."

There *were* a couple of fine prospects: the duet between Barbra and Kris, "Lost Inside of You"; a scorching "Woman in the Moon"; even Barbra's rendition of "Watch Closely Now" (Kris's was released without much success). For whatever reason, none was released. Still, the quadruple platinum *A Star Is Born* was Barbra's most popular contemporary album; unchallenged in worldwide sales until *Guity.*

In February of 1978, more than a year after its release, the soundtrack received five Grammy nominations: Record and Song of the Year, Best Arrangement Accompanying Vocalists, Best Pop Vocal Performance—Female, and Best Original Score. Although Streisand and Williams had already been honored with an Academy Award and a Golden Globe, Barbra figured their work "would be forgotten" up against its impressive competition. Prior to her arrival that evening, Ian Freebairn-Smith won a Grammy for his arrangement of "Evergreen." In what has to be one of the great ironies of her professional life, Barbra tied for her third major award (the New York Critics Poll *Wholesale* nod and the 1969 Oscars were the others). She and Paul shared the Song of the Year Grammy with Joe Brooks ("You Light Up My Life"). But the Pop Female award was all hers. Not having won since 1966, she was genuinely surprised. "I thought all the other girls [Linda Rondstadt, Dolly Parton, Carly Simon and Debby Boone] were way over me," she expressed excitedly backstage. "I always have a feeling of self-doubt."

Streisand Superman(JC 34830)

Produced by Gary Klein

Arranged by Nick De Caro, Jack Nitzche, Charlie Calello and Larry Carlton
Engineered by Armin Steiner and Tom Vicari

In 1977, shortly after the release of *A Star Is Born*, Barbra walked onstage at the Grammy Awards (to present Record of the Year) and was greeted with an instantaneous ovation. In her acknowledgment of the audience she admitted that only recently had she begun to feel a real part of the music community. One of the major changes to happen during that period was her subsequent alignment with The Entertainment Company, headed by Charles Koppelman, formerly of CBS Records. Koppelman's monied partner was businessman Samuel J. Lefrak—once the teenaged Streisand's landlord in Brooklyn. Although Barbra doesn't remember the booking, Lefrak also claims credit for arranging a one-night stand ("for $50 and car fare") at an exclusive men's club called the Lotos Club. "I knew she was going to be a superstar," he said.

Seeking to capitalize on the momentum in Barbra's career by keeping her on the pop charts during 1977—and not just the easy listening or MOR charts—Koppelman assigned Barbra's next album to producer Gary Klein. Klein, "a real song man," had gained the respect of both Streisand and Peters when he was asked by Koppelman to critique *ButterFly* for them. "I went over the album cut by cut, and I was very specific about what I thought was wrong with it," he told James Spada, writing for *Billboard* magazine. "People are afraid to tell her the truth because she's BARBRA STREISAND. But I never felt intimidated by her, and we got along for that reason. But she does have to have an *explanation* when you tell her something—because she'll give *you* one."

Since then, *A Star Is Born* had managed not only to spawn a new generation of young fans, but to reveal a youthful, girlish Streisand. One special humorous sidelight to the film was the moment when Barbra, dressed in white shorts and a T-shirt with the Superman insignia, triumphantly staked out her territory in the Arizona desert. It always got a chuckle from audiences: Streisand as Superwoman ("Clark Kent, eat your heart out!"). The tongue-in-cheek gesture was also an expression of confidence and assurance. *Streisand Superman* would incorporate her feelings about the conflict of public opinion versus the largely negative image conjured up by the press—in the process becoming a venue for addressing supporters and detractors alike.

In the midst of song selection, Barbra became particularly incensed over an item in *Los Angeles* magazine intimating that she had become a Howard Hughes-esque figure who was more concerned that her birds (two parakeets) be allowed to fly indoors than for the comfort of her guests. "I find it such a waste of time to have to constantly refute these idiotic statements," she wrote in the *Superman* liner notes. She chose to enlist the help of writers Ron Nagle and Scott Matthews to paint her side of the gossip war musically: "Dinner and a movie/I'll just show my face in town/Rumors fly so fast that I/Don't try to live 'em down...Don't believe it/Don't believe what you read/Don't believe it/'bout the life that I lead."

Although, as an artist, she usually prefers to work "totally in the present," Barbra commissioned new arrangements from Nick DeCaro for *Star Is Born*'s "Woman in the Moon" and "With One More Look at You." Both songs were recorded when she went into the studio in April, but fell by the wayside to make room for two compositions that didn't make it into *Star*. "Answer Me" was another collaboration between Barbra and Paul Williams and was meant to underscore the film's first love scene. But, once "Lost Inside of You" was completed, everyone agreed the latter provided a better musical link. Nick DeCaro thought "Answer Me" was "a wonderful song, but it's not a real 'accessible song' (to use a Robert Hilburn term). It's kind of complex, musically, and when I first heard it I thought, 'My God, I shouldn't be doing this.' In fact, I mentioned to Barbra that she would be doing it with someone like Claus Ogerman...and she said, 'Well, if I don't like the way you do it, I'll do it again with Claus!' But she did like the way I arranged it."

Other gems on the album would include a song which had recently own the grand prize at the American Song Festival, "Love Comes from Unexpected Places" by Kim Carnes and Dave Ellingson, and Billy Joel's "New York State of Mind" —in Barbra's words, "marvelous, old-fashioned horn blowing blues." Moderately successful songwriters up until then, both Carnes and Joel were on the verge of major breakthroughs. But nothing fazed Joel's mother until Barbra recorded one of her son's songs—*then* she paid attention. "It was amazing," he said in *Playboy*. "[Barbra] sent me an album and inscribed it: 'Dear Billy, thanks for the song. Hope you like it. Love, Barbra.' I still have it in a frame. My mother came over and saw it; all of a sudden, I became legitimate in her mind."

The album was recorded in Hollywood at Sound Labs, Capitol and United-Western Recorders. Backed by a solid group of musicians (including Jeff Porcaro and David Paich of Toto, future NARAS president Michael Melvoin, and David Foster), Barbra seemed to be enjoying herself. Even if the pressure to produce *Superman* wasn't intense, late nights remained a staple part of the schedule—prompting

With Charles Koppelman (L) and Jon Peters, 1978.
(Photo courtesy of the Richard Giammanco
collection)   51

A dramatic teaming: Barbra and Neil on "You Don't Bring Me Flowers."

"Was, du willst nicht?" (Do You Want to Fight?) The German single of "The Main Event"/"Fight."

her to thank all the musicians and friends "who stayed up with me till the wee hours of the morning and still laughed!" "She works herself the hardest," Klein added. "Sometimes, I had to stop her. She'd say, 'I feel fine, my voice is fine,' but I could see on the meters that she was losing steam—if she sang for another hour, she'd hurt her voice."

There were no signs of strain on "My Heart Belongs to Me." The single was released on May 13, 1977, and rushed onto turntables. The sudden release took a lot of fans (who hadn't expected a new musical offering so soon) by surprise. When "Heart" peaked at number 4, it was the first time Barbra had strung two major hits together back-to-back. *Streisand Superman* showed its mettle subsequent to its June release when it climbed to the number 3 position on the *Billboard* chart. It was Barbra's second platinum album.

Reviews:

"On *Streisand Superman*, Streisand has mostly chosen songs with intelligent lyrics. Nothing deep, but nothing ridiculous, either.... Just how much of this album's quality comes from vocal style, rather than material, is made clear by the relatively undistinguished 'I Found You Love,' which she fills with little pleasures of phrasing—plastic pop, yes, but it works. Two songs above all sum up the best of *Streisand Superman*. One is a light and sophisticated 1930's Cole Porterish piece by Billy Joel called 'New York State of Mind,' the other is a wise and ironic number about the paradoxes of human need, 'Lullaby for Myself.' Marvelous songs, sung marvelously."

—*High Fidelity*

Songbird (JC 35375)

Produced by Gary Klein
Orchestral arrangements by Nick DeCaro, Lee Holdridge, Gene Page and James Newton Howard
Rhythm arrangements by Nick DeCaro, David Wolfert, Larry Carlton and Jon Tropea
Engineered by Armin Steiner

Eyes of Laura Mars Original motion picture soundtrack (JS 35487)

Produced by Gary Klein
Remixed by Armin Steiner
Executive Producers: Jon Peters and Charles Koppelman

Leaving Columbia Records was the furthest thing from Barbra's mind when her recording contract came up for renewal in late 1977. In November,

she had, as a matter of fact, gone back into the studio with producer Gary Klein. "This should be a fairly typical Streisand album," the producer stated. "There won't be any radical changes in her style or in the kind of material she sings." The only difference was that the first six cuts were recorded at Media Sound Studios in New York City, her first East Coast-based project in several years. A movie brought her back to New York—not hers, but Jon's production of *Eyes of Laura Mars*. On December 22, Columbia threw a party in her honor to celebrate her resigning.

The songbird returned to Los Angeles at the end of January to complete her 34th LP (counting *Wholesale, Pins and Needles* and *Harold Sings Arlen*). She was confident, relaxed and encouraged by the genuine respect between musicians. But had anything actually changed with regard to her work in the studio? "There is a no more sentimental group of people than musicians," Peter Reilly observes. "I think in the past what they have always found missing in Barbra was what they would call 'soul.' She wasn't considered to have paid her human dues. I call that pure maudlin nonsense." Personal problems—major personal problems à la those that plagued Judy Garland, Billie Holiday, and Aretha Franklin—are thought to be a great leveler for an extraordinary talent. But Barbra never seems to communicate any; her severest crises have simply been the comparatively minor controversies raised between critics and fans: Is she shy or aloof? A sensitive artist or a ruthless perfectionist? She is, they say, all of these things. She is also, invariably, busy.

Peter Reilly: "Barbra isn't one to hang out at the recording studio for no reason. Imagine the look on these musician's faces when she goes in and does the job and then leaves! They'd go, 'Is that all?' and she'd say, 'Yeah, that's all.' It's just two different ways of approaching the profession: your profession as your life or your profession as your profession. The glitz and glamour of it doesn't really appeal to her." Nick DeCaro believes most musicians don't really expect her to socialize much. "Everybody knows they're going to make a lot of money when they play on a Streisand date and have to go into overtime. They might get a little crazed if they've got their part down and she's still going for this performance...but it's always tempered by the fact that she's a fabulous singer and they're making good money. Barbra has more respect among musicians than 'people in the know' think."

"There are times when she does push too hard, but only because she's trying so hard," elaborated Gary Klein. "Once we were working until 3:00 or 4:00 in the morning and one of the string guys walked out. She felt bad, but it's just her way of working. A lot of people don't want to put out as much as she does, but they lose because she can bring out a lot more in a person than anyone else."

Starting with *Songbird* she began to assemble a group of creative people who responded to that challenge. The material ranged from Stephen Bishop and Kim Carnes to "Tomorrow" from the hit Broadway show *Annie,* and Michalski and Oosterveen's eerie "A Man I Loved." (M&O were discoveries of Jon Peters'; they also contributed to the *Eyes of Laura Mars* and *Main Event* soundtracks.) Klein heard Bruce Roberts' "I Don't Break Easily" and asked Roberts if Barbra could record it. "He knew I would be thrilled, so that was his way of surprising me," Roberts says. "When I got up off the floor I said yes." The title tune, according to DeCaro, was rewritten to reflect a more intimate point of view from Barbra.

Although "Songbird" was the emotional centerpiece of the LP, the side that inevitably stole its thunder was "You Don't Bring Me Flowers." Gary Klein: "[Barbra] looks at a lyric as a script. She said to me, 'If you give me a great script, I'll give you a great performance.' And she has a lot to say about lyrics. It's murder to find material good enough for her." Critic Stephen Holden would venture that "Streisand's gift—one that Liza Minnelli, Bette Midler, Jane Olivor and a host of theatrically-bent chanteuses vainly try to capture—is to elevate the old-fashioned romantic clichés of pop to near-operatic pitch, then to sustain that pitch with a combination of pyro-technical skill and sheer chutzpah." No single Streisand recording would seem to illustrate this better than her understated performance (relative to the melodramatic material) on "You Don't Bring Me Flowers."

As work on *Songbird* was being completed, Barbra went back into the studio to record one more number, the "Love Theme from *Eyes of Laura Mars* (Prisoner)." The tune was written by Karen Lawrence and John Desautels, former members of the L.A. Jets. The band had opened the '76 *Star Is Born* concert in Tempe; later, when Jon and Barbra caught them in performance at the Roxy Theater in Los Angeles, they heard a rough version of "Prisoner." After the Jets signed with Charles Koppelman's publishing company, the completed composition was submitted to Peters as a possible theme song for *Eyes.* (Jon had tried to encourage Barbra to write the theme herself, but she decided against it.) "Some people have said they were disappointed I had Barbra sing the title track," Jon reported to *Variety,* "but she's a great singer and the song fit her perfectly." "I thought Barbra would be able to do a great job on the song. She can sing full blast, flat out, but she's sensitive, too. Now that she's really doing it, it's just a mind-

blower," Karen Lawrence enthused in *Record World.* "They even kept the little piano intro I wrote."

On May 22, 1978, Columbia released "Songbird" backed with "Honey, Can I Put On Your Clothes." *Record World* characterized the "A" side as "a quiet ballad [which] makes its point without theatrics, but with style," while *Billboard's* review stated "this is a pretty MOR-ish tune from one of the best female vocalists around...Streisand's forte is her beautiful, far-ranging voice and here it excels." The album, featuring Barbra and her dog, Sadie, on the cover, was released the same week. Both the single and the LP were slow to moderate climbers on the charts. On July 6, just as the title track eased into the Top 30, "Prisoner" was released along with its companion soundtrack.

"'Prisoner' is a booming, dramatic ballad with a compelling rock undercurrent in the fiery instrumentation. It also features some of Streisand's gutiest singing to date," *Billboard* said. It was, in fact, Barbra's most commanding rock performance and as such rated prominent attention on radio stations. Early trade reports indicated this could be a giant single for her. Ultimately, both "Songbird" and "Prisoner" suffered in the tug of war over airplay. "There may have been some confusion," says *Billboard's* chart analyst Paul Grein. "With 'Songbird' already out, Columbia was undercutting its own record considerably by putting another Streisand single out so soon."

The final tally? "Songbird" 25 (but it was number 1 on Easy Listening), and "Prisoner" 21 (much bigger on rock stations and a Top 10 hit in the South); *Songbird* (the platinum LP) 12, and *Eyes...* a dismal 125.

Reviews:

(Songbird)

"Streisand's latest album reinforces her status as perhaps America's most acclaimed pop singer but it also supports the argument of those who question her judgment as a record-maker. Streisand is singing better than ever. Her sense of soul (that's right—*soul)* is beginning to match her mastery of dramatics and vocalese. But it will take a less mundane approach to song selection and considerably less of a conglomerate-type production effort to lift her to a still-higher plateau of pop glory....*Songbird* is down-the-pike Streisand, safety negotiating the lanes to the right of the middle of the road. She mastered that course years ago. From someone of such scope, we expect more."

—*Los Angeles Times*

Posing with Donna Summer, 1979.

(*Eyes of Laura Mars*)

"The chief selling point on this soundtrack of the new Faye Dunaway thriller is the title track, sung by Barbra Streisand and not available on her latest LP."

—*Billboard*

FINAL NOTE: 1979 Grammy nominations included Best Pop Vocal Performance—Female, for Barbra's solo rendering of "You Don't Bring Me Flowers;" Neil Diamond and the Bergmans were nominated for Best Song. Barbra's most interesting acknowledgment, however, came from the prestigious *Playboy* Music Poll—as their female jazz vocalist of 1978 (her fourth such nod).

Barbra Streisand's Greatest Hits/Volume 2 (FC 35679)

"You Don't Bring Me Flowers" (duet with Neil Diamond)
Produced by Bob Gaudio
Arranged by Alan Lindgren
Other cuts previously released 1970-1978
Produced by Barbra Streisand, Phil Ramone, Gary Klein, Charlie Calello, Marty Paich, Richard Perry and Tommy LiPuma

There was another possible explanation for "Songbird's" and "Prisoner's" inability to move higher on the charts: some radio stations were playing a *third* single that was eliciting an incredible response from listeners. Program director Gary Guthrie of WAKY, Louisville, Kentucky, was on the verge of an amicable divorce from his wife when *Songbird* came out. Neil Diamond's "You Don't Bring Me Flowers" had made a profound impression on his wife Becky, but he always thought there was something missing. When he had heard Barbra's rendition, everything fell into place. He decided to create a "duet of superstars" as a going-away gift to his soon-to-be ex. It took him six hours in the 4-track studio to put a rough tape together. "I had to vary the speed of her voice just a hair because it was a little out of sync with his," Guthrie informed *Radio & Records*. "Then I took Neil's first verse and followed it with her second verse and came back with both of them doing the chorus and reprise." After a couple of polishing sessions, Guthrie gave the mix to WAKY's morning man. "All of a sudden, the phones started going bananas," he recalled in the *Los Angeles Times*. "Then, all the record stores in town began calling. They said, 'What are you doing? Every husband and wife is asking where they can buy this record!' Somebody told me there were 24,000 re-

quests for the single in this area alone. I went, 'Oh, no. We've created a monster!'"

Guthrie reported his success to the industry trades and pretty soon WGN in Chicago, WJR in Detroit and other stations had produced copycat versions. In July, Guthrie sent a tape to a local CBS promotion man who brought it to Los Angeles to play for the president of the record division, Bruce Lundvall, at Columbia's annual convention. While Barbra was accepting her platinum album for *Songbird*, Lundvall was looking into getting two of his top artists into the studio. "It was a difficult situation to deal with at first because Barbra's singles were still charting," promotion VP Bob Sherwood said. Public response, however, demanded a real-life teaming. A copy of the synthetic duet was forwarded to Charles Koppelman.

"Jon, Barbra and myself were listening to the tape at the beach house, when who walks in but Neil Diamond. So together we listened," Koppelman told *Record World*. "I don't think this duet could have happened if Neil and Barbra hadn't been good friends." In September, just before Rosh Hashanah, Streisand and Diamond held some infomal rehearsals at her home in Malibu. "We talked it over and decided that the best way to potential approach [the duet] would be nose to nose," said producer Bob Gaudio, "meaning the two of them in front of the microphone singing a love song to each other, with a piano [backing]."

Musician Mike Pinera was recording an album at Cherokee Studios in Hollywood when the duo went into the studio to cut their song: "The funniest thing happened: one of the guys from the other session came over and said, 'Barbra wants to know if there's a couch in here that she could borrow.' The couch at Cherokee is just gigantic. I mean, it would take a crane to lift it into the next room. And I said, 'No. If there was, I'd gladly give it to her.' Then my keyboard player says, 'Well, I don't live too far from here...two or three blocks away. I'd be glad to go get [mine] for her.' This was really wild. So we went in the van to pick up his couch...because for this particular track she wanted to sit down and sing. I just thought that was the coolest thing I'd ever heard. You know. 'Bring me a couch 'cause I want to get the right feel for this.' I walked in there after she was done...and there was the couch with a little vase and a flower [next to] it, and the whole bit. Talk about inspiration and having things just right!"

The CBS promotion staff had no trouble picking up on *this* collaboration. Sherwood was clearly "nuts about the whole idea.... 'Flowers' is more than a classic song—it's an event," he said. "Streisand and Diamond are two of the world's biggest multi-media

A cool, sensual pose illustrates the Spanish picture sleeve for "I Ain't Gonna Cry Tonight."

stars and I've got to believe that radio will treat the single like a monster because of the tremendous demographics they both share. Another important factor is the familiarity of their individual voices to the listening audience.... You don't find superstars of their magnitude recording together, and I don't think we'll ever see it again."

The single was mixed and pressed so quickly the vinyl was still warm when it arrived at Top 40 stations on October 17 of '78. KRTH, Los Angeles, played it straight out of the box "and within a half hour we had 55 requests, just from one play, so we knew we had a blockbuster." Eighty percent of the stations reporting to *Radio & Records* had added the record within the first ten days. *Record World* dubbed it their Powerhouse Pick of the Week: "Explosive is the word for this disc. It is taking excellent jumps everywhere while the heavies keep coming in. Breakout sales are being reported across the country." A programmer's newsletter said it was time to "Get the Grammys polished... MVP for 1978...females 18–44, males 25–44 solid...still number 1 phone riot, females go berserko and will wait all day to hear this." The single debuted at

number 48 on *Billboard*'s Hot 100. Six weeks later, it was crowned the top pop single in the country, making Barbra Columbia's only act to snag more than one number 1 single in the '70s. (It was her third such hit.) Barbra & Neil were the top new duo of the year.

"Sweetheart Pop" also made some headway on the country charts. To capitalize on the song's success, RCA Records rushed out a duet between country artists Jim Ed Brown and Helen Cornelius. Some stations, however, had already added the Streisand/Diamond version, not suspecting there would be a country cover. Barbra and Neil's single was number 7 at WHN in New York, number 3 in requests. "It's a mass appeal song that shouldn't be limited to a pop format," stated the station's music director. At WHOO in Orlando, Florida, the program director decided to test both songs on the air and asked his listeners to vote on their favorite. Barbra and Neil won by a 2 to 1 margin. Other stations were less adventuresome. The Brown/Cornelius rendition was a Top 10 country hit; Streisand/Diamond reached number 70. Still, it was Barbra's only charting country single.

An enjoyable piece of "ear candy": Barbra and Barry Gibb team up for Guilty, 1980. The all-white theme was conceived by Barbra to be an acknowledgment of Gibb's unique contribution and on the day of the in-studio photography session she asked him to bring an extra white shirt—for her.

One complication caused by the single was that Barbra hadn't planned another major release until 1979. Columbia had previously denied reports that they intended to put a greatest hits package together for her anytime in the near future. Neil Diamond, on the other hand, was already in the studio so the new single fit conveniently into his plans. The only other option which allowed Streisand to take advantage of the situation was to actually record an entire LP with Diamond. Her work on *The Main Event* precluded any such undertaking; the compilation was okayed.

In December, the ads hit the periodicals and the LP hit the stores. "For the person who thought they had *everything*...everything *Volume 2*." Barbra's second greatest hits package entered the charts higher (a whopping number 7 in *Billboard*) than Volume 1 had peaked. *Greatest Hits/Volume 2*, in fact, remains Barbra's highest debuting LP. The album went quadruple platinum domestically and won several platinum certificates abroad.

Reviews:

"There's added pleasure in this album—the expertise with which Barbra shapes a ballad. Several tracks seem perfection, like the sad 'You Don't Bring Me Flowers' —which she shares with Neil Diamond—and the sweet 'Songbird.' Others, like the fervent gospel 'Sweet Inspiration'/'Where You Lead' or the sentiment of 'My Heart Belongs to Me,' don't reach incandescent levels, but the impact is exciting."

—*Seventeen*

"This is a terrific 'Best of' package from the golden-throated girl, including many of her big single successes in recent years like 'The Way We Were,' 'Stoney End' and the incomparable 'Evergreen.' It all kind of serves to say Streisand has a lot more to sing about and we can expect an endless flow of material from here. Recommended."

—*Hollywood Reporter*

FINAL NOTE: Good news and bad news. Good news first. "You Don't Bring Me Flowers" was nominated by NARAS for Record of the Year and Best Pop Vocal Performance by a Duo, Group or Chorus. Perhaps if Grammy voters had been allowed to cast their votes *after* Barbra and Neil's thrilling performance on the 1980 Awards show, the duo would have walked home with at least one citation.

In 1979, Gary Guthrie found it necessary to sue CBS Records. His only acknowledgment thus far for his work had been flowers from Barbra and a telegram from Neil when the tune hit number 1. The record company had considered offering a "finder's fee" but reportedly felt any exorbitant payment might be construed as payola. The dispute was settled out of court.

The most intriguing item to surface post-"Flowers" was the rumor of a motion picture pairing of Streisand and Diamond. Several scenarios were discussed, but none ever saw fruition.

The Main Event/Original motion picture soundtrack (JS 36115)

"The Main Event" / "Fight"
Produced, arranged and conducted by Bob Esty
Engineered and co-produced by Larry Emerine
Executive producer: Gary LeMel

In 1974, a young composer saw the dream of a lifetime crushed on the shores of negative criticism when his musical *My Name is Rachel Lily Rosenbloom and Don't You Ever Forget It* opened—and closed—off-Broadway. The subject of the musical? A fan's obsession with Barbra Streisand. "I've been in love with her since I was fifteen. I must have seen *Funny Girl* 43 times," Paul Jabara told the *Los Angeles Times*. "I knew her every breath on every song." As a teen, he'd even written a song about it: "Dear Miss Streisand." Devastated by the failure of his show, Jabara moved to Los Angeles to get work as an actor and he continued writing. At an audition for a bit part in *A Star Is Born*, he dropped off a tape of his music with the casting director. The next thing he knew he was signed with First Artists Publishing, hoping against all hope to one day get Barbra to sing one of his songs.

His introduction to Streisand didn't come directly from First Artists, however. A relentless promoter of his own material, Jabara cornered Donna Summer by locking her in the bathroom of a Puerto Rican hotel and not letting her out until she agreed to record his "Last Dance." Based on the immediate popular response to that song, First Artists' Gary LeMel asked Jabara to write something appropriate for *The Main Event*, the catch being that Barbra wasn't sure she wanted to sing another motion picture theme. In November of 1978, Jabara joined forces with Bruce Roberts to write and produce a demo of a song called "The Main Event," which LeMel played for Barbra "and she really didn't like it," he said. "She still hadn't decided to sing in the film, but if she was going to, that wasn't the song she wanted to do."

In fact, she had already composed a theme for *The Main Event* (a ballad) herself. Producer/arranger Bob Esty says that, in addition, David Shire worked with the Bergmans on a "Way We Were"-type ballad for the movie. Ultimately, Barbra felt, as Jon did, that a comedy about boxing should have an uptempo theme and that this was an ideal opportunity for her to tackle a contemporary dance tune. Fortified by Jabara's recent Oscar nomination for "Last Dance," Peters talked her into reconsidering the rejected Jabara/Roberts demo.

Barbra finally agreed to meet with the songwriters, but requested that the arranger of "Last Dance," Bob Esty, be invited as well. For various personal and professional reasons, Esty was a bit hesitant about working on the project. But he did want to meet Barbra, so, somewhat begrudgingly, he went along with his friends to her house. The meeting in Malibu did the trick for everyone. The Streisand fan got his introduction— "I was crazed," Jabara admitted. "When I got the map to her house, it was like getting the final clue in a treasure hunt." The reluctant arranger, who had expected "a tough, difficult lady to get to know," found instead that "she was very sweet, very nice, very accommodating…anything she could do…the opposite of what I had expected." And the producer and star got their song. "We played the song for her, and Jason, her son, started singing the song upstairs," Roberts recalls. "He was the one who really sold it [because] he loved it and [Barbra] listened to him."

Esty: "Then we got down to trying to make this 'Main Event' song work. The main thing Barbra felt was that this movie was about boxing and yet there wasn't a single word in the song about fighting or boxing or anything like that.…Paul and I had been working on a song called 'Fight,' which we intended to be a parody of the Village People. We'd just put it on the shelf, so [when Barbra articulated her objection] we both looked at each other and said, 'Have we got a song for you!' I played a few bars of it and she loved it. She said, 'This is what I want to do. Forget "Main Event"!'" Esty advocated combining both songs in a medley. That way, he said, "'You could use both songs as singles if you wanted to…and then have a longer, extended version for the clubs.' 'Oh,' she said, 'that's a great idea.'"

After mixing both "Main Event" and "Fight" as separate singles, plus an 11:35 dance cut and a 4:52 medley, the producer concurred with Columbia that the strongest single was the short medley. "The Main Event" / "Fight" was released on June 5, 1979. "A light, breezy opening moves into a fast-paced pop disco number, as Streisand handles the cute lyrics with her usual charm," Cashbox said. "It's no 'People,' but neither was it intended to be," opined Billboard. "Barbra is at her trendiest on this sizzling discotized track.…"

"Main Event" / "Fight" was an instant radio favorite. In Los Angeles it scaled over all other competition to become the most requested song at two power stations during its first week in release. One trade even speculated that it would be a top contender for "Record of the Year." The song, which hit number 3 in Billboard, was Barbra's fourth gold single and did indeed play an important part in the continued visibility for The Main Event. The album was released two weeks later and probably did as well as might be expected considering Barbra's limited involvement (her only contribution was the title tune). It, too, was certified gold, but it stopped at number 20.

Reviews:

"The showcase of this interesting soundtrack LP is the title tune which is written by Paul Jabara and Bruce Roberts. Streisand interprets it both as a ballad and a disco tune, and once again shows her enormous vocal range and versatility."

—Cashbox

Wet (FC 36258)

Produced by Gary Klein
Arranged by Lee Holdridge, Greg Mathieson, David Foster, Lalo Schifrin, Nick DeCaro and Charlie Calello
Recorded and mixed by John Arrias

In discussing the way in which she attacks recording an album, Barbra readily admits that sometimes the concept begins with the cover. With Wet, she saw herself in the outdoor jacuzzi Jon built in Malibu, surrounded by shades of lavender. The concept evolved into a selection of songs using water—tears, rain—as a backdrop. While Barbra started writing a tune incorporating some of these ideas, word was put out in June of 1979 that Streisand was looking for "wet" songs.

Ecstatic over an Academy Award for "Last Dance" and the golden status of "The Main Event," Paul Jabara set a new goal for himself: he wanted to bring his two favorite artists, Barbra Streisand and Donna Summer—the top-selling female vocalists of 1978—together on a project. "That would be the ultimate, having the two divas meet and work together. If anyone can arrange it, I can, and I think I can," he bragged to the Los Angeles Times. Jabara was already working on one song for the album, "Hurricane Joe." His partner, Bruce Roberts, had joined Carole Bayer Sager and Marvin Hamlisch on "Niagara," but Jabara thought they had a better card up their sleeves.

"Paul came over to my house and said, 'We've got to write something else. Let's write something for

The Grammy Award-winning team (for their duet on Guilty) celebrates with Billy Joel and Jon Peters at a party thrown by Columbia Records at the Four Seasons restaurant in New York, 1981.

Barbra and Donna.' It was a natural [impulse] to see if we could put those two together," Roberts says, "but pulling the thing off seemed so far-fetched that I didn't take it seriously [in terms of] writing the song under any kind of pressure. I just went to the piano and played the chords and we started to sing it. It was written in a very short period of time." In their enthusiasm, however, the songwriters had neglected to include the integral "wet" element, so they added a new verse: "It's raining/It's pouring/My lovelife is boring me to tears..." plus an occasional lyric declaring "pack his raincoat, show him out" and "no more rain/no more tears."

Part One of the plan was getting The Entertainment Company to consider the song; Part Two was bringing Streisand and Summer together. It is no secret that once again Jason Gould (then twelve-and-a-half) played a key role—because *he* wanted to meet the queen of the disco charts. For the second time, Jabara and Roberts traveled to the Malibu ranch to sell a song of theirs. "We went into a little tiny bedroom with a Fender Rhodes piano...Barbra, Jon Peters, Charles Koppelman, Donna, me and Paul," Roberts recalls. "I started to sing it as Barbra—I tried not to, but it came out that way. I didn't know what their reaction would be. You never know when you play a song for a producer or artist what the reaction will be. But they loved it. Some things are just meant to happen and here there were no stumbling blocks."

Wet was already in production. Although she had initially hoped for a change of pace by involving new producers (Bob Esty or Joe Wissert), Barbra stuck with The Entertainment Company's Gary Klein. Through Klein, she found a new engineer. John Arrias had been warned that with Streisand "you really have to be on your toes." His inauguration was a live date with a 55-piece orchestra (on "Wet," the song she co-wrote with David Wolfert and Sue

Barbra Streisand
MEMORY

"Memory" was embraced as an artistic triumph. "[It] is one of those achievements that have the unmistakable stamp of the classic on them," Peter Reilly wrote.

Sheridan). "Barbra walked in as we were rehearsing the orchestra—this is one moment she can't remember—dressed in purple, and she went straight into the vocal booth where I had everything set up for her. Right away, we had a headphone problem....It turned out it was because I gave her a mono mix and she likes to hear it in stereo; she likes to hear the 'openness' in her headphones. (Mono sounds much smaller.) So I worked out a technical way of giving her stereo and she said, 'Oh, there it is. Wonderful.' And from that day to today she has never raised her voice to me, never said a harsh word, she's always been super kind."

If there were any changes regarding her attitude in the studio, arranger Nick DeCaro says that, by the time they worked together on *Wet*, she probably was more trusting. "By then she was taking things more in stride. She'd worked with enough people to find producers, arrangers and musicians she trusted; therefore, she could let them do what they did best." One of the cuts DeCaro worked on was the Bruce

Roberts/Carole Bayer Sager/Marvin Hamlisch collaboration, "Niagara" —another live session. "There's something intangible that happens when you record live that doesn't happen when you overdub," he says.

Roberts laughs when he recalls that "When we wrote 'Niagara,' Barbra's response was 'Is anybody going to know what that means? And is it wet enough?' We said, 'Barbra , it's Niagara Falls. Its very popular and very wet.' On the day of the session itself, Barbra was late so Marvin asked me to sing the song. I got into the vocal booth and, with my back to the window, started doing a perfect impression of her....The string players thought I was crazy, everybody did. When the thing was over, I turned around and there she was in the control booth. Arms folded, glaring. I just panicked, and she put the speaker on and said, 'You do me better than I do.' She was very sweet. I was totally mortified."

The "Niagara" section yielded an even more memorable moment, says Roberts, when Barbra went to the piano with Hamlisch and he began to play "Over the Rainbow" as a tone poem. "And she just sat there with Marvin playing these odd, avant-garde, strange chords for 'Over the Rainbow' and sang the melody like a bird. It's really unfortunate there wasn't a tape recorder going because it was *the* most stunning performance I've ever heard. Ever. It was just one of those brilliant moments where all her artistry came together…and I feel very fortunate to have been there." It remained a private moment. Barbra was adamant about not recording the Garland standard.

The composer never found Barbra to be a prima donna. "I never experienced screaming fits," Roberts emphasizes. "I experienced extreme professionalism. She knew what she wanted, and if she saw that you couldn't give it, if you exposed an Achilles heel [by] lying or trying to make believe you could do something you couldn't, then she'd totally destroy that. There's nothing wrong with that. That's just being with it and saying 'Don't screw around.' She expected you to be professional, too.…I found her extremely bright, and her first instincts were always great. The very first feeling she would have would be right, and then she would go around asking everybody what their opinion was. Many artists do that. Getting 55,000 answers and being totally confused when *she* knows what's right for her."

In August, the creative team tackled the complexities of "Enough Is Enough." The sessions had all the forebodings of a logistics nightmare. On the evening before Streisand and Summer were to report to Crimson Recording Studios in Santa Monica, Donna Summer's engineer, Juergen Koppers, was recording the rhythm track at The Brothers' studio. After the musicians were dismissed it was discovered that one of the machines had fluctuated during recording and stretched the tape, rendering an important instrumental section completely useless. The entire track had to be re-recorded before Barbra and Donna showed up at 11:00 a.m. the following day. Then there was the problem of who was going to sing what. "The parts were not that well defined," Roberts admits. "They defined themselves in the mix of the record." Both singers were inevitably required to sing all the parts of the song.

An especially important ingredient to the success of the teaming was the respect the two artists gained for each other in the studio. Deflated somewhat by the "Yes-Barbra Syndrome," Barbra turned to Donna Summer for some quick pointers on singing dance tunes. Summers was taken aback. "You're Barbra Streisand," she said. "You're asking *me* how to sing?" John Arrias says the main obstacle was that Barbra tends to "back phrase" things. "She doesn't

sing on the beat, she sings after the downbeat. But for disco you have to be on top of the beat and that's what Donna was trying to impress on her." Because his friends were involved and he wanted to make sure everything was okay, Bob Esty also gave her a little unofficial coaching (much to the chagrin of Paul Jabara, who still blamed Esty for keeping him out of the "Main Event" sessions). "I was doing a Cher album and Barbra called me and said, 'What's going on? Something's weird here and I don't know what to do. Singing-wise, this duet is very strange and I don't know what to sing.' She was kind of disjointed…so I came in to help her get over that initial confusion."

By the end of the first day, with two producers, two engineers and assorted members of the two entourages in attendance, it became apparent that things would have to be streamlined in order for the duet to come off. "They never could quite feed off each other," Arrias states, "so they decided, 'Okay, let's try it individually. Donna singing to Barbra's scratch part and Barbra singing to Donna's.'" The separation spurred rumors of a political melodrama unfolding in the recording studio between the two camps. "I never felt Barbra and Donna were enemies at all. It was good, juicy gossip [but] it was not the artists, the women, who were responsible for this craziness," Roberts says. "I think it was everything that was going on around them, people trying to protect them. It turned out to be more of a business than an artistic venture, and you have to take that into consideration." Esty remembers coming into the studio and seeing "this guy smoking a cigar in the control room and just being obnoxious and saying, 'Doesn't matter what Streisand sings, it's a hit.' It was that kind of mentality.…People feeding off the situation."

Both singers being highly competitive, a little healthy rivalry was to be expected—but it did have its humorous moments. First, there were the "Lunch Wars" with Barbra and Donna taking charge of the catering and ordering elaborate gourmet spreads for the crew. The competition spread to who could hold the longest, hit the highest, note. "During one particular vocal session, Barbra and Donna were in the studio at the same time," Arrias reminisces. "At the end of the ballad section, they were going to simultaneously hit this note and it builds and builds for about seventeen bars. So they went for the note and held it and suddenly Donna falls right off her chair, right on her back and lay passed out on the ground— and Barbra was still holding the note. She stopped and we all went, 'What happened?' Barbra started laughing and then she thought, 'Oh, my God, she's really out!' Everyone was stunned. We all went rushing into the studio to see how she was. And then

Barbra and Alan and Marilyn Bergman watch Michel Legrand take the orchestra through a rehearsal during the Yentl *recording sessions, 1982.*

Donna started laughing. We still don't know to this day if it was a joke by Donna or if she actually hyperventilated." Barbra believes it was a joke. John Arrias isn't so sure; not only was Summer exhausted from her multi-day engagement at the Universal Amphitheatre, but she was also suffering from a cold. "If it was a joke, she did a great impersonation of someone passing out."

The situation progressed to the point where, when the two singers were recording separately, one would come in and lay down a track—and, listening to that track, the other singer would decide she needed to overdub a few lines in order to clarify *her* part. Bruce Roberts also brought in some friends (Luther Vandross, David Lasley) to add some punch to the background vocals by Julia, Maxine and Luther Waters. All in all, the actual recording, mixing and mastering of the 4:39 single, 8:19 album cut and 11:40 12-inch (re-mixed by Giorgio Moroder) at

a series of studios in Hollywood, Santa Monica and Malibu, cost an estimated $100,000 and took over 150 hours to complete. "I spent hours and hours and hours and hours mixing the song at Village Recorders' Studio D," Arrias confirms. To further illustrate the complexities, he says that at one point, "I turned around and counted fourteen people in the control room who all had to approve the mix: Walter Yetnikoff, Jon Peters, Gary Klein, Giorgio Moroder, Barbra and Donna, Paul Jabara, Bruce Roberts...everyone involved in the project was there during the mix."

Within the industry, the shrewd packaging of "No More Tears (Enough is Enough)" would be termed "high concept." But there were those who felt that although it might look great on paper, it wasn't necessarily what was best for either artist. The struggle between business people continued into the shooting of a photo for the picture sleeve. But the success of the single (released October 5, 1979) and the 12-inch (October 9, 1979) far overshadowed any conflict. *Record World* called the duet "an awesome tag team vocal exhibition." *Billboard*: "The two hottest female stars of the year combine talents here, taking turns on lead vocal and also dueting. The opening is a soft ballad, favoring Streisand's booming delivery; the ending is a frenetic disco rocker, giving Summer a bit more of the spotlight." It took very little time for the collaboration, which many have called the epitome of disco (and a harbinger of the format's ignominious fall from grace), to top charts internationally. It also earned a place on the charts as a Top 20 black hit.

In February of 1980, "Enough Is Enough" set another precedent. It was the first song to be certified separately for its gold single and 12-inch, each reaping over 1,000,000 units. *Wet* was released in mid-October. Recapturing Barbra's platinum status amidst the industry's worst recession on record, the album reached number 7 in *Billboard*. A second "wet" single, "Kiss Me in the Rain" backed with "I Ain't Gonna Cry Tonight" reached number 37 on the pop chart.

Reviews:

"On the surface, one might have figured that Miss Streisand, with her Broadway-schlock ballad background, was a long way from Miss Summer's low-life disco cum progressive-synthesizer sound. Yet not only do the two blend well on their duet, but the pairing also illuminates things about each of them....The Streisand album is a compendium of emotive ballads, only partly redeemed by Miss Streisand's undeniable gifts as a vocalist: her throbbing vibrato, her way of reaching up yearningly for high notes, her melodramatically confessional intimacies of style. The material sticks mostly to the watery metaphorical conceit of the title, and the arrangements are everything you ever wanted in the way of syrupy strings and tired movie-music clichés. Clearly, enough people have wanted such things to make Miss Streisand a millionaire many times over."
—*The New York Times*

Guilty (FC 36750)

Produced by Barry Gibb, Albhy Galuten and Karl Richardson
Arranged by Albhy Galuten, Barry Gibb and Peter Graves
Engineered and mixed by Karl Richardson and Don Gehman

Surprisingly, the Streisand/Summer teaming failed to receive any acknowlegement from NARAS. One reason could have been disco backlash. More to the point, though, was the fact that Barbra managed to top herself within that same voting year with an equally formidable collaboration.

If *Wet* wasn't as adventurous as one might have hoped, neither was it a throw-away effort, and the popular success of "Enough Is Enough" indicated there was still a great deal of latitude for experimentation within Barbra Streisand's career. By 1980, Barbra had spent nearly a decade reconciling the division between the traditional music of her early years and the contemporary rock-oriented music that threatened to pass her by. But even with the enormous success of the '70s and her acceptance by young music fans, most people felt she represented pop music's Old Guard.

Guilty placed her firmly on the cutting edge of today's music. It would be the definitive pop statement fans had been waiting for since *A Star Is Born*. Needless to say, no small part of its success was due to the commitment of its other key participant, Barry Gibb, who was still basking in the spotlight provided by the phenomenal success of the *Saturday Night Fever* soundtrack.

Joining the two artists had taken almost two years of political negotiations between Walter Yetnikoff, head of the CBS Record Group, The Entertainment Company's Charles Koppelman, the Robert Stigwood Organization, representing the Bee Gees, and Gibb's lawyers, who hoped to establish their client as a freelance producer and songwriter apart from his sibling group. Intimidated by the usual stories about the demanding, temperamental perfectionist, Gibb wasn't sure at first if he was making the right move. "I even called Neil Diamond to ask what it was like to work with her," Gibb told James Spada for *Billboard* magazine. "He had nothing but glowing reports, so I felt a little less scared." Another crucial factor was that "My wife told me to do it or she'd divorce me!"

Koppelman saw nothing wrong with another superstar teaming. He likened it to the movies where the right chemistry between stars can make "one + one = three." His Entertainment Company sent five demos to Gibb for consideration. "The songs had been chosen for Barbra ," said Gibb, "but my brother Robin and I didn't think any of them had the little bit extra that it takes to make a hit. We told her publisher that and they asked us to write five [new] songs." Two weeks later the pair submitted their tunes to Barbra and she liked them. "It was as easy as that. We hit it off straight away." With Barbra's encouragement, Gibb also worked on four additional songs for the second side; and out of his trunk he pulled a recent composition he thought fit her perfectly, "The Love Inside." Principal recording was to take place in New York, Hollywood and Miami. "Just call me when you're ready for me to sing," she said.

The call came in February of 1980. "We treaded on eggs until we actually got to know one another," Gibb said, "[but] working with her turned out to be wonderful. She wanted my ideas and she gave me a lot of leeway—but she also wanted me to listen to her ideas, which I was glad to do.... And she was a hard worker. She'd work from 7:00 a.m. until late into the night and during the breaks she'd be working on the script of *Yentl.*" Apart from her questioning a line from "Woman in Love" ("It's a right I defend") which she thought was much too strong for a pop song, Gibb confessed his major problem with Barbra was "[keeping] her away from the food so she'd keep singing!"

"This project could have been a disaster," Koppelman told *Billboard*'s Paul Grein. "You're dealing with a lot of egos here, mine included. And this wasn't one song, it was an entire album. But it went much smoother than any of us anticipated.... As the album progressed, it became more and more of a collective effort between Barbra and Barry."

That isn't to say that during the six months of work there weren't concerns that the album would present Barbra as the fourth Bee Gee or that she might overcompensate for that by insisting that her vocals dominate everything. But, as producer Phil Ramone notes, "a good producer knows how to leave Barbra's stamp on the record and not his own." Gibb's strength was that he crafted melodies where the arrangement didn't interfere with the artist's unique phrasing. With the exception of an occasional intrusion of the trademark Bee Gees falsettos (most glaringly on "What Kind of Fool"), *Guilty* retains a kind of timeless quality. It is, without a doubt, state-of-the-art pop and Columbia was quick to recognize its commercial value. "We could tell about halfway through that we had something very different than what she'd been doing and that it could be an extremely big album," Gibb told Paul Grein. They could also tell that two songs, "Carried Away" and "Secrets," weren't as strong as the rest of the material. Barbra asked for a replacement—and Gibb obliged with the album's title cut, "Guilty."

Wary of not overdoing the duet approach, the principals agreed that the first single should place Barbra securely out front. Ironically, one of the hooks of "Woman in Love" is the haunting background vocals by Denise Maynelli, Myrna Matthews and Marti McCall. The highly-anticipated single was released on August 29, 1980, and was an instant "add" at 60 percent of pop stations across the country. Early retail reports also indicated the teaming met with record-buyers' expectations. "Streisand's last two gold hits were manic discotized throw-aways," *Billboard* reported, "but here she soft-

ens the tempo for a restrained mid-tempo ballad. The Gibb sound is much in evidence, giving the record a dreamy pop feel."

More legal complications presented themselves before the LP could be released some five weeks later; Gibb was at odds with The Stigwood Organization over the split on royalties. That settled, *Guilty*—with its front and back cover portraits by Mario Casilli proudly announcing Barry Gibb's prominent participation—hit record stores in late September. On October 25, the album and single simultaneously topped charts nationwide (the LP alone was selling 400,000 units a week). A dozen countries from Norway to New Zealand would soon follow suit. Even as "Woman in Love," which sold almost two million singles domestically, approached number 1, Columbia planned a quick follow-up. "Guilty"/"Life Story" was released on October 21; three weeks later, it passed the 500,000 unit mark. "The brothers Gibb have come up with another surefire melody that sounds better with each listen," *Billboard* declared. The duet with Barry Gibb climbed to number 3 in the Hot 100 and was Barbra's second gold single from the album. "Woman in Love" spent 24 weeks on the chart (three at number 1), "Guilty" 22.

In January 1981, Walter Yetnikoff told the *Los Angeles Times* that the Streisand-Gibb collaboration had sold close to seven million LP's worldwide "and we still have more singles to put out." "What Kind of Fool"/"The Love Inside," the next Top 10 hit (and number 1 on the Easy Listening charts), was released on January 20, 1981. It became Barbra's eighth gold single. Eight months after the initial single release, "Promises" found its way to retailers; it peaked at number 48— but *Guilty*, by then certified quadruple platinum, was still in the Top 30. Between the album and the various singles, Columbia Records projected they'd sell 20 million units internationally. The LP even wound up a Top 10 favorite in the U.S.S.R.

Truly a charmed project in terms of industry, critical and public response, *Guilty*, was Streisand's biggest album ever.... until *The Broadway Album* challenged its position five years later.

Reviews:

"A triumph of star packaging... *Guilty* proves to be a sensational blending of talents, since the pair fill in each other's weaknesses while reinforcing their strengths. On the two duets they share, Mr. Gibb's breathy baritone, with its quivering falsetto, supports Miss Streisand's belting soprano, instead of competing with it. Miss Streisand responds to Mr. Gibb's gentleness by not pushing too hard, for a change, and as a result she strikes a much more

Listening to her performance of "The Way He Makes Me Feel."

listenable balance between crooning and belting than usual. It's her most human singing in years....As a pop confection celebrating the giddiest extremes of their star ethos, *Guilty* is just about perfect."

—*The New York Times*

FINAL NOTE: Grammy Award nominations were announced on January 13, 1981. *Guilty* was nominated for Album of the Year; "Woman in Love" for Record and Song of the Year, "Guilty" for Best Pop Vocal Performance by a Duo or Group. Industry observers considered *Guilty* a solid contender in each of the five categories. In a dead heat with the Kenny Rogers/Lionel Richie collaboration "Lady" and Frank Sinatra's rendition of "New York, New York," however, Adult Contemporary's "Old Guard" made way for newcomer Christopher Cross, who "sailed" away with Record, Album and Song honors. Bette Midler took home her second Grammy for her effecting performance of "The Rose." Barbra and Barry took home one Grammy (awarded off camera) for their duet.

"I wanted to produce [Barbra's] best-selling album, and I accomplished that," Gibb stated in 1983. "But, to me, none of the songs on [*Guilty*] match the greatness of some of the songs she's done with the Bergmans or 'People' or 'Evergreen.' I would love to work with her again. I have a lot of ideas for her [and] I'm pretty sure we could follow it with an even better album because we know each other better."

Memories (TC 37678)

"Memory" and "Comin' In and Out of Your Life"
Produced and arranged by Andrew Lloyd Webber

Other cuts previously released 1974-1980
Produced by Bob Gaudio, Gary Klein, Charlie Cal-

ello, Barbra Streisand, Phil Ramone, Barry Gibb, Albhy Galuten, Karl Richardson and Marty Paich

Regardless of whether or not critics felt *Guilty* was a truer test for Gibb or Streisand, continued activity surrounding the album helped to place Barbra on *Record World*'s poll as 1981's top female vocalist as well as top female crossover artist. And yet, if given her choice, she wouldn't have released any new product that year. After many heartbreaking setbacks and delays, *Yentl* was due to begin production early in '82 and Barbra was understandably concerned about concentrating her energies in that area. In the late summer of 1981, however, she received an urgent plea from her record company to consider a year-end offering; Columbia was reported to be "scrambling for superstar product" in the wake of a disappointing year commercially. "With Barbra, the complaint among the more stupid record company people is that she uses us," Peter Reilly states. "What is she using us for? To make money for us." She heeded Columbia's call. In the interest of time, both artist and record company settled on a package of previously-released ballads, plus "Enough Is Enough" (which in all likelihood wouldn't fit into a *Greatest Hits/Volume Three* compilation), a new solo rendition of "Lost Inside of You" (the song she wrote with Leon Russell for *A Star Is Born)*, and two new sides to be produced by Andrew Lloyd Webber in London that September.

"Comin' In and Out of Your Life," a no-holds-barred, power ballad in the tradition of "My Heart Belongs to Me," was one of several songs submitted to Barbra via The Entertainment Company. The other new composition was a poignant ballad from Webber's latest smash musical, *Cats,* then playing exclusively in London. After four years of speculation regarding whether or not Barbra would star in *Evita* (which he wrote with former partner Tim Rice), Streisand and Webber finally met at a performance of *Cats.* Before long, they were talking about a collaboration in the recording studio and "Memory," with lyrics drawn from T.S. Eliot's "Rhapsody on a Windy Night" and "Preludes," was selected as one cut she'd like to sing. From its majestic evocations to the purity of its emotion, the song had all the elements of a great Streisand song, and Barbra exploited it to its fullest. "She is sheer magic," Webber enthused.

Indeed, her recording of "Memory" was magical and one of the finest tests of her vocal range and ability. In his *Stereo Review* critique, Peter Reilly wrote that the song was a classic return to her roots. "In this performance, she seizes upon [the song] with the kind of hypnotic intensity that has been her particular strength from the first days of singing old standards in scuzzy Greenwich Village clubs....Proof of her musical taste, dramatic judgment and galvanic acting ability runs through the whole like a gold thread through russet velvet." The critic concluded that single performance expanded on her early excitement and stripped away the "high gloss lacquer" that had been laid down over much of her work in the '70s. "There is a lot of good music on those albums, and Barbra was enough of a professional to carry it off, but they were just adding to a body of work," he elaborates. "They weren't *events.*"

"Streisand is a great artist who is also a truly popular artist," he adds. "She needs to be heard like everybody else." "Memory" would give her the chance to reaffirm her standing with her early supporters as well as display to the newer ones what qualities differentiate her from the average pop singer.

"Comin' In and Out of Your Life," backed with the alternate version of "Lost Inside of You" produced by Gary Klein, was released on November 3, 1981. "Once the stores started stocking it," composer Bobby Whiteside observes, "you couldn't go into a record shop and find it. It went that fast." "Within three weeks the song was in the Top 30, but it lost momentum when the album was released in late November. The song, which many felt to be "a shoo-in" for the Top 10, stopped at number 11 in *Billboard*'s Hot 100 (considered the industry's most reliable chart) but made it to number 9 in *Cashbox*. In all likelihood, it was the album that did the single in: once fans had "Memory" there was decreasing interest in buying 45's of "Comin' In and Out of Your Life," which by comparison was perceived as a lesser effort.

Ironically, "Memory," the single supporters had demanded, struggled to a lackluster number 52 in *Billboard*. A Top 10 hit in England—as recorded by Elaine Page—it couldn't even best "Comin' In and Out" on the Easy Listening charts. The latter topped *Record World*'s chart; the former reached number 9. Airplay was the principal villain; radio apparently didn't know where to slot the song. Fans calling Top 40 radio stations found they weren't even serviced with the single and that critics had neglected to review it.

The good news was that *Memories* spent an impressive 100 weeks on the charts. The LP attracted much more than Streisand's substantial core audience as record buyers—in fact, casual admirers were more likely to buy the album because they didn't have all of the songs. "*Greatest Hits/Volume 2* sold four million; that still leaves countless millions of potential record buyers," *Billboard*'s Paul Grein reminds. "People often forget that point when they're

The promo sleeve for the first single from Yentl, *1983.*

talking about a multi-platinum record. They think that's covering the universe, and it really isn't. There are millions of people who are into pop music who don't necessarily have *Thriller* or *Rumours* or *Saturday Night Fever.*" Although it barely grazed the Top 10, domestically *Memories* was a double platinum album, nonetheless, and one of the bestsellers of the Christmas season.

In the United Kingdom—without the aid of a hit single—the compilation positioned itself on top of the charts as *Love Songs.* The foreign LP had four additional cuts: "Kiss Me in the Rain," "I Don't Break Easily," "Wet" and "A Man I Loved.

Reviews:

"This is superstar holiday product whose sole reason for being is that Streisand is a superstar, these are holidays and CBS needed product. Thus, we have the fourth CBS album appearance of 'The Way We Were'; the third of 'You Don't Bring Me Flowers,' 'My Heart Belongs to Me' and 'Evergreen.' The concept seems to be love songs, but Streisand's quin-

tessential love song, 'People' is not here, while her trendy disco foray, 'No More Tears' is (for those fans of the song who don't own Streisand's *Wet* album, Donna Summer's *On the Radio* LP, the seven-inch Columbia single or the 12-inch Casablanca disco disk). Streisand's singing is superb, the cover photo is striking, the two new cuts are lovely, but, to quote a line from a hit within, 'enough is enough.'"

—Billboard

FINAL NOTE: Despite a weak attempt by Barry Manilow to popularize the song, "Memory" is undoubtedly associated, first and foremost, with *Cats* and Barbra Streisand; it was the ideal pairing of the singer and the song. Further evidence of this surfaced in 1986 when, at the height of *The Broadway Album*'s success, *Memories* re-entered the Top 200. However, like "The Way We Were," Barbra's exquisite vocal was mysteriously overlooked by NARAS at Grammy nomination time.

Yentl (JS 39152)

Produced by Barbra Streisand, Alan and Marilyn

69

Although Barbra had recorded songs by Kim Carnes before, "Make No Mistake" was the only time they actually worked together in the studio.

Bergman
Associate producer: Michel Legrand
Post-production supervised by Phil Ramone

Soundtrack arranged and conducted by Michel Legrand
Engineered by Keith Grant

"The Way He Makes Me Feel" and "No Matter What Happens" (studio versions)
Produced by Phil Ramone and Dave Grusin
Arranged by Dave Grusin
Engineered by Don Hahn

Throughout 1982 and 1983, Barbra was refining the actual elements of her directorial debut, but her work on the *Yentl* soundtrack dates back even further. The dramatic property had undergone many subtle changes since she acquired it late in 1968. One transformation she had studiously avoided—perhaps because of her desire to be known as more than a musical performer—was a musical one. What's more, the author Isaac Bashevis Singer was adamant in his belief that the inclusion of *any* music would be an intrusion. "As a matter of fact, I never imagined Yentl singing songs," he wrote in *The New York Times*. "The passion for learning and the passion for singing are not much related in my mind. There is almost no singing in my works." By the time Barbra pacted with Orion Pictures in November of 1979, however, a decision had been made to add music.

"From the start we felt that music was the best way to heighten the emotion of Singer's short story," Marilyn Bergman said, "because Yentl is a character with a secret...[and] after her father dies, there is nobody to whom she can reveal her essential self. [But] we thought about it for a long time before making the suggestion to Barbra." According to Barbra, the Bergmans were the first people she asked to read the story. Because of their mutual attraction to it, as well as their interest in Jewish tradition and culture, they were among the first people invited to join the project. "The idea of working on material we felt close to with people we felt close to was something we could not pass up," Bergman continued.

Work on the music began in earnest in 1980 when Michel Legrand was brought in to write the score. "I don't know anyone who writes better for Barbra's voice than Michel," Alan Bergman said. "He flies at the same altitude, he takes chances." Legrand is also a prolific writer of sophisticated romantic music—not the first composer one might think of in terms of writing traditional ethnic music, but someone fully capable of researching the period to discover what elements of Middle European folk and Hebraic music might be incorporated in his work.

The foursome experimented with music that was recognizably Jewish in character. Some of this music was intended for the background (pentatonic chanting in a synagogue, folk songs sung in a tavern, the wedding music). Some, such as a reprise of "Where Is It Written," with Barbra singing a cantorial refrain, would not make it into the finished score; but the prayer preceding "Papa, Can You Hear Me?" did. "What Barbra was looking for was a feeling of magic, a fairytale-like quality," Legrand explained. "Our emotions do not belong to a particular century—happiness, sadness, whatever...they are timeless experiences."

In the past, Barbra has been accused of taking a very difficult approach to something that can be accomplished with relative ease. Few of the delays leading up to production on *Yentl* were of her own making—yet they worked to her advantage, both on film and in the soundtrack. Streisand, Legrand and the Bergmans "met with the same attitude" on *Yentl*, dedicating themselves to working through each and every problem until they were satisfied with the entire piece of work. What evolved was a musically diverse score that matched Yentl's soul *and* Barbra Streisand's.

"None of us wanted to make a conventional musical," Marilyn Bergman stated. With the inevitability of Yentl as the sole narrator of the story, a number of possibilities began to present themselves. The interior monologue expanded to an even more innovative concept: when Yentl was alone and free to express herself as a woman she sang aloud; when she was out in public, her thoughts could only be heard by the audience. In addition, the action wouldn't stop to make way for song. Instead, the music was woven into the fabric of the narrative. "We worried at first about how audiences would react to this device," Barbra admitted, "but there was really no better way to reveal Yentl's unique perspective." Later, with the casting of Mandy Patinkin, a tenor with "the voice of an angel," the collaborators did contemplate utilizing his abilities more fully. But, he later said, "The original conceit was better....I felt a little frustrated at first...then I realized that if I sang, *everybody* in the movie should sing. You would have the bookseller singing and the father singing and the guys in the yeshiva singing, 'Oh, we love to learn, learn, learn...'"

The work progressed quickly. There were four or five scenes within the story that seemed to demand a musical point of view. "We would work up a scenario or a little for [those] songs," Alan Bergman told James Spada, reporting for *Billboard* magazine, "and [then] Michel would come up with five or six melodies." The first day the threesome met at the

Emotion, *1984.*

Bergman's home, Legrand played several melodies he'd already written for them; one of them became "Where Is It Written." With the exception of "This Is One of Those Moments" (which was a statement the Bergman's felt strongly about making and a late addition to the score), most of the lyrics were dictated by the uniquely vivid construction of Legrand's music. "In the case of 'Papa, Can You Hear Me?'...I know that phrase was never used until those notes were played," Bergman added.

"To give you an idea of how the concepts for the songs came about," Barbra related, "on one occasion I observed a couple I know and felt, 'This man is so lucky. He has a wonderful woman who adores him, takes care of his needs, handles his business and brings him eggs rancheros in bed. Why wouldn't a man want a woman like that. If I were a man, I would, too!' And that was the beginning of the song, 'No Wonder.'"

While Barbra struggled to find a home for her orphan production, she found that she could always go upstairs to the Bergman's music room and hear the latest revisions to her score. There is no doubt that this was one period of her life she derived great pleasure out of singing. Often, their sessions together were recorded—for future reference and for posterity. Preserved on these tapes are discarded songs such as "Several Sins a Day," a song which juxtaposed the dramatic versus comic sides of Yentl's predicament ("As God is watching/I'm committing several sins a day/And I commit them/Even as I'm sitting down to pray"); a slow, dreamy version of "Tomorrow Night," sung to Hadass; and "The Moon and I" ("The moon and I/We know each other well/I'm safe beneath its light), which was later replaced in the sequence of songs by "No Matter What Happens."

The soundtrack was recorded at Olympic Recording Studios in London prior to the April 1982 start date for principal photography on the film. By then, the song score had evolved into a full musical score, including background elements such as traditional cantorial singing and two new folk songs (one tavern round featured Mandy Patinkin in the background). The sessions allowed Barbra a great deal of flexibility in her vocals because each new performance was sung live to a new orchestral track. It was an unusual way to record—the economics of recording usually requires that the orchestral track be set first (and the musicians sent home) and *then* the singer is left to try and create a free, spontaneous vocal.

Following the film into post-production in Fall of '82, Legrand spent two weeks digitally re-recording the orchestra at EMI-Elstree in order to deliver quality audio for the album that could approximate the movie's lush soundtrack. The experiment didn't work. Meticulous to the end, in 1983 Barbra hired Phil Ramone to supervise post-production work on the soundtrack (at Lion's Share Studios in Los Angeles) and to produce a series of pop singles. Ramone, 1981's Producer of the Year, hadn't worked with Barbra since they shared the commercial breakthrough of *A Star Is Born* in 1976. Although the work he did in the intervening years was extremely satisfying, he looked forward to the chance of working with Barbra again. "She called me a couple of times from London to discuss things that were going on with *Yentl* and how deeply she was involved as director/producer," he says. "I stopped several projects I was working on and said I'd like to help her in any way I could."

The problem the record company found with the soundtrack was that there was no single release to hook promotion of the album on to. In the interest of historical authenticity, the producers had taken care not to use any instruments that weren't in existence prior to 1903. "That's okay for the movie," Ramone told the *Los Angeles Times,* "but Barbra wants to put some of these songs on the pop market—obviously, they have to be updated [and] produced in a way that fits the current market." Ramone and his co-producer, Dave Grusin, saw their work as styling an "encore," so to speak, for Barbra to come back and do a few songs as the mature, contemporary vocalist. "We did not want to destroy the wondrous things that happened to Yentl throughout her growth in the picture. I hope we succeeded," he said. "Besides checking all the ads and everything else she had to do, it's amazing we got this record out of her."

Early in October '83, Don Hahn was paged to engineer the new cuts at A&M Studios. "Papa, Can You Hear Me?", "The Way He Makes Me Feel," "No Matter What Happens" and "Piece of Sky" all had new arrangements by Dave Grusin. (Legrand had elected to remain in Paris.) Hahn was immediately impressed by the incredible control Barbra exercised over her voice. "You don't need a limiter [an electronic device that catches the voice as it gets louder or softer] with her," he says. "I'm not sure which song it was—maybe 'No Matter What Happens'—but I remember she came into the control room and wanted to know why her voice disappeared on the climactic phrase. She asked, 'Have you got a limiter on me?' I told her no. 'Okay,' she said, 'I'll fix it.' And she did, because she'd just backed off too much before. She knows how to control the microphone."

Since *Yentl* was such a passionate expression of herself, one thing Barbra couldn't always control was her own emotions. "'Papa, Can You Hear Me?' was a very emotional song; the lyric meant so much to her,"

Hahn elaborates. "When she got to the end of the song ['Papa, how I miss you/Kissing me goodnight'], she just started crying. She really broke up. I looked up at her and closed the mike, and then someone (Jon or the Bergmans) went into the studio to comfort her. It was very, very emotional. We left her alone. Half an hour later, she was ready to continue and we went on to the next thing."

Unfortunately, neither "Papa, Can You Hear Me?" nor "Piece of Sky," with its jazzy, uptempo arrangement, made the final cut. "The Way He Makes Me Feel" was released October 12, 1983. "This love song in the classic MOR ballad tradition gives no hint at the offbeat nature of the movie's plot," *Billboard* said in its critique. "It does give the singer a vehicle for an achingly wistful performance on her first single release in over a year." After seven weeks on the charts, the single stalled at number 40—though on Adult Contemporary stations "The Way He Makes Me Feel" was a definite charttopper. *Billboard*'s Paul Grein feels that the song may have been held back by the fact that it lacked the sort of rock undercurrent that's such a part of Contemporary Hit Radio "and by the fact that *Yentl* was perceived—rightly or wrongly—as an unsuccessful project. It might have done better if it had simply been the first single from her new album."

The LP, with its double-gate packaging and dedication "to my mother for understanding the dedication to my father," did much better. According to the *Hollywood Reporter,* the album's first pressing of 600,000 copies sold out during its first week in the nation's record stores. In 1984, *Yentl* would break into the Top 10, resting at the ninth position long enough for a platinum certification and a NARM nomination for Best-selling Soundtrack. In an era of Michael Jackson, The Police and "Total Eclipse of the Heart," Barbra's risky, "offbeat" venture still managed to propel her into the Top 5 listing of Female Pop Album Artists (with Cyndi Lauper, Linda Ronstadt, Madonna and Tina Turner). The album's second single, the fervent soundtrack version of "Papa, Can You Hear Me?", was released in February. It never got into the Hot 100.

Reviews:

"Some Streisand records are so self-conscious in their commerciality that she seems to be slumming; here, she's aiming higher and reaching deeper inside herself than she ever has before, with smashing results. More artists should follow their hearts as Streisand has here."

—*Billboard*

"Composer Michel Legrand and Lyricists Mar-

ilyn and Alan Bergman have constructed the score as Yentl's running Talmudic commentary on the genesis of her womanly desires. (That's why Patinkin doesn't sing.) The songs begin in a liturgical mode, heavy on recitative and minor chords. As Yentl enters the real world of passion and deceit, the melodies become more secular, and by midpoint, when Yentl's thoughts turn from intellectual to sexual love, the songs are swimming strongly in the American pop mainstream. It is the most romantic, coherent and sophisticated original movie score since *Gigi* a quarter-century ago; and its treacherous glissandi and searching wit find their ideal interpreter in Streisand's incredible Flexible Flyer of a voice. After two decades of hard work, that voice is still as smooth as mercury poured over dry ice."

—*Time*

FINAL NOTE: Ironically, the most criticized area of *Yentl* was the one that had the least problem being recognized by the motion picture industry. The musical score, "The Way He Makes Me Feel" and "Papa, Can You Hear Me?" were all nominated for Academy Awards. *Yentl* took home its only Oscar for Best Original Song Score. "I'm very grateful for this," Marilyn Bergman said in her speech. "I'm very grateful, too, for the privilege and experience of having worked on *Yentl* which is a story of a woman with a dream, a woman with a struggle. And life has a way of imitating art in very interesting ways. We worked in an atmosphere of creativity, of collaboration, of excitement, energy, synergy…that allowed us to do our best work, I think. And for that I thank Barbra Streisand." Enthused Michel Legrand: "We spent years of love, and I'm ready to do it again anytime."

Emotion (OC 39480)

Produced by Maurice White, Barbra Streisand, Richard Baskin, Charles Koppelman, Albhy Galuten, Richard Perry, Bill Cuomo, Kim Carnes and Jim Steinman
Arrangements by Maurice White, Robbie Buchanan, Martin Page, Brian Fairweather, Michel Colombier, Bill Cuomo, Bobby Whiteside, Jim Steinman, Albhy Galuten, James Newton Howard and Lee Holdridge

Recorded and/or engineered by Jeremy Smith, Dennis McCade, John Arrias, Jack Joseph Puig, Gary Skardina, Niko Bolas, Jim Dorfsman, Mick Guzauski and Ed Cherney

"Most people dream of romance while listening to music, but I think of other artists who could sing the same song better."

—Charles Koppelman

Collaborating with Stephen Sondheim on seven out of eleven cuts for The Broadway Album, *Barbra encountered an artist whose concern for detail was as acutely tuned as her own.*

With Somewhere *producer David Foster, 1985.*

"There are people out there who actually respect Streisand as an artist, but this should cure them."

—Joel Selvin
San Francisco Chronicle

Barbra wanted her next recording project to be something totally different from the all-consuming *Yentl.* Throughout 1983, rumors ran rampant that her next album would be produced by longtime friend Quincy Jones, and include a duet with Michael Jackson. Culture Club's Boy George was also reported to be working on material for her. In 1984, the Quincy Jones angle appeared to bear fruit when Liz Smith told her readers Barbra had recorded "Grace," the specially-commissioned theme Jones had written for the Olympic gymnasts. The truth was that not only did Barbra *not* record the composition, but the very much in-demand producer was unable to clear up his schedule in time and had to turn The Entertainment Company deal down.

The music company already had another kind of adventure in mind. Why not surround Barbra with a colorful assortment of producers, songwriters and arrangers and put a diversity of feelings and emotions on vinyl? Artists from Joni Mitchell to Dennis De-Young of Styx were invited to submit material. One of the first producers brought into the project was Earth, Wind & Fire's Maurice White, then fresh from producing Jennifer Holliday's debut LP. He was asked to produce three sides. In November of '83 Barbra met composer Richard Baskin *(Nashville, Welcome to L.A.).* He would contribute to one Maurice White production ("When I Dream") and co-produce and co-write "Here We Are At Last" with Barbra . Following their success with "Comin' In and Out of Your Life," Bobby Whiteside and Richard Parker sent two or three new tunes to Charles Koppelman. Streisand's first pop album in four years gave Koppelman the opportunity to re-submit these to her; Barbra chose "Best I Could."

At the suggestion of Jon Peters, John Cougar Mellencamp was brought in to help Barbra flesh out her lyrical idea on a song. A few days after their first meeting, Mellencamp delivered a melody and urged her to complete the lyrics. It was, admittedly, not her forte, but she thought it might be fun to try. Other superstar talents asked to work on the album included Richard Perry, then enjoying renewed success with the Pointer Sisters; producer/songwriter Jim

Steinman, also riding a wave of success with "Total Eclipse of the Heart" (Bonnie Tyler) and "Making Love Out of Nothing at All" (Air Supply); Kim Carnes; and Bee Gees producer Albhy Galuten.

With vocal and rhythm tracks being recorded and mixed at a dozen studios—eleven in the Los Angeles area and two in New York—and the complications of nine different producers and countless musicians, composers, arrangers and engineers, *Emotion* easily ran the risk of allowing "too many cooks" to spoil the broth. Ultimately, it became Barbra's responsibility to provide the continuity. After every recording session she took home cassettes on each vocal. "She always wants to hear all of the vocals she's done," engineer John Arrias says. "Every time she does a vocal you make a cassette....If she does eighteen vocals, I put each on the cassette and then she listens to every one on the way home. And she has such perfect recall that she remembers every take, every inflection. That's why she likes working with me—because I also have a good memory when it comes to her vocals, the different instrumental tracks and how to put things together." Arrias took it upon himself to assume the unofficial position of "executive engineer," because, he says, "someone had to coordinate all of that material in order to compile and master the album, and make all of the cuts sound like they were recorded at the same place."

After the album had been mixed, Barbra decided there was a section on "Heart Don't Change My Mind" she wanted to change. "Maurice (White) was in San Francisco working on another project," the engineer recalls, "and he couldn't come down to work on it, so we called him [instead]. Barbra wanted a certain section of the song to have a short string passage...and at the end of the song she wanted her vocal to continue with the orchestra—Maurice had turned her vocal off." Arrias re-mixed the song with Jeff Lorber adding some strings on the synthesizer. "Barbra has a very sensitive ear. Her ability to hear things amazes me sometimes," Arrias smiles. "Like she'll hear in her vocal a pitch bend. 'Don't you hear that? It's out of tune.' And I'm listening to the whole note whereas she's listening to the last itty-bitty part of the note...a little trill or inflection that goes by so fast it's nearly impossible to tune your ears to it. So you end up just trusting her. You say, 'If *you* hear it, if it bothers you, let's try another one and do it until it's right. Until it doesn't bother you anymore.'

"I've seen her take an arrangement that she's never heard before, go out and sing it with the whole orchestra there, and then stop and say, 'I hate it. Let's re-do it.' And she'll go over to the piano with the producer or arranger and sing all the parts she wants the orchestra to play. She'll tell them, 'The violins should be soaring right here [and she'll sing something]; the cellos should be doing this and moving very fast; and the drums like this.' It's done in a general sense with very descriptive terms: airy, light...She'll paint you a picture."

The all-star *Emotion* was "an enormously expensive album to produce" for all the obvious reasons. Witness a sampling of the "studio musicians" employed on various cuts: Paulinho da Costa, Leland Sklar, Michel Colombier, Roy Bittan, Max Weinberg, Rick Derringer, Russ Kunkel, Steve Lukather, Don Felder, James Newton Howard, Jeff Porcaro...plus the Pointer Sisters as back-up. The cost did not bridle the Columbia Records hierarchy, though. They were sure Barbra had brought home another multi-hit album á la *Guilty*. Salesmen took demos out into the field declaring the LP to be even better than the first single, Jim Steinman's "Left in the Dark," revealed. A confident Streisand and her new beau, Richard Baskin, previewed the album at New York's Hard Rock Cafe to enthusiastic response from the patrons. "Overall, there appears to be little doubt that *Emotion* is destined for tremendous retail and radio success," *Cashbox* confirmed.

On September 5, 1985, "Left in the Dark" ominously trumpeted the album's imminent release. Its "B" side was "Here We Are At Last," the ballad Barbra had written for *The Main Event*, with new lyrics by Richard Baskin. (It would back the album's third single, too.) The single debuted at number 81 on *Billboard*'s Hot 100. With strong sales but little airplay, it hit a premature peak (number 50) five weeks later—the video, shot in late September, got its broadcast premiere the week "Left in the Dark" lost its bullet in the trades.

Emotion was released the first week in October 1984 and, contrary to the sluggish performance of the single, made the expected jumps up the chart—until it snagged at number 19. A strong second single would have given it the push it needed to break into the Top 10. There was some discussion about releasing the title track (Barbra had already left to shoot the accompanying video in London), but the general feeling was that "Make No Mistake, He's Mine," the duet with Kim Carnes, was a better choice. That selection, *Billboard*'s Paul Grein points out, may have been seen as vital to give Streisand's core Adult Contemporary audience "a record that they would be comfortable with." What that thinking overlooked was the strong critical and popular sentiment for the Maurice White material: "Heart Don't Change My Mind" for CHR, "Time Machine" as a dance single and/or the jazz fusion of "When I Dream" for more sophisticated A/C stations. Equally perplexing was the unexplained delay between the demise of "Left in the Dark" and the release of "Make No Mistake" on November 28. The single followed its predecessor's path to a dismal showing at 51.

The third and final single, the Richard Perry-produced title cut, was released on February 13, 1985. Supported by an energetic video—which was a requested favorite on MTV (but, unfortunately, exclusive to that cable outlet for several weeks)—and Barbra's solo 12-inch (another belated release), the single crawled to an unspectacular number 79, spending two weeks on the charts. All in all, it was Barbra's worst chart performance since her commercial transition in the early '70s. Surprisingly, the LP still managed a platinum certification. "Barbra has the capacity to be a very 'hip,' contemporary artist," composer Bruce Roberts insists. "She still is. The material is not, and the way the records sound certainly isn't as contemporary as it could be...the proof of which is in the sale of *Emotion*. Naturally, she'll sell platinum. But you don't expect that from Barbra Streisand; you expect her to sell *five* million—not stretch to get one."

Reviews:

"[*Emotion*] makes up in diversity what it lacks in consistency....The common thread holding the album together is Streisand's imagination....The album's classiest cut is 'Here We Are at Last,' a wide-screen ballad that Streisand wrote and produced with her companion, Richard Baskin. The song has a romantic, after-hours mood and a sophisticated melody that signals Streisand's maturation as a composer....The album's gravest misjudgment is 'Left in the Dark,' a bloated melodrama written and produced by Jim Steinman....Streisand should be setting trends in pop, not merely following the charts and working with whoever lands a hit record. It may be time for Streisand to settle on one producer...and pour her time and talents into an album that will be her *Thriller*, a bold artistic statement to push her into the leadership role in pop that's hers if she decides to take it."

—*Los Angeles Times*

FINAL NOTE: If *Emotion* was perceived as a "formularized, predictable pop effort" from Streisand, the same cannot be said for Columbia's peculiar handling of the album. Totally lacking in coordination, and always two or three weeks off in their timing, the sales force appeared to lose steam around the same time as the first single did. "There *were* some strange laws in effect for the promotion of that album," Grein agrees. But the chart analyst doesn't think there was any conspiracy on the record company's part to bury it. "A record company will promote anything they think will make money for them," he says. "They don't care if it's Michael Jackson or REO Speedwagon. That's not a significant factor when you talk about Streisand. I think the biggest problem with *Emotion* was the failure of the first single. And that could have been predicted if the people who chose it as the first single were more aware of the declining pattern of Jim Steinman's record releases. 'Total Eclipse' went number 1. 'Making Love Out of Nothing at All' went to 2—that's still real strong. But then 'Read 'Em and Weep' by Barry Manilow went to 18. That's quite a drop-off...and Bonnie Tyler's 'Holding Out for a Hero' went to 34; it was the least successful of his first six singles. So I think radio programmers and the public had just tired of those melodramatic, bombastic epics—especially coming this time from *the* superstar in pop music. You expect more [from her] than being fifth in line on a formula. It wasn't a totally unreasonable assumption to think 'Left in the Dark' would be a hit, but what was the point of Barbra Streisand doing tired Bonnie Tyler retreads?"

Grein feels this was additionally complicated by a loss of interest in superstar teamings. "Whatever you think of 'No More Tears,' there was a tremendous appeal to it just because it paired this almost legendary figure with the current hot singer. But after Barbra did it with Donna and Neil and Barry, the teaming itself was no longer enough to insure success because it was no longer considered novel. Especially when she paired with Kim Carnes three years after Kim's career had peaked (and Carnes had recently exploited that gimmick herself with Kenny Rogers and James Ingram on 'What About Me?')....A lot had changed in pop music betwen 1980, the year of *Guilty*, and 1984. I mean, there was a revolution—namely MTV. In 1980, the hottest trend in music was Adult Contemporary: Kenny Rogers, Barbra Streisand and Christopher Cross were the biggest acts in pop that year. But the market changed radically and was much less sympathetic to the midstream artist in '84. And with the enormous impact that MTV had, Barbra was really out in the cold in terms of the most important single promotional vehicle there is today."

Above and beyond these changes in the marketplace, there was, perhaps, a growing feeling that Streisand was more of a reactor than an innovator. "I guess it's Barbra's fate to be popular in the rock era," Grein concludes, "when all artists are sort of judged by rock standards—which isn't fair, of course. I wonder how Bing Crosby and Frank Sinatra would fare in a market where 95 percent of the critics are rock critics, not pop and certainly not A/C. They have little understanding of or appreciation for Adult Contemporary, and not a whole lot for pop....Strei-

A heartfelt reading of "If I Loved You."

sand does take some critical abuse because she isn't Prince or Bruce Springsteen."

"Streisand is practically the Picasso of pop singers,"Robert Kemnitz of the *Los Angeles Herald-Examiner* wrote in 1977. "She alternates her blue periods with a unique impressionism that becomes a refreshing balance of the abstract and the obvious....And although her huge success might make her seem cold and impersonal to some people, she had a streak of the truth in her as big as her voice....She is almost incapable of making a bad album. [My] only gripe is that she hasn't really made a great album in a long, long time."

The Broadway Album (OC 40092)

Produced by Barbra Streisand, Peter Matz, Richard Baskin, Bob Esty, Paul Jabara and David Foster
Orchestrated and arranged by Peter Matz, Barbra Streisand, Richard Baskin, Randy Waldman, Jeremy Lubbock, Bob Esty, Paul Jabara, Alexander Courage, David Foster and Sid Ramin
Recorded, engineered and/or re-mixed by Don Hahn, John Arrias and Humberto Gatica

Executive producers: Barbra Streisand and Peter Matz

The one advantage of Barbra's predicament in early 1985 was that she no longer had to be a slave to the demands of Contemporary Hit Radio. "She can do whatever she wants now and not worry about radio so much," says Grein. As the failure of *Emotion* became all too apparent, critics and admirers pushed for Streisand to exhibit some of the brilliance and commitment that had characterized her early career.

"Here's what she needs," David Tipmore speculated in a 1976 *Village Voice* review, "a hot album conceived as a total embrace of B. when she made her first round of auditions in New York. The album *must* include the reintroduction of the perfect Peter Matz as her arranger-conductor and a small cover shot of B. exactly as she appeared at her high school graduation. Nothing else. Ambition intact with absolutely no glamour."

The irony was that she had been trying to get such an album off the ground for years. But Columbia Records was very happy with her positioning in the contemporary market and had no interest in an album of show tunes. Although she certainly could have forced the issue, Barbra chose not to for the time being. She continued to make records that added to her commercial reputation—if not her personal one. *Emotion* gave her sufficient reason—and leverage—to make a change. Her artistic integrity was in question. "Anybody could have done the songs on [that] album as well or better than I could have done them," she told Stephen Holden. "It was time for me to do something I truly believed in."

79

Her point was won even before returns on the album were in. "At that time in her life, Barbra really had very little direct dialogue with Walter Yetnikoff and Al Teller or anyone like that," Marty Erlichman states. "Jon was doing these things. But she picked up the phone and called them to say that she really disliked 'Left in the Dark.' She didn't like it on the album and certainly felt it shouldn't be a single. She wanted it removed. CBS told her that they [Yetnikoff and Teller] not only loved the song, but the whole company loved it: A&R, everyone. And they were so emphatic in their belief in the song that she said, 'Okay. But I'm doing it under duress.' Because she was wrong about 'Woman in Love' and it became a big hit, so she conceded that maybe she was wrong again and she allowed the single to come out. [Its non-acceptance] was the motivating force for her going back to *The Broadway Album*."

"We were at her house at Christmas," Peter Matz told Paul Grein, "and she said she was going to go ahead with the project. I always felt very strongly that she was right to do it and that it was a good idea." Once she made up her mind that a new direction was in order, there was to be no compromise; her next album would be a return to the music of her youth. "This is the music I love, it is where I came from, it is my roots," she said.

The news did not excite Columbia executives, who were equally adamant in their belief that the only thing Streisand's last album lacked was top-notch material. It is no secret that people who had formerly been up-front in their public support of Barbra threw up their hands in light of her decision. Two ideas seemed to be at the heart of their thinking: 1) Despite record-buyers' acceptance of *What's New*, Linda Ronstadt's album of Big Band standards, there were many people in the industry who considered it strictly a "non-recurring phenomenon" —as evidenced by the disappointing support for Ronstadt's follow-up LP, *Lush Life;* and 2) Barbra was something of a non-recurring phenomenon herself. The many elements that went into her success were too complicated to explain, let alone try to duplicate. But the temptation to distill these intangibles into a formula was enormous. Columbia felt that what both the record company and artist needed more than anything was a good, solid superstar teaming.

Obviously, Barbra wasn't having any of it—not any more. Her forthrightness in taking the responsibility upon herself to make a change (as opposed to manipulating the record company into thinking it was *their* idea), coupled with the feeling by some that *Emotion*'s demise had signalled a number of layoffs within the company (and that Streisand didn't care what happened at Columbia as long as her film career was going well), undoubtedly stirred up some resentment in Columbia's mid-to-lower staff ranks. Many more surprises were in store for them before the year was through.

In March, Barbra officially invited Peter Matz to join the project as executive producer, conductor and arranger. His first task would be to help her sort through the selections. "Barbra had already gone through a tremendous amount of material trying to find the right songs," he remembers, "so there was a strange kind of abstract shape to the album before I came in. There was a stack of albums and sheet music a mile high in the house—all of the music from all of the shows as far back as you could think. Cole Porter, the Gershwins, Harold Arlen, Rodgers & Hart, Rodgers & Hammerstein, Lerner & Loewe…plus lesser-known shows and composers. When I got involved with the project, it was down to maybe a hundred songs and then it got down to fifty. It was a complete range of songs covering many different styles. If you looked at them and said, 'What has this one got to do with that one?' they have nothing in common except that they are all songs she feels in some way attracted to or touched by.

"The thing that really determined whether or not there was something magical about a song was Barbra saying, 'What is this song about? Let's look at this.' And then we'd go to the piano and I'd play it and she'd would say, 'Yeah. Let's pursue that. Let's investigate that song.' And we'd put it in Pile A. And we'd go through maybe twenty others. Sometimes she just wasn't affected by them and they were discarded. On the other hand, there were some songs we spent months trying to find a way to do them.

"A good example is 'Some People.' *Gypsy* is one of Barbra's favorite shows and it's certainly one of mine. We must have spent two months turning that song inside out. Liza Minnelli does it in her act and we listened to a recording of that—not only for how good it is, but for how *not* to do it; we needed to find a different way. (During that search Barbra also phoned Liza to discuss the song in further detail.) Then we put it together with 'Rose's Turn'…that was Barbra's idea, actually. We played it on the piano and sang it and then left it for three days and came back to it and tried a different rhythm. We never did figure out a way to do 'Some People' so that it sounded fresh. Everybody had too much respect for Ethel Merman to just duplicate the way she did it in the original show."

The single most important influence on the album was the selection of ten songs from Stephen Sondheim's catalogue. As the composer of a diverse array of musically and lyrically complex work, from *West Side Story* (lyrics only) to *Sweeney Todd* (words and music), Sondheim is considered the most important voice in contemporary musical theater. Barbra had recorded only two Sondheim songs in the past; "There Won't Be Trumpets," a last-minute deletion from *Anyone Can Whistle*, didn't make it into her catalogue of releases, but a snippet of "Small World" from *Gypsy*—co-written with Jule Styne—did (in one of the *Color Me Barbra* medleys). In 1984, the composer says, she called him to discuss a possible motion picture collaboration. The following January she told him she planned to record several of his songs for *The Broadway Album*. "I was thrilled and expressed my delight," he said. "I was also curious to see the way she worked. Knowing that a lot of artists do not like people in on the recording sessions, I shyly inquired if it would be possible to attend one of the recording sessions when I was in California [to oversee the West Coast production of *Merrily We Roll Along*]. To my exultant surprise she said, 'Oh, I'd love it.' She welcomed the prospect of my being present."

In fact, her work with the producers, composers and arrangers of *The Broadway Album* was to be a collaborative process in every sense of the word. Prior to Sondheim's arrival in California, he and Barbra conducted detailed telephone conversations regarding four songs in particular: "Putting It Together" from his most recent musical, *Sunday in the Park with George;* "Pretty Women" from *Sweeney Todd;* "The Ladies Who Lunch" from *Company;* and "Send in the Clowns," the popular standard from *A Little Night Music.*

The last tune was actually written as "a little song for a little voice" and was meant to provide a poignant counterpoint to the romantic misadventures of the play's leading actress. It is a short chorus on stage, followed by a monologue, and then a repeat of the first verse which reflects ironically on what's just happened. "Every time it's been recorded people have had to sing that version because there was no second release written," the composer admitted. In addition, Barbra noted, because the song was originally written for an English actress there were certain phrases that sounded a bit fancy: "Sorry *my dear*"; "My fault *I fear.*" She wanted to hear directly from Sondheim how to approach these embellishments and to clarify the sentiment of the line, "Well, maybe next year." She asked him what he felt about ending the song with "Don't bother, they're here" instead.

"I didn't know how he would react," she told Holden, "but he was so cute. He said a lot of people had asked him what the song meant—now they would understand it." Sondheim felt Barbra's instinct was "very shrewd.... If I were writing this as just one

song which was a chorus and a half long, of course I would end it with 'Don't bother, they're here.'"

There was more. "I also thought that the bridge was absolutely exquisite and wanted musically to return to [it]," Barbra stated, "but I didn't want to sing the same lyric again. So I asked Steve how he would feel writing a new lyric. What is so *extraordinary* about him is that he said he would try; that he believes, as I do, that art is a very living process. Even though he wrote that song twelve years ago, he was willing to examine it again ['Not as easy a job as it looks, let me tell you,' says he]...I just thought it was so incredible of him not to say, 'This piece of work will never change'—because it was such a wonderful piece to begin with."

Similarly, Streisand had always been attracted to the melody of "Pretty Women," though in the play it was sung by two men. Since she didn't feel comfortable singing it from a male point-of-view, she discussed the various ways to broach a musical solution with Peter Matz. She wondered if the song could be done in tandem with "The Ladies Who Lunch." "There's something about these idolent women," she told him, "women who essentially have nothing more to do than to be beautiful objects of a man's desire." Matz created a dense, multi-tiered arrangement joining the two compositions together; when Sondheim came to town, he added new lyrics to complete the transition. "Then we took [the medley] out, put it back in, took it out, shifted bars around," Matz describes, "and finally ended up with something that was really unusual. It took a month to do it."

"Putting It Together" represented an equally formidable challenge. Basically a patter song, in *Sunday in the Park with George* the number is used to delineate an artist's frustration over selling himself to patrons who really have no idea what it is he does. They try to suppress the things that are unique about his work. It was a dilemma Barbra could easily identify with—the stick-to-what-you-know-works mentality. "Nobody's too big a star to ever not have to audition and sell yourself for something you truly believe in," she emphasized in a conversation with director William Friedkin. Echoing the sentiment of artists like Judy Garland, she offered that much of the struggle comes down to the simple fact "that the establishment wants to be you. Wants to be the artist. They are secretly very jealous of the artist and, in a way, sometimes they actually cut off their noses to spite their faces." Again Sondheim agreed to revise his lyrics, this time to adapt a song about the visual arts into commentary on the contemporary recording industry.

The opportunity to work so closely with some-

With Stevie Wonder (left) and Lionel Richie (right).

one within her peer group—someone who definitely commanded her respect—"turned into a process that was so exhilirating, there were moments I was screaming with joy," said Barbra. Other collaborations were not quite as easy. Arranger Sid Ramin, who worked with her on *I Can Get It for You Wholesale* and *The Third Album,* was invited to orchestrate two selections: "Adelaide's Lament" from *Guys and Dolls* and "Being Good Isn't Good Enough" from *Hallelujah, Baby!* On the latter song, lyricists Betty Comden and Adolph Green submitted some suggestions regarding updating one of the choruses in the Jule Styne composition. Weeks later, Ramin ran into Green in New York, "and I gleefully told him, 'You know, I've just come back from Hollywood where I recorded "Being Good" with Barbra.' He looked at me rather balefully, so I said, 'Whoops! What's wrong?' He said, 'We had to write another lyric for the last half of the chorus. We wrote two lyrics and neither satisfied Barbra. So it's out of the album.' I felt so terrible because [what I had heard] sounded damned good."

Other selections fell into place. Sondheim's "There Won't Be Trumpets" would once again be attempted in a medley with "A Quiet Thing" from *Flora, The Red Menace.* (Barbra had recorded the medley once before in the late 1960's.) The depth of the material ranged from "Home" from *The Wiz* to *Nine's* "Unusual Way"; "Can't Help Lovin' That Man" *(Showboat);* "I Know Him So Well" from the as-yet-unproduced *Chess;* "Show Me" *(My Fair Lady);* a medley of tunes from *Porgy and Bess;* plus other Sondheim tunes, including the spectacularly theatrical "Being Alive" *(Company),* "Not While I'm Around," a lesser-known gem from *Sweeney Todd,* and "Somewhere" from *West Side Story* (music by Leonard Bernstein). It was enough to fill a double album.

As Barbra narrowed down her list of choices, she also got feedback from friends and associates. The Bergmans recommended "Adelaide's Lament." Richard Baskin always loved *West Side Story* and began writing an overture, based on its well-known themes, to open the album. Paul Jabara talked to her about *The King and I* and, with a little encouragement, decided to develop something with producer/ arranger Bob Esty. She called Rupert Holmes in New York to get his opinion and even tried to track down a hard-to-reach Peter Daniels (then on his way to England).

Much as the process of making *Yentl* had put her in touch with the goals and ideals of her early years, *The Broadway Album* brought her back to the artists and musicians who knew these standards better than anyone—and to the people who'd always

provided solid support. As the rehearsals proceeded, Streisand and Matz discussed other people they'd like to bring in. "Do you think we could get Sid?" she asked, meaning Sid Ramin. "All we have to do is try," he responded. Ramin was in Europe, but jumped at the chance to work with Barbra again, "because I thought it would be fun," he said. "And when they sent me the demo of Barbra singing 'Adelaide's Lament,' she'd enclosed the nicest note, saying that it was great that we were finally working together again, that we'd really come full circle....Later, when we met in L.A., I could tell her smile was not a perfunctory smile. It was something she really meant, and that was important [to me]. She didn't forget. It's very rare for somebody who's been as famous as she is to remember that way."

At 10:00 a.m. on Monday, July 22, 1985, Streisand, Matz & Co. entered A&M Recording Studios in Hollywood to commence "Putting It Together." Barbra had decided she didn't want to sing more than three days a week; the remaining days were set aside for reviewing and mixing material. First on the schedule was the intricate recording of Randy Waldman's synthesizer track. It was to be the driving force of the orchestration and it was especially important to Barbra to get it right. On the 25th, they made some minor alterations in anticipation of the big session the following day. Everyone was in agreement that live recording, although expensive, was the only way to capture the truest reading of the material by the orchestra and by Barbra.

The "Putting It Together" sessions would feature an orchestral setting of some 48 pieces, several played by musicians who backed Barbra up on Broadway. In addition, she brought in Sydney Pollack, David Geffen and Ken Sylk "to come and play with me." Also in attendance were Richard Baskin and Stephen Sondheim. " 'Putting It Together' was the most complicated song to record," says engineer Don Hahn. "The thing that I remember most about it was that Barbra didn't want the orchestra overpowering the electronic effects. She wanted the synthesizer, and her voice supported by the orchestra—which is a turn-around in the way most artists would want to do a song like this—and it worked." Sondheim continued to make minor revisions in his lyrical drama as it was rediscovered during production. Barbra supervised the Executive Chorus (writing many of their lines herself). "She is a consummate artist," the composer marveled later. "Her work is exactly what 'Putting It Together' is all about. [Barbra] works exactly the way Seurat worked on his painting: dot by dot, moment by moment, bar by bar and note by note. The only thing that surprised me was that she paid as much exquisite attention to detail in the orchestra as she did with her own singing. Nothing escapes her attention."

After nearly a year of inactivity—and countless years of simply calling upon the voice whenever she needed it—getting in shape for the complex vocal gymnastics of Sondheim's musical monologue was more demanding than Barbra expected. "She was a little concerned at the beginning of the album that maybe the voice wasn't there," says Matz. "Any person who depends on their voice gets very sensitive to the reliability of that voice. It becomes almost like another person: 'Can I trust you?'...In addition, Barbra felt a certain amount of constraint from not having used her voice. It's like going out to play tennis when you haven't played for five years."

"One thing I've never done is pay attention to my voice," she explained to Stephen Holden. "I've never pampered it or thought about it. It just served me. Now I realize I'm at an age when it's not automatically going to serve me for much longer." A month of rehearsing, however, had warmed her up considerably. "There's just a wonderful kind of mellowness to the voice now," says Matz. "You heard that in *Yentl*, I think. Her singing in *Yentl* was very grown-up, very adult, and I think that maturity is gonna make this album more interesting to people..... The fact that she's now developing the lower end of her range just means that when she does go for that high note, it's coming from somewhere important." Later in the week, the producer and his crew would witness just such a happening. "One of the most beautiful songs on the album is Rodger & Hammerstein's 'If I Loved You'...which is treated with absolute simplicity," he says. "She stuck it on the piano one day and I started playing a quiet, very simple kind of accompaniment. We both started feeling the tingles up the back and said, 'Oh, yeah. That's it.' The song rises to an incredible crescendo at the end. [During the recording session] Barbra went for a note that nobody had ever sung before. I think it surprised her as much as it did us—it just broke our hearts."

During her subsequent HBO special, Barbra would explain why the opportunity to sing this collection of songs from the theater was so invigorating: "I'm drawn to songs that have a place to go. They have a beginning, a middle and an end. They're like little plays. You know, you start a song like 'If I Loved You.' It's a character singing to another character, 'This is only if I loved you. This is what would happen *if* I loved you.' You can't take these words for granted. In other words, if you really look at that lyric, there's an enormous thing to act."

While Matz was confronting "the hardest work" of his recent career, Barbra's subtle musical discoveries were leading her in a new direction—arranging. Her work on *The Broadway Album* had less to do with writing charts and determining keys than it did with knowing instinctively what would work for her. "I watched her talk to Peter," states Hahn, "and she said, 'Peter, there's something wrong with this chord.' Now, it wasn't the chord, it was the voicing or the instrumentation. It was too fat or too thin or too shrill. That's what she means, and if you work with her enough you know what she's talking about. Then Peter would say, 'Okay, let's take this one out and put this one in and do this.' He could turn an orchestra upside down for her, and she'd say, 'Yeah, that's better.' Of course, he's always said that Barbra will give him comments that he as a musician or an arranger would never think of trying because it's one of those left-field curves—you're not supposed to do it. But Peter would try it and say, 'Yeah, I really like that. That's fun.'"

"My experience with her has always been high quality is in order. Give it your best shot," Matz emphasizes. "I've never heard her say, 'That chord is too complex. *They* won't understand it.' She never talks like that....The key, for me, is always to find out what she's looking for. When the situation involves multiple takes, I frequently find myself not even listening to the take so much as trying to figure out what it is she's hearing. There's something here that she likes better than what's there. What is it? Is it an emotional quality or the timing or what? It's not always an objectively measured thing....And from her point-of-view, it often is something that isn't easily verbalized. Sometimes, it simply comes down to, 'I like that one better'—and she's entitled."

At most recording sessions, Hahn adds, everyone—including the artist—watches the conductor. With Streisand, the orchestra watches the conductor but the conductor watches Barbra. Matz: "In order to evaluate her properly, in my opinion, in order to conduct for her, you have to drop the idea that you're working with a singer. You're working with an actress and you have to interpret the music as an actor would. It's not like conducting for Ella Fitzgerald or Peggy Lee where you know there are certain musical things that are gonna be adhered to. With Barbra, you're adhering to dramatic content. She's an acting performer. Whether it comes up in humor or love songs, that's her strong suit. And if you really examine it from a professional point-of-view, what you see is an actor at work."

On July 26, they also recorded "Can't Help Lovin' That Man" for the first time. The jazz-oriented rendition featured her singing against a hot trumpet line. Even before she had finished her first pass at the vocal Barbra sensed something was wrong. "I thought the trumpet made it feel a little too jazzy," she said. Future experimentation with the arrangement didn't yield anything substantial. "Then I remembered that I had seen in the 1950's Ava Gardner in the movie *Showboat*...And I remembered being moved by that version." Gardner didn't sing the song in the film (MGM wouldn't allow it), but she did sing on the soundtrack album and Barbra had her staff search for the record. "Thirty dollars, it cost," she smiled, but she found what she was looking for. The Conrad Salinger arrangement "was so simple and had the most gorgeous harmonies on the strings....It was really hard to improve on it."

In August, the production associates talked about adding another instrument to the arrangement to give it a new perspective. Baskin suggested using a harmonica and the distinctive touch of Stevie Wonder. "So I called Stevie up and said, 'Would you consider playing the harmonica on my song?' And he said, 'Absolutely. What time? Where?'...He just came in and listened to the song a few times and started playing. I didn't want to stop him because each time he did it, it came from his soul." In an affectionate nod to the artist/producer, Wonder ended each of his takes with a variation on the "People/People who need people" musical line.

During the first week, Barbra also tackled the "Pretty Women"/"Ladies Who Lunch" medley. In her interview with Friedkin, she spoke of what the songs meant to her: "When you first sing about 'Pretty Women' and create those pictures of how lovely they are, that's one vision of them. Then I started to change the reading a bit....On 'breathing lightly' I started to sort of make a little fun of those women who are just pictures on the arms of their husbands. They dress beautifully and they stand before mirrors and brush their hair...because they have nothing else to do. How interesting to have been one of those pretty women who gets taken care of just for being pretty. In a deep, secret part of me when I was fifteen years old, when I would have loved to have been voted the prettiest girl in high school—and I wasn't—perhaps that was something I wanted. In other words, I could express a lot of feelings in that song, 'Pretty Women.' It's not just a superficial song for me. It has a lot of resonance....In the end, I'm glad I'm not one of them; in the beginning, I perhaps envy them a bit."

Although Sondheim had to return to New York, Barbra's dialogue with him continued. "I witnessed a lot of conversations between them where she would be playing parts of a song over the phone and he'd tell her whether he liked it or not," Arrias says. "On 'Send in the Clowns,' which she produced, there

was one section ['in my *ca*reer'] where Barbra changed the inflection in it by going up on a note instead of down. She sent the completed tape to him and he called her back and said, 'I hate it.' So she changed it back. Then we finished mixing the song and he called her up and said—not kidding— 'You know, I listened to that again and I love it.' Barbra said, 'It's *too late*. It's going to go the other way."

"As far as the notes themselves [are concerned], I asked her to always sing them as written on the first statement of the chorus," Sondheim said, "simply because the listener is unfamiliar with them. But in the second chorus, she could do her jazz thing and make her own embellishments and occasional changes in the notes. Like many composers, I suspect, I prefer always to have the notes sung exactly as written. But, an artist has to feel some way into the material and to personalize it. You can't expect a good jazz musician to only play the tune; thus, too, with a good jazz singer. And Barbra, understanding the principle perfectly, always held off until the second chorus."

"She treated him with so much respect it was practically Mr. Sondheim," Arrias notes. "She would stop everything for him. I remember once she even let Walter Yetnikoff and Al Teller wait in the studio while she was on the phone with him."

On August 2 and 5, after months of trying to negotiate the different male and female roles in "I Loves You Porgy" and "Bess, You Is My Woman Now," Barbra finally committed her medley from the Gershwin classic to vinyl. She wanted to record *Porgy and Bess* for years but never had an appropriate setting for it. "There was one thing that kind of impressed me," says Sid Ramin. "The medley was orchestrated by a wonderful arranger by the name of Alexander Courage. When Barbra heard his arrangement, there was a certain note right at the top (during the first eight bars) that she thought should be here. 'The note will probably work, but it's not Gershwin,' Sandy said to me. 'He didn't write that note.' But Barbra heard it and she wanted to try it, so she went over to the piano and played what she wanted and then Sandy and Pete fixed it....I thought that was very revealing: that she hears so much that she'll hear a fill that will be obtrusive or she'll hear a harmony that's not correct. With great artists like Sinatra and Streisand, their instincts are just so damned good that it's hard to fault them when they say something. You may not agree with them at the moment and you may sulk away and say, 'Damn it. They don't know what they're talking about.' But in retrospect, they usually have a pretty good idea what the average person expects or what will work [for them] and what won't work." The *Porgy and Bess*

"Somewhere," 1985.

sessions incorporated *The Broadway Album*'s largest string section, as well as the largest orchestra (60 pieces).

On "Something's Coming," Richard Baskin played a demo for Barbra that he'd produced in an all-night session at Randy Waldman's home studio. She liked the track so much she asked them not to re-cut it; she wanted to add her vocal to their "rough cut." The two minute tape was brought to John Arrias to remix into an extended 2:54 cut with a horn arrangement by Jerry Hey. The selection was to be the only part of Baskin's *West Side Story* tribute to make it to the album—but not the only cut from the Bernstein/Sondheim musical. A high-tech version of "Somewhere" was selected to close the album. "[Barbra] asked me to produce the entire *Broadway Album*," producer/arranger David Foster revealed to *USA Today,* "and I said no because I was too busy with other projects....I think I made perhaps the worst mistake of my career."

Foster did find the time to produce one additional cut (the unreleased "I Know Him So Well"), but *West Side Story*'s hopeful anthem provided the main challenge. In addressing the youth of the 1980's, much as the original standard addressed the 1950's, the producers allowed themselves to take certain liberties. "Barbra had the idea of making 'Somewhere' ethereal. The way she put it was that it should sound like it was coming from another world," the producer stated.

In the final mix, Barbra would craft her performance to fit the arrangement. "The panning thing at the beginning of her vocal was her idea," Foster recalled. "Her entrance was very tricky, too, because the click track was erased during her first vocal." After putting in approximately 150 hours of studio time, the producer/arranger admitted still hearing flaws: a drum fill here, a pitch bend there. But he was pleased to have Leonard Bernstein wire his congratulations to Barbra upon hearing the new track.

While production continued at A&M Studios, Paul Jabara and Bob Esty toiled in a "no man's land" of never being quite sure if their material would be heard, let alone make it to vinyl. Jabara had suggested "Shall We Dance"; Barbra liked "I Have Dreamed" and "Something Wonderful." The team's concept optimistically expanded to fill out a complete side of the projected two-record set including "Broadway, I Love You," an original ballad Jabara had written for Barbra; a disco arrangement of "Shall We Dance"; a few lines from "Hello, Young Lovers"; followed by a dream sequence which pitted Barbra's voice against a lush synthesizer arrangement of "We Kiss in a Shadow" and "I Have Dreamed"; capped by a full orchestral version of "Something Wonderful." "We wanted to create something beautiful for her," Esty says, noting that this was also an ideal opportunity for the pair to establish themselves as something more than disco songwriters. The final medley would encompass the last three songs. "Bob and I worked for days trying to put the tape together so Barbra could get a feeling for the piece as a whole," Arrias says.

She did like it. Her only problem was "Where am I going to put it?" Ironically, instead of narrowing her options, Barbra asked them for more. There was something about the "Shall We Dance" arrangement that made her think that if those ideas could be transferred to "Some People" or "Show Me," those tunes should not be ruled out as possiblities. Unfortunately, both numbers were to remain as elusive as ever.

Sid Ramin's experience turned out to be equally frustrating—and thrilling. "The direction I got from Pete on 'Adelaide's Lament' was that they loved some of my orchestrations for [the original production of] *Gypsy*, especially 'You Gotta Have a Gimmick.'...So I wrote what I'd say is a very busy background— much busier than I would have ever written for the theater—expecting some things to be left out. But they didn't leave anything out." The actual recording session was a lot of fun, Ramin says, with Barbra ad libbing new comic dialogue to restate the case for Frank Loesser's anxious-to-be-wed heroine. "The thing that gave me a big charge was looking over at some of these musicians who had played for everybody in the world. They've played the most beautiful music in the world, and they were totally overwhelmed by what they heard Barbra doing. There was one trombonist, Dick Nash, who practically stopped playing. He was so overwhelmed by the sound he heard coming from Barbra that he couldn't even play...and that was something that I had never seen before."

"Adelaide's Lament" was slated as the comic intermission following the *King and I* medley. But, when the double album Streisand and Matz had hoped for became a single sleeve LP (Columbia Records wouldn't even okay the cost of producing an attractive double-gate package), the producers realized there was no room for it. Happily, the compact disc did not have the same space restrictions and the comedy song found a home there.

Now began the painful process of piecing together the vocals and eliminating the excess baggage. Although recording live with the orchestra, Barbra was much more concerned about getting the basic track right at that time than finalizing her own vocals. After the initial sessions, not everyone agreed that piecing together a "perfect" vocal was required. "With any other artist you risk losing spontaneity [during such a process]," Arrias argues, "but not with her. Barbra looks for imperfections—and out of that she wants perfection. And emotion.

"I've *never* seen her so possessed. She *had* to do it and it had to be right. She'd get inspired in the middle of the night and call me. I usually record those conversations because I couldn't write fast enough to keep up with her. She'd say, 'On take sixteen, this section was much better than take seventeen, so let's use sixteen instead.' And then I'd say, 'Why are you doing this? That first vocal was great!' Then when it was all finished, we'd play it back and it sounded so spontaneous, so perfect, with all the notes in there and all the inflections exactly the way she wanted it. 'Okay,' I'd say, 'now let's go back and listen to the original.' We'd always go back to the original vocal for reference—and there was no contest, the edited vocal was much better. And she continually proved that to me throughout the production of this album." "Don't you remember what we did on *Yentl*?" she might ask Don Hahn. "Barbra, I have a hard enough time remembering what you said four minutes ago."

Arrias was to coin the motto that would stick with the project through its final stages. So many tracks had been recorded that in order to experiment further, an agreement had to be reached regarding what could be erased—and nobody wanted to make it. "It got to the point where I finally said, 'Look, guys, no more procrastination. There comes a time when you have to go for it—No guts, no glory.'" With tapes being re-mixed at nearly every recording studio in town and Barbra jockeying from one studio to another, things did get a bit confused. "I just remember having a real good laugh with her one time," the engineer continues. "We both made a very obvious mistake. We were listening to vocal tracks.

We'd listen to one vocal, then listen to another, and then go back to the first one...and the second one...and back and forth. And when we listened to each track we definitely heard a difference. Together, we chose the one we liked best. Then we asked Richard to choose and he chose the same vocal. I was curious about something so I put both vocals up together—and it turned out they were *both the same vocal*. We couldn't stop laughing. We were hysterical...holding onto each other to keep from falling to the ground...tears rolling down our faces. 'Well, we better go home now because we've been at this too long,' we said. 'When two identical tracks sound different, it's time to go home.' But that laugh with her is a moment I'll always cherish."

At last, Barbra was ready to play the album for Yetnikoff and Teller—and they were visibly moved. "When they start talking about how much they like it, that means they *loved* it," she told Arrias. One argument that stayed alive up through the mastering of the album was the sequencing of songs. No one except Barbra believed "Putting It Together" should be placed first. "They were practically on their knees pleading. 'Please don't do it, Barbra. It's a mistake.' They felt that if you put that song on first, you were apologizing for the album," Arrias recalls. "But I sat and talked with her about it and she said, 'You've got to understand why I did this song. It was rewritten just for this album....I'm not apologizing. I'm just saying you may not like it, but listen. Don't be turned off by this music, you haven't heard it yet.' And she stuck to her guns. I couldn't believe it. Anyone else would have folded under that pressure; God bless her for doing it *her* way."

With the album being readied for release, Streisand had a special reason for wanting it to succeed. "Barbra's contract with Columbia says she has to deliver *X* number of albums," Marty Erlichman states, "but they have to be approved albums—meaning most of them have to be contemporary albums. CBS never approved this album; it was not considered to be a pop album. Therefore, she didn't get the advance she was entitled to (she only got half her usual advance) and it wasn't going to count as an approved album contract. Except if it sold 2.5 million copies—at that point it would automatically become an approved album whether they okayed it in advance or not."

While some industry insiders were expressing doubt that "even somebody as superlative as Barbra" could bring the Old Broadway standards back, CBS reversed its predictable hit single mentality and began planning its strategy. "Whatever Columbia's initial interest might have been, once they heard it, they really got behind it," Matz told *Billboard*'s Paul Grein. "Plus, the timing was just great. We were very fortunate."

The Broadway Album was released on November 4, 1985. In a nod to her first Broadway show, both the front and back cover portraits featured Barbra in a secretary's chair (the sheet music she's holding is the Bergdorf-Goodman medley—arranged by Peter Matz—from *My Name Is Barbra*). The photograph was shot at New York's Plymouth Theatre prior to the actual recording sessions. Unable to talk the record company into a fold-out package, Barbra did manage to slip in a separate sheet of liner notes by the Bergmans and a sleeve which included complete lyrics to each song or medley.

The LP debuted on *Billboard*'s Top Pop chart at number 59. It jumped 35 places in its second week on the charts. "Place this reaction record in as many places as you can and grab your calculator...you'll need it to track sales!" *The Album Network*, an industry trade, enthused. "At Tower Records-Sunset, Barbra is selling like 'Barbra Springsteen-sand'! We're moving an amazing 100 + pieces a day since its release," the store's buyer said. At the Tower Records in New York, *The Broadway Album* sold more than 300 copies its first day out, breaking the store's previous record on *USA for Africa*. At Licorice Pizza she was outselling other artists three to one. "We've had reports from stores about people buying ten and twenty copies," Peter Fletcher, Barbra's product manager at Columbia, told *USA Today*.

At its height, the album was selling 80,000 copies a day. *Radio and Records*' editor Ken Barnes saw it as an important commercial breakthrough for Adult Contemporary: "This proves there's a big, untapped adult market out there that wants to buy records, but can't find anything they like." Music publishers disagreed. "They're buying a legend," one publisher told *Billboard*.

On January 25, 1986, the already double platinum *Broadway Album* hit number 1—and stayed on top of the charts for three weeks. It was her highest charting album since *Guilty*. "This album gave me a chance to *live up* to the greatness of the material," she expressed to Friedkin. "I never understood the opposition to this album. I still don't."

Reviews:

"Her voice has the sustained power of a waterfall, the vivid colors of a rainbow. Streisand's roots go deep into the tar and concrete of Broadway; in this thrilling collection of show tunes, the melodic plums include 'Can't Help Lovn' That Man' from *Showboat;* 'Something's Coming' from *West Side Story; Carousel*'s 'If I Loved You'; and 'Send in the Clowns' from *A Little Night Music.*"

—*Seventeen*

FINAL NOTE: Barbra's sixth chart-topping album established a new record of longevity for her. The twenty-one years and three months between her first and last number 1 LP's represented the longest span in the forty-one year history of *Billboard*'s Top Pop Albums chart. It would also make her one of the few artists of the '70s or '80s to have a number 1 album without a Top 40 hit.

On November 20 Columbia had released "Somewhere" backed with "Not While I'm Around." Barbra pledged to donate all the proceeds from the single to PRO-Peace (the ill-fated group which organized 1986's anti-nuclear Great Peace March) and the American Foundation for AIDS Research. Since the single was relegated primarily to Adult Contemporary stations, however, its success was severely limited. Once again, Top 40 radio was confused about what to do with the latest Streisand song; instead of doing something creative, they didn't do anything at all. Stations that properly analyzed the song's audience found they had a Top 30 Adult hit; 90 percent of their target audience was 25 years and older. The single peaked at number 43 nationally (number 6 on the Adult Contemporary chart). "Send in the Clowns"/"Being Alive," released in February, received no chart action at all.

While the singles floundered, *The Broadway Album* continued to linger in the Top 10. The CD, for which Barbra spent weeks supervising digital remastering, was the number 2 compact disc in the country for several weeks. To date, the international sales reports on the album are shaping up like *Memories* (aka *Love Songs*), maintaining steady sales all around with varying degrees of success on the charts themselves. Worldwide sales now exceed six million (including three million U.S.) and CBS Records believes the album has the potential of becoming Barbra's best-selling album.

In 1986, her search for her roots brought Barbra back to her original manager, Martin Erlichman. They are currently planning several projects together.

THE FUTURE

"Sometimes I listen to myself and say, 'Oh, God, is that me?' It sounds awful—like a nasal voice," Streisand told *Playboy* in 1977. "Other times I'll hear it and I'll think, 'Jesus, is that my voice? Sounds pretty damned good to me.' A pretty sound, like an instrument. Sometimes I'll just love it, sometimes I'll hate it."

"Barbra's is a very big, solid, thickly textured-voice—especially now," Stephen Holden offers. "When she started out, it used to be more reedy. It has acquired some body and timbre as the years have gone by. Now it's very steel-like…. Hers is one of the few voices I've heard that can really take a large, large orchestra and soar above it."

In 1986, *Radio and Records* did a survey of radio station programmers and record store managers and buyers. Streisand rated number 7 in the retail area (below Bruce Springsteen, Lionel Richie, Phil Collins, Michael Jackson, Billy Joel and Bryan Adams) and number 5 in the Adult Contemporary market (Richie, Wonder, Collins and Joel) with a number 11 rating overall. She was the number 1 Contemporary Female Artist. "Barbra Streisand may have a major hit album now, but she's been totally consistent for us for years," one retail store manager responded. "For us, a new Streisand album is an event." Indeed, a predictable annual event is her naming as Favorite Female Vocalist in a variety of publications, including *People* magazine's Readers' Poll.

So what's in store for her now? Next on the agenda is a new pop album. There is talk of a *Broadway, Act II* or an album dedicated to film music. Although many of her ideas for *Life Cycle of a Woman*, a project she began in 1974, were eloquently re-stated in *Yentl*, that Legrand/Bergman collaboration still stands as a possible project. "All of the songs are written," Legrand revealed to columnist Joyce Haber in 1975. "The first songs deal with birth, the last with death. In between are songs about childhood, adolescence, a first love at age sixteen, marriage, motherhood. The songs are intense." Thus far, five songs have been recorded: "Between Yesterday and Tomorrow," "Can You Tell The Moment?" and "Mother and Child." "Once You've Been In Love" and "the Smile I've Never Smiled," two songs reported to be part of that work, were actually recorded for entirely different projects (but never released). In 1987, Columbia Records is planning a multiple record set tentatively titled *Legacy*, to commemorate Barbra's 25th anniversary in recording.

1987 also marks twenty years since her arrival in Hollywood. "*The Broadway Album* has kept me away from directing for eight months," Barbra told Rod McKuen early in 1986. "I have to get back to making movies. It's a question of how many battles you can gear up for every year."

Funny Girl *to* Funny Lady

IN CONCERT/ON TELEVISION

"Less is more, but this is ridiculous!" Or so say many seasoned Streisand supporters who miss Barbra as a performance artist or as a producer of quality product for television. Unfortunately for them, her live performances during the late '70s and early '80s can be counted on one hand, and most of her television work has been limited to promotional appearances. In an era when almost any soap opera star is as easily recognized in public as Streisand, what admirers seem to be missing most is a chance to see a real *Star* at work.

"Miss Streisand is that rarity that has both cult and crowd appeal, probably because she caters to neither. A one-of-a-kind talent, her stage image is a mixed bag of paradoxes—she is fresh and sophisticated, subtle and straightforward, and complex and direct. Above all, she is a consummate performer, both free and self-aware and mixing improvisational flair with an effortless control of her songery and audience." *Variety*'s review referred to her 1963 engagement at Mr. Kelly's, but the observations are equally appropriate for the Forum in 1972 or Sun Devil Stadium in 1976. Conversely, has there ever been a recording artist whose greatest successes were so inexplicably detached from concert performing? Everyone hits the road or guests on variety specials occasionally to support their product. Streisand doesn't. And while it's hard to measure what effect touring would have on her album sales, decreased public exposure has not tarnished the (multi) platinum sheen of every LP since her last concert in 1980.

Barbra's appearances during the past decade have been so infrequent that each has been treated, perhaps unfairly (for the artist and the audience), as a rarefied event—which makes one's expectations even greater. Could Garbo ever live up to a comeback? Therein lies the rub. Because, like that enigmatic star, Barbra would probably be the first to say her recession from concerts and, to a lesser degree, television was never part of any Grand Plan. In fact, ambitious projects in both areas continue to be discussed. Sometimes things fall into place as quickly as HBO's *Putting It Together* documentary/special, which was virtually assembled after *The Broadway Album* had been completed. On the other hand, for years Jon Peters tried to coordinate the details of a major concert tour—it would have been Barbra's first international outing—and was unsuccessful.

Astronomical sums have been offered to lure her from her California home base: British promoter Malcolm Feld reportedly offered $1,000,000 for one two-hour concert at Wembley Stadium, and when Barbra's representatives turned that down, he doubled the pot *and* added the chartering of a Concorde jet for her staff. An oil-rich prince tendered a cashier's check for a like sum to entice her to sing birthday greetings over the phone to his son. Following *A Star Is Born* and *Yentl*, rumors persisted regarding a possible tour—but the closest she actually came to a commitment was in 1979.

In July, Barbra and Jon took their sons to see the Bee Gees play Dodger Stadium "...because we were talking about doing an album together and I said to Jon, 'God, can you imagine filling up this many seats?' I mean, 56,000 people came to see them," she told Mike Walsh for his Australian TV show. "And I really thought to myself 56,000 people would never come to see me—that's what I thought, you know? Then when we walked in and sat down, the audience sort of spotted me and started to applaud [and cheer]. I was in shock, I couldn't believe they would respond to me that way. It was really thrilling, really nice. I had a good feeling. Later, I said to Jon, 'You know, maybe I'll do a concert tour in the next few years.' Because I'd love to see more of the world and sing for people.... It's just that I'm frightened. So it's funny that just as I was saying to myself, 'I could think about this seriously,' the next night on TV someone on the news said I would never appear in concert again. And I said, 'What?...Who is this person and where do they get their information?'"

If anything challenged her enough to make her go out and prove people wrong, it was then-recent newspaper and magazine articles depicting her as a recluse who was so paranoid about performing that she remembered darting about the stage in Central Park to avoid harm [she didn't]. At the end of July, Jon Peters' organization announced tentative plans for a 1980/81 worldwide tour. In the meantime, Barbra found the financing for *Yentl*; pre-production on that film took precedence over finalizing any dates on the schedule. Thankfully, her commitment to liberal causes would insure at least two concert appearances in Los Angeles. And, of course, there was always television.

Funny Girl to Funny Lady (ABC-TV)
Broadcast March 9, 1975

Produced by Gary Smith and Dwight Hemion
Directed by Dwight Hemion
Executive Producer: Ray Stark
Written by Herb Sargent
Additional Material by Marty Farrell
Musical Conductor: Peter Matz
Audio Consultant: Phil Ramone

Washington, D.C., was selected as the site of the World Premiere for *Funny Lady*. The opening, organized by Eunice Kennedy Shriver, was a benefit for her favorite charity, the Special Olympics. Ray Stark, a master showman and promoter, sold ABC-

TV on the idea of a live television event: An exhilarating mixture of Hollywood, represented by *Funny Lady*, Washington (the Kennedys, President Ford) and the sports world (Muhammad Ali, Frank Gifford, Rafer Johnson)—and, above all, a veritable command performance from Barbra. Streisand's first concert appearance in three years could be attended not by thousands but by millions via the miracle of modern technology. It was an exciting concept, and with the additional involvement of the Special Olympics, many VIP's agreed to donate their time.

The show was prepped in L.A. over a three-month period. On Friday, March 11, the principals flew to the nation's capital. "*The Carol Burnett Show* taped on Friday nights, so after the show I got on a plane with four or five musicians I was bringing with me...and when we got off in D.C. early the next morning we discovered the music didn't make the trip with us," Peter Matz says. "Nobody was interested. We couldn't find anybody from TWA who was interested in helping us to find our music that day. We kept getting referred from one office to another. They wanted time to track it down and we were saying, 'Wait a minute. We have an orchestra rehearsal at the Kennedy Center this afternoon, and tomorrow we're going on the air *live*! These are major folks we're dealing with—Columbia Pictures, James Caan, Barbra Streisand...' And the general attitude at TWA was 'Take it easy.' I finally had to call Ray [Stark] at home. Thank God he had the clout to put a tracer on it and they found the music in Las Vegas or Denver. He got a plane to pick it up and take it to Chicago where TWA agreed to bring it the rest of the way."

The music didn't arrive until the day of the show. Lacking any charts or arrangements, the musicians and crew "faked" their way through a camera rehearsal on Saturday. On Sunday, with all the craziness of preparing for a live event and having to film the opening interview segment between Barbra and host Dick Cavett, they got in a couple of hours worth of rehearsal before the theater had to be cleared. The Special Olympics involvement is what made it worth it. "I remember when Barbra did the dress rehearsal, a lot of kids were let in to sit and watch what was going on," Marty Erlichman says. "Barbra walked up and down the aisles with them, signing autographs and talking with them. It was very touching for everybody concerned."

Everyone, with the possible exception of Muhammad Ali, was nervous. Barbra experienced "a three-way scare". 1) Because the fate of her new film was at stake and the premiere itself was held in the chilly political world of Washington, 2) Because the idea of having to put on a happy face and perform during what could be an excruciating moment for

An informal chat with Barbara Walters for Funny Lady, *1975.*

her (and Jimmy Caan, whose brief musical moments from the film were to be recreated onstage) was far from thrilling, and 3) Because it was a "live…live!" event—no skillful editor would be available to maneuver around technically flawed moments. "It's very risky to do live television, because if anyone stretches it [by] adding a line or anything, then your timing goes in the toilet," Matz explains. "One thing we didn't calculate correctly was the reaction to Barbra. When Dick Cavett introduced her, it was assumed that she would come out and say, 'Hi. Thank you for joining us tonight,' etc. But when she walked out onstage there was a standing ovation that lasted two minutes—and this was supposed to be a very fine, kind of austere audience. I don't think anyone ever figured that that would happen. It was thrilling, but totally unexpected…and it immediately put us in the dumper."

The response to "The Way We Were" was even warmer. "If you applaud too much we'll run out of time," Barbra nervously reminded the audience. Matz: "You don't stop an audience from cheering. If they're glad to see you, they want to let you know." Following "Don't Rain on My Parade and a smashingly eloquent "My Man," James Caan joined her for "It's Only a Paper Moon"/"I Like Her (Him)". The duet was staged with Barbra—adorned by very straight, very long blond hair—circling Caan à la Sonny & Cher. She even got in a little "zinger."

Complimenting Caan on his acting transition "from a crook to a producer" she remarked, "That's quite a difference…or is it? [A guilty look] I don't want to mention any names!" Her co-star then set the scene for her final musical number, the only public performance of "How Lucky Can You Get?"

Barbra would subsequently be the focus of some criticism (including snipes at whether or not she was paid) for her central participation in what turned out to be an extended plug (60 minutes) for the film. In all fairness, even big money-raisers like Jerry Lewis recognize the importance of a high entertainment-to-charity-promotion ratio. Both times *Funny Girl to Funny Lady* shifted its sights to the Special Olympics, the segments were smartly positioned to avoid viewer tune-out (lest they miss a Streisand performance). Nearing the home stretch, Muhammad Ali introduced two young representatives of the Special Olympics who presented Barbra with a gold medal for her efforts. The schedule called for her to sing "People" as a tribute to all the children and volunteers who took part in the program. But they ran out of time. "Oh, that's it? [she laughed] That's a live show for you! We weren't kidding around." They didn't even have time for the credits. Instead, a much more relaxed Streisand sang "People" to the two thousand-plus dignitaries assembled in the Eisenhower Theatre. The official screening of *Funny Lady* began as soon as the stage was cleared.

95

Reviews:

"Live television? What's that? What you saw last night at 7:30 p.m. on ABC, when Barbra Streisand turned a Special Olympics benefit for mentally retarded children at the Kennedy Center in Washington, D.C., into a super, sensational plug for her new movie, *Funny Lady*.

"The telecast...covered a ten-year period in which the famed singer learned one thing: 'How to kiss better,' she told Cavett.... Any benefit has to benefit from Miss Streisand's singing, even if one cringes at the promoting of a movie along with such a worthy cause. But in all honesty, looking at Streisand film clips and hearing her sing is a slice of good entertainment."

—*New York Daily News*

The Tonight Show

Since her success in *Funny Girl,* Barbra had continued to make sporadic appearances on television variety shows. But it had been over twelve years since she last guested on a talk show. (She had taped a two-part David Frost interview in 1971 but it never aired. It was reportedly pulled due to her exclusive CBS contract; the contract expired in 1975.) All of that was due to change on Wednesday, July 9, 1975, when she was scheduled to reunite with Johnny Carson on *The Tonight Show*. Her last appearance on the show had been in March of 1963. Carson had built up such a solid viewership in the intervening years that most industry analysts considered him unbeatable in the late-night time slot, and he negotiated a staggering multi-million dollar contract to prove it.

For months, Ray Stark's office had been pressing Barbra to agree to a *Tonight Show* appearance in support of *Funny Lady*. Barbra, who had already taped a *Today Show* interview with Barbara Walters, performed live on *Funny Girl to Funny Lady* and attended press conferences in New York and London, thought she had done enough. Weary of the talk show circuit of her youth, she allowed herself to be coerced into making one final appearance. "In the early stages of Barbra's career, she was able to get herself up to do all this. As she got more successful, a lot of anxieties came with it," Marty explains. "There was tremendous anxiety over *The Tonight Show*. 'I don't want to do it. I don't want to do it.' 'Okay, I'll do it.' And a lot of people saying, 'Do it. It's good for this.... It's good for that.'"

A full week prior to the show, NBC began heralding their "exclusive" during daytime and primetime programming. No guest of the popular talk show had *ever* been publicized that far in advance, and never to that extent. The advance promotion—and speculation about what Barbra might sing, if anything—created much public excitement.

On Tuesday the 8th, *The Tonight Show* office received word that Streisand would not be available for the Wednesday taping. No reason for her withdrawal was given. Although last-minute substitutions and cancellations are an everyday part of talk show programming, Carson took Barbra's change of heart personally. "I was informed prior to going on the air that we'll have a cancellation tomorrow night," he told the audience. "Barbra Streisand will not be with us. We don't know why. Nobody has been able to reach her.... Although she doesn't owe the show anything in particular, we thought it only fair to tell you, so when you tune in you don't get mad at us—I would rather you get mad at her. Streisand will not be here Wednesday night nor will she be here in the future. Over the years, we've had the reputation for delivering. We'll be here, though, and that's all there is to it."

The host returned on Wednesday with the promise of "the star of Hollywood's biggest movie." The star turned out to be a man in a shark's suit (*Jaws* was the year's sensation). Carson teased the viewing audience further as he introduced an internationally-acclaimed singing star with the initials B.S. Out of the curtains came a curly-headed look-a-like singing "People." "I'm sorry, we're booked. We can't use you for the show," Carson told the singer (Madlyn Rhue) as she was pulled back into the curtains. Turning to sidekick Ed McMahon he shrugged, "When you're booked, you're booked." His real guest was opera star Beverly Sills.

The petty, one-sided feud made gossip columns and news wires around the world. "It was just a little joke, nothing vicious," Carson claimed in a 1979 *Rolling Stone* interview. Denying that there was any real resentment on his part, he said he was "just taking advantage of what was going on."

During one of her final *Tonight Show* appearances in 1963, Barbra talked about how her uneasiness over performing often manifested itself backstage in a brief outbreak of hives. When the same condition plagued her *days* before the actual event, everyone knew it was a bad sign. "You're better off saying no at that moment in time than you are going on the show and not being able to handle it in front of ten, twelve million people," Marty defends. But Carson, who admitted ignorance of any specifics, didn't agree. "Instead of alienating millions of people, it would have been nice if she came on the show and shown millions of people that she's also a human being," he told a largely supportive audience on Wednesday evening. The trouble was that the host *didn't* see the conflict in human terms. His behavior suggested that he could only see Streisand the diva damaging the credibility of his show.

Discussing a very difficult, traumatic period years later, Erlichman notes that "It happens to all of us on a daily, weekly or monthly basis where we make decisions that we know we just can't follow through on even though we said we'd do it.... Barbra understood all of the effort that had gone into the promotion of her appearance—which NBC had gone above and beyond what they should have, and that's their own problem for doing that. But she had to make a decision predicated on her own well-being. Hers was a very severe emotional reaction that translated into a physical one. Barbra knew at the time she said, 'I can't do it,' that there would be repercussions. It wasn't like any of us hid from her the damage that it could cause. It created a problem in the public's eye and with Johnny directly, but she didn't know to what extent it would go.... Ten years later people are still talking about it. These things happen in life. They just happen."

If Streisand stood to lose some admirers over the incident, so, too, did Johnny Carson. He continued to vent his frustration on the show and in his nightclub act (with occasional allusions to playing frisbee with Barbra's records). "I was barely able to sympathize with Carson's attitude the night before Barbra was due to appear," one viewer wrote into a Dallas newspaper. "My patience totally vanished the next evening.... I have been a Carson fan and a Streisand fan for many years. If Johnny made this cancellation a regular part of his opening monologue...he could not hurt Barbra's career, but his own smallness is certainly showing."

Concert—Tempe, Arizona
March 20, 1976

She didn't find it too "demeaning" (as one columnist surmised earlier) to salute a former employer on March 14, 1976. Promising to make her speech brief, "unlike those we had on the set," Barbra appeared on the televised *AFI Salute to William Wyler.* (And quietly donated her honorarium back to the America Film Institute to help establish an exchange program with the Soviet Film Industry.) The tribute actually took place five days earlier; by Sunday, Barbra was in Arizona shooting *A Star Is Born* and gearing up for the day-long concert at Arizona State University's Sun Devil Stadium in Tempe.

Once again, it was an event choreographed to serve a dual purpose. While the crowd was drawn by names like Peter Frampton, Santana and an oppor-

tunity to see Barbra Streisand and Kris Kristofferson in person, they also provided a realistic, and very spectacular, backdrop for *A Star Is Born.* Veteran rock promoter Bill Graham coordinated the event with Jon Peters. "I began booking acts, making it clear there were certain unique problems—like having to arrive at the stadium between 7:00 and 9:00 in the morning and be ready to perform. All of this contact work," he said, "had to be done in only eleven days. Normally, it would have taken me two months to put together an outdoor show of this magnitude."

Streisand and Peters arrived at the stadium around 4:30 the morning of March 20 and, much to their amazement, were greeted by thousands of fans who had come hours before the gates were scheduled to open. By the time Barbra went onstage at 8:45 a.m., the stadium was nearly filled to capacity (estimates of the crowd size vary; 70,000 is the most often quoted figure). Donald von Wiedenman described in *The Advocate* her first appearance before the crowd: "Everyone is in a state of sensual undress, taken with the heat and the music and the thrill of it all. Streisand walks out onto the stage and the entire audience is on its feet, applauding and cheering and stomping their feet at the tiny white dot between the huge black speakers. It's wave after wave of sweeping adulation, a tribute indeed to her remarkable gifts and power. I am surprised. I did not realize she had this much appeal to the young."

"Do you recognize me with my short, curly hair?" Barbra kidded. "I didn't think you'd remember who I was!" Then she told the crowd about her film. "We fight, we scream and yell at each other, we talk dirty, we smoke *grass*....We're going to rock'n'roll today! So, in the lingo of the movie, all you motherfuckers have a great time!" Some members of press in attendance would find her rap condescending—but the crowd loved it.

Despite the advance promotion concerning the film and Streisand and Kristofferson's appearances, there was legitimate concern that the kids had come to hear rock'n'roll. As with the Forum in '72, Barbra was more than somewhat "petrified and insecure about performing"; she was afraid she'd be booed off the stage by this audience she'd always been told wasn't hers. "I hope she doesn't fail," a member of the crew muttered backstage. But, having taken command of the situation, she was to discover she was, in fact, the star attraction. "Barbra lit up when she connected with that crowd," Jon Peters remembers.

Later in the day, she reappeared dressed in a new outfit. "The Way We Were" was being piped in over the loudspeakers. "Now, if you'd like" [as if she had to ask], "I'll have them turn off the vocal track and I'll sing to the accompaniment—I didn't bring any strings with me today." After a roar of approval, she casually proceeded to mesmerize the gathering. This was followed by "Woman in the Moon," a new song from *Star.*

"Working with Barbra in that vast stadium with 70,000 people," Phil Ramone states, "and watching her perform in front of them and taking them to heights I don't think most performers could ever do, in a sweltering, hot situation with bad acid and other drugs being distributed....To see her take control of that audience was an amazing moment. She was compelling."

The day ended on an "up" note. After another costume change, Barbra came out for the last time. "I'm going to test something out on you," she said. "This is a song I wrote, and if you don't like it—I'll be crushed." After her warm rendition of "Evergreen" and the audience's enthusiastic response ("Did you

Sun Devil Stadium, March 1976. (Photo courtesy of the Richard Giammanco collection)

really like it?" she queried happily), she delivered a touching performance of "People" that had even the most stubborn of those in attendance cheering. "It was a once-in-a-lifetime view of a woman many call the greatest talent of this generation," the *Hollywood Reporter* proclaimed. Later, ill-informed, poorly observant cynics would insist that Barbra had been lip-syncing.

Barbra: With One More Look at You

Produced by Andrew J Kuehn and Jeff Werner
Designed and Edited by Jeff Werner
Directed by Andrew J. Kuehn
Cinematography by Jose Luis Mignone, Erik Daarsted and Steve Poster

In February of 1975, Barbra taped an interview with Barbara Walters for *The Today Show.* Both women were pleased to find the person they met to be contrary to their images. A year and a half later, when Walters was putting together her first special for ABC-TV, she landed the first primetime interview with Barbra and Jon—still the focus of much controversy with the embattled *A Star Is Born* set to open in

December. The couple shared the bill with another illustrious couple, President-elect Jimmy Carter and his wife Rosalynn. The special aired on December 14, 1976; Barbra and Jon's half hour attracted a 40 share of the national viewing audience, a 30 share went to the Carters. Six weeks later, Geraldo Rivera's *Good Night America* took viewers to the post-premiere party at New York's Tavern on the Green restaurant, stealing the guests of honor (Streisand, Peters, Kristofferson) away for his "private" tête-à-tête.

By far the most thorough look at Barbra and her movie was furnished by Kaleidoscope Films, a documentary outfit which was responsible for chronicling the filmmaking process. Jon had hoped to give *With One More Look at You* to one of the networks. It was, admittedly, a promotional item, perhaps even indulgent, but it was not lacking in value. The special was syndicated to local TV stations in February 1977. "It probably didn't get picked up by any network because its form is not as attractive as its substance," Jon Bream ventured in the *Minneapolis Star*. "The one-hour program has no real focus except, of course, its omnipresent star. Much of *One More Look* is a behind-the-scenes look at the making of Streisand's film, *A Star Is Born*, whereas other portions are historical glimpses of the great entertainer and revealing interviews in which she discusses her philosophies of womanhood, acting, stardom, audiences and critics and *A Star Is Born*....The editing of the program is rather choppy, but Streisand fans will be fascinated, nonetheless."

1977 Academy Awards
March 28, 1977

In March, Barbra made what the *Los Angeles Times* would term a "dramatic bit of contrition in the grand manner" when she agreed to return from a foreign promotional tour for *A Star Is Born* in time to sing "Evergreen" on the 1977 Academy Awards. (*Star's* few nominations were in the technical areas.) Still a little off-balance due to an inner ear infection, Barbra was the only performer to run through her entire number, testing lights and camera angles the day before the telecast. Ian Freebairn-Smith had written a new arrangement especially for her Oscars performance. "We talked about changing the chart a little bit [by] opening it up and adding an instrumental section in the middle," he recalls. "I actually wrote it that way...and we rehearsed it...She listened to it and decided to play it safe. Everybody knew and loved the record version; she just didn't want to fool around with it."

Barbra's arresting, somewhat tremulous performance on March 28 was greeted with unre-strained applause from the Academy audience. Next, Jane Fonda introduced "the boy from the baritone section," Neil Diamond, to announce the award for Best Original Song. "Before I mention the winner," he said in an unusual aside, "about three weeks ago I was talking to Barbra and I said, 'You know, I love your song so much that no matter who wins I'm going to read your name,' but I have to cancel out on that, Barbra. So, if I call your name out you actually won it, and if I don't...you wrote a terrific song the first time out." He need not have worried. The envelope beckoned an ebullient Streisand and lyricist Paul Williams to center stage.

The Stars Salute Israel at 30 (ABC-TV)
Broadcast May 8, 1978

Produced and Directed by Marty Pasetta
Executive Producers: James Lipton and Charles Fishman
Written by Buz Kohan, Bob Arnst and James Lipton
Special Musical Material by Earl Brown
Art Director: Charles Lisanby
Miss Streisand's music arranged by Peter Matz

None of Barbra's post-Vegas concert performances have been engineered to fill her own pockets. Most were designed to call attention to worthy causes. In 1978, the American Committee to Celebrate Israel's 30th Anniversary arranged a "gala birthday party" in Los Angeles. Joining the celebration were a host of celebrities including Anne Bancroft, Mikhail Baryshnikov, Debby Boone, Carol Burnett, Sammy Davis, Jr., Kirk Douglas, Henry Fonda, Gene Kelly, Barry Manilow, Paul Newman, Jean Stapleton, Cicely Tyson, Ben Vereen, Natalie Wood—and Barbra Streisand accompanied by Zubin Mehta and the Los Angeles Philharmonic. The gala took place on the afternoon of May 7, 1978; a two-hour condensation of the event, including a satellite feed from Israel and a poorly edited video/phone conversation between Barbra and Golda Meir, aired the following evening.

Streisand's appearance was choreographed to provide "a powerful and emotional finish" to the evening. Dressed in an antique white lace gown and moving across the stage as if it were her living room, she did just that with immaculate grace and control. Her repertoire ("Tomorrow," "People," "Happy Days Are Here Again") was chosen to reflect hope and unity. Contrary to some press reports, her segment did not go overtime. It is true, however, that ABC was most interested in keeping her performance intact—and because they had so much material, some appearances were abbreviated (or cut out entirely).

Reviews:

"Every once in a great while a program comes along with a balance so perfect it never fails to connect. *The Stars Salute Israel at 30*...has that rare winning combination. Whether in song, dance, dramatic rendition or comedy, the tribute was a profoundly moving one with the sincerity of the participants evident throughout....The triumph continued to accumulate as Barbra Streisand, in a rare public appearance, belted out a closing medley of songs....Rounding out the highly successful birthday celebration was 'Hatikva' (Hope) sung as the only Streisand can, to the audience of lighted candles at the Dorothy Chandler Pavilion while the event was simultaneously being celebrated in the Grand Ballroom of the Hilton Hotel in Jerusalem."

—*Hollywood Reporter*

1980 Grammy Awards
February 27, 1980

"The rush is so high, it's like I'm going to faint."

Barbra's sole domestic television appearance during 1979 was in another "Making of..." documentary entitled *Getting in Shape for The Main Event.* (Australia also received an exclusive three-part personal interview via *The Mike Walsh Show.*) The half-hour syndicated special featured outtakes from the film, clips from Hollywood's classic battle of the sexes comedies, plus dual interviews with Barbra and Ryan and screenwriters Gail Parent and Andrew Smith.

She made up for the inactivity in 1980 with two appearances of some historical significance. Marty Pasetta, who also produces and directs most of the Grammy Awards shows, had talked nominees Streisand and Diamond into singing their "You Don't Bring Me Flowers" duet live on TV. It was a surprise teaming; Barbra's only performance on the Grammy show was kept secret from the media until a day prior to the telecast. Jon Peters called in one of his trusted assistants, Rusty Lemorande, to stay with her throughout this "mini-ordeal." "There was an incredible rallying of the forces to help make it happen and support Barbra's decision," Lemorande conveys. "Which meant, literally, within something like a 24-hour period it all had to be done: musical arrangements had to be worked out...rehearsals had to be accomplished. It was quite extraordinary."

On February 27, Lemorande accompanied Barbra to Los Angeles' Shrine Auditorium—and watched her discuss the dynamics of the song (how they should approach their characters) with Diamond, talk through the arrangement with the conductor, work with the musicians and, of course, go over the staging with Pasetta. The director's original concept involved three stools (one with flowers) on a bare stage. "What was later desribed as being very appropriate blocking of the number, where Barbra and Neil came out from opposite ends of the stage and slowly walked toward each other, was actually Barbra's idea," Lemorande says. "And I witnessed what she would later be criticized for quite often—which was, to have an idea, be diplomatic in the way she presented it to the director, probably be right about it, but have others (the ancillary people who have a lot of time on their hands) view it as if she were pushing people around. It was very interesting because Barbra was the only performer I was aware of who said, 'Gee, could we roll a little tape on this camera rehearsal and take a look at it?', which is a very intelligent and professionally conscious thing to do, and the director couldn't have been more positive. But as they went into the van to look at the tape, I was standing off to the side and got to hear all the mumblings and grumblings about her taking over. It couldn't have been more untrue."

The rehearsal went very well and Barbra and Neil retired to their dressing rooms to get ready for the show (which is broadcast live on the east coast). Lemorande: "Then it got bad. Barbra put on her costume and started getting nervous, so she taught me how to play backgammon (she's very good at it and loves the game)....We got to the point of no return. I was holding her hand...there offstage and I'm thinking, 'You know, this woman has *ruled* the stage. She has re-distinguished in our generation what it is to be a stage performer in a world where film and television are what it's all about. And here she is sweating bullets, not able to breathe, very hypertensive....' And she's saying, 'I can't go on, I can't go on.' In my own naive way, I just tried to talk her through it."

Meanwhile, Neil Diamond was on the other end of the stage so he couldn't offer much support and Lemorande began to think it would be his fault if Barbra passed out before she was supposed to go onstage. "At the same time, I realized that she was a trouper and didn't need me at all. Even with nobody there, at the moment of truth she would have gotten it together and gone out. Yet the performance was magically colored by that obvious panic: Putting her hand in her pocket and catching her breath...the audience was mesmerized."

"But nervousness is great," Barbra underlined in a 1975 interview. "It shows you're alive. It makes your adrenaline flow and your sensitivity higher. It even makes your voice higher—when you're frightened your voice can soar. It's just a matter of using

During Barbra's final performance of the day she sang "Evergreen" and "People."

the fear."

Indeed, much of the charm of the performance was that the facade wasn't working and both Streisand and Diamond appeared very human in their nervousness. They walked onstage unannounced. A roar filled the auditorium as soon as the duo was recognized—and cheers continued throughout the performance, culminated by the audience's approval of Barbra affectionately touching Neil's cheek (in much the same manner as her final moments with Redford at the end of *The Way We Were*). The adulatory response took even the camera crew by surprise as they stumbled to recreate the blocking that had been set in rehearsals. Although "You Don't Bring Me Flowers" went unrewarded for the evening, the performance very neatly eclipsed any excitement over the major winners that night.

ACLU Tribute to the Bergmans
June 1, 1980

Discouraged that Streisand had yet to finalize a concert tour, supporters had at least come to expect that she would perform for an occasional charity. In June, Angelenos had one more chance to catch Barbra in concert, this time at a tribute to her friends, the Bergmans, benefiting the American Civil Liberties Union. It was another celebrity-studded event—onstage and in the audience. The concert was produced and directed by Joe Layton; Peter Matz was the musical director; Marvin Hamlisch arranged the overture; Billy Goldenberg, Michel Legrand, Dave Grusin, Lee Holdridge and David Shire were among the others providing orchestrations.

As the unofficial mistress of ceremonies, Barbra opened and closed the show. In her report on the event, *Herald-Examiner* society columnist Wanda McDaniel made some fun of the audience ("Well, at least they wore shoes"), but when the curtain rose to reveal Barbra at center stage, bathed in a golden light, quite a few VIP's were on their feet as well. The applause after a rather tentative "The Way We Were" was deafening. As usual, Streisand paced her performance so that she didn't have to stop between numbers. "I never really stop long enough for the applause," she told the BBC's Iain Johnstone. "I always go into another song because [the response] makes me feel a little uncomfortable." This time, however, the crowd was difficult to ignore. "We love you, Barbra!" fans screamed from the rafters. "Thank you. I love you, too," she responded, then asking for a chance to hear the intro to her next song, "After the Rain." Upon its conclusion, she assured the audience she'd be back in a little bit, "but right now have a wonderful, wonderful time." Having

Barbra open the tribute with two selections—however brief—allowed the audience to enjoy the rest of the show without the unbearable anticipation regarding her upcoming appearance.

Ninety minutes later she was back onstage in a lavender version of the outfit she wore on the Grammys. She sang "Summer Me, Winter Me," accompanied by Michel Legrand at the piano. "Michel," she said, "you write the most extraordinary melodies. If you were only Jewish, they'd have an evening like this for you, too!" After an exquisite "What Are You Doing the Rest of Your Life?" she teased the audience with a taste of "The Way We Weren't": "We were wistful, we were young/All the smiles of love were waiting in our eyes/And we were neither innocent nor wise/As we are now." "Did we make a mistake, Sydney?" Barbra winked at her former director (seated in the audience) before launching

The first Barbara Walters special, December 1976. (Photo courtesy of the Richard Giammanco collection)

Chumming it up with "Good Night America" host, Geraldo Rivera (L), Kris Kristofferson and Jon Peters.

into a fervent reprise of "The Way We Were."

Prior to the show, alert concert-goers spotted Neil Diamond in the audience and, although he wasn't listed on the bill, hoped for an encore of Barbra and Neil's electrifying Grammy Awards duet. When Barbra came to his opening line, however, she continued singing and he remained seated....Three phrases later, Diamond started making his way toward the stage and the audience was in ecstasy. "I don't think they recognize you, Neil," she kidded. "The [Dorothy Chandler Pavilion] has never heard such a rave reaction from any audience in which we've been present," Army Archerd wrote in *Daily Variety*. "Streisand was never in better/greater voice."

Onstage, Barbra appeared to have pulled her act together for her friends, graciously dealing with raucous fans and sounding warmer than ever. Backstage was another story. The nerves had gotten so bad she was physically ill before (and during) the concert. Throughout the show, the Bergmans and Jon Peters rushed from their seats to comfort her prior to her performances. (She brought a yoga teacher with her, said columnist Liz Smith—but he only succeeded in making matters worse, according to other reports.) "I saw her after the show," Bob Esty says,

"and she was almost catatonic. 'Was I okay?'"

"In concerts it's a nice feeling to realize that there are [thousands of] people there to see you," Barbra said in a 1968 radio interview, "but it was more fun when I was sharing the bill and could take the play away from the star." What had changed since the early '60s was her ability to hide behind the bravado of the characters she created in her songs.

The essence of pop stardom requires that one give of oneself, that the audience be made to feel they are sharing a personal statement—whatever that may be. But who was "La Streisand," the mythic diva created not only by the scope of Barbra's work (and the importance she gave it) but also amplified by the variety of images projected in the press? Everything that BARBRA STREISAND is to the public has become so large, the expectations—and *her* perception of those expectations—have become so great that living up to that image has become impossibly problematic. It was one thing to imagine the rejected lover who sang "Cry Me a River." How does one *act* the part of Barbra Streisand?

"Barbra was much more relaxed [in the smaller clubs]," Marty says. "She was looser then. She enjoyed walking on the stage and toying with an audience; playing with them, winning them and losing them. Performing was much more difficult as she became more successful [because] she felt that the audience's demands had changed." "I'll tell you what

103

happens," she explained to Lawrence Grobel, "I feel [people] listening so hard, I feel my own power, and it frightens me."

Progressive stage fright isn't a new phenomenon. Even respected veterans such as Katharine Hepburn and Laurence Olivier experience it. Hepburn admitted to Dick Cavett that sometimes one becomes even more terrified as one gets older "...because you know so much more. You know all the horrible things that can happen and go wrong. And by that time you really know yourself pretty well and what a real *bore* you are. So you think, 'Are they going to accept this ridiculous object that I am?'"

In the past, it wasn't uncommon for journalists to exclaim that Streisand could recite listings from the telephone book and make it sing. In places like the Bon Soir it was easy to get away with such experimentation. But fill Madison Square Garden with 25,000 fans who haven't seen her perform in at least 16 years (if at all)—and how many of these admirers would quiet down for an obscure selection from *Je m'appelle* or *Classical Barbra?* How many aficionados of *Color Me Barbra* would want to hear "Enough Is Enough?" How many young fans would sit still for "Here We Are At Last" or "On Rainy Afternoons" instead of "Woman in Love?"

Barbra has never been a traditional performance artist. She never toured; she never became part of the social scene that attracts most young people to music. Though the "rush" provided by an audience's approval is undeniable, her motivation has always been internally focused. She is an artist, in much the same way that a painter is considered an artist, as opposed to a performer. "In the early days, when I first met her and she was a cabaret performer," Peter Matz states, "the truth was that Barbra couldn't *wait* to leave. I mean, she loved it if somebody famous came to the club. She'd be like a kid with her responses. 'Wow! Did they really come to see me?' It was very nice. But the fact was that she didn't get anything from that mass outpouring of love. It can be a powerful energy source, but Barbra never felt a need to be renewed in that way."

The argument over whether or not Streisand owes it to her fans to perform live continues. Is the work enough? It should be, but that simple point only complicates the frustrations and the justifications. Because, while Barbra refuses to rule out the possiblity, the ACLU Tribute to the Bergmans on June 1, 1980, was her final public performance.

I Love Liberty (ABC-TV)
Broadcast March 21, 1982

Created and developed by Norman Lear

"Barbra: With One More Look at You" provided a bird's eye view of production on A Star Is Born...

Executive producers: Bud Yorkin and Norman Lear
Produced and directed by Bill Carruthers
Written by Richard Alfieri, Rita Mae Brown, Rick Mitz, Arthur Allan Seidelman and Norman Lear
Musical director: Peter Matz
Barbra Streisand's segment produced by Joe Layton

The stunning success of *Guilty* brought about Barbra's only 1981 appearance: onstage with Barry Gibb at the Grammy Awards (which were telecast from New York for the first time in years). Any hopes for a surprise duet at Radio City Music Hall were quickly squelched, but the brief comic exchange between the duo delighted the audience; it prompted spontaneous cheering that was as vocal as that for any teen idol.

...and some humorous moments, as well. Here, Barbra supplies a little comic relief during an intense editorial meeting.

The year 1982 saw the realization of Barbra's dream to make *Yentl*. Prior to the commencement of principal photography, she filmed two videos: "America the Beautiful" and "Memory." The former was shot expressly for *I Love Liberty*, a two-hour special from Norman Lear and People for the American Way. PAW felt that Reverend Jerry Falwell's Moral Majority and the new Religious Right were seeking to infringe on the freedom of speech and diversity of opinion. Falwell and Lear had been antagonists since the Moral Majority started publicly criticizing such Lear-produced series as *All in the Family* and *Maude* for emphasizing sexuality and undermining traditional American values. With so much news time devoted to Falwell's work, PAW hoped *I Love Liberty* would help "reclaim patriotism from the convervatives and give it back to the people."

Lear very wisely selected former President Gerald Ford, Lady Bird Johnson and Walter Cronkite to co-chair the event. The program was taped on February 22; attendance was free. The final version of the show, which featured such luminaries as Senator Barry Goldwater, Jane Fonda, Walter Matthau, Kristy McNichol, Mary Tyler Moore, Melissa Manchester, Christopher Reeve, Kenny Rogers and Robin Williams, was splashy, colorful, sometimes corny, sometimes heavy-handed in its presentation. Barbra's "special guest taped appearance" was produced in London by Joe Layton. Using the U.S. Air Force marching band as back-up, Barbra was very

simply presented; the focus of the piece being the sincerity projected in her vocal. Although infinitesimally out of sync with the vocal track, she brought the song to a thrilling climax and provided one of the show's few highlights.

Reviews:

"With Barbra Streisand singing 'America the Beautiful,' Gregory Hines tap-dancing to 'This Land Is Your Land' and Melissa Manchester backed by 120 voices on 'Amazing Grace,' it may sound like a cross between *The Night of 100 Stars* and *Up with People*. But when the performers include Jane Fonda and Barry Goldwater, the co-chairmen include Gerald Ford and Walter Cronkite, and the writers include Rita Mae Brown, better to forget the labels and reach for the popcorn."

—*New York Daily News*

"Memory"
Directed by Jack Semmens
Produced by Chips Chipperfield

There had been other Streisand promotional videos. CBS Records International put together film footage and photo montages for *A Star Is Born* and *Guilty*. An interesting but rarely seen video was "My Heart Belongs to Me," which was produced exclusively for the 1977 Columbia Records convention. Shot in close-up with wisps of "clouds" drifting by

Backstage at the 1976 Grammys with Best Record winner George Benson.

her, Barbra made a humorous jab at such effects by coughing comically throughout the musical bridge; at the end of the video, she casually took her bow to a solitary handclap.

"Memory," on the other hand, was shot to resemble an actual recording session. The only props were a microphone, music stand and a stool. Edited into that basic performance footage (two angles, sometimes reversed) were vintage shots of a city skyline at night and nostalgic glimpses of a New Year's Eve celebration. Memorable moments included a mid-section where Barbra (with her straight chestnut hair hidden under a knit cap) pretends to conduct the orchestra, and the denouement as she leans out of the spotlight. The 4:15 video was released by CBS Records International in England

(where *Love Songs*, as *Memories* was titled in Great Britain, hit number 1) in April of 1982. It was never officially released in the States.

20/20 (ABC-TV)
"Barbra Streisand: Papa, Watch Me Fly"
Broadcast November, 17, 1983

Senior producer and writer/correspondent: Geraldo Rivera
Produced by Craig and Sheri Rivera
Associate producer: Michael P. Smith
Edited by Robert J. Brandt

With the exception of a brief respite when she presented Best Picture to Richard Attenborough and *Gandhi* at the 1983 British Film Awards, the remainder of Barbra's 1982 and 1983 schedule was set aside for *Yentl*. On November 17, 1983, ABC's news/magazine show *20/20* set a precedent by devoting an

"Right on, Barbra Streisand!" Jane Fonda exclaimed as she announced the singer of the next Oscar-nominated song. The '77 Academy Awards featured a burnished image of Barbra from head to toe. The rusty theme even followed through on details such as the color of her microphone and a star-burst spot which highlighted her bronzed skin.

Streisand's "Concert for Israel" segment (1978) began with the optimism of "Tomorrow." "Do I have time to introduce all the members of the band?" she joked about her "back-up band," the Los Angeles Philharmonic. (Photo credit: Bob Scott)

entire program to a show business personality. It was the beginning of Barbra's largest promotional push ever in support of her directorial debut. The hour-long show included a behind-the-scenes look at the film, post-production work on the film and soundtrack, a tour of the Malibu ranch and interviews with Barbra and Jon (recently separated). Her friendly relationship with correspondent Geraldo Rivera allowed viewers to get an intimate feel of a woman caught at an important crossroads in her life. Rivera had been filming segments since August of 1982. "Usually I'm very impatient to get things on the air," he told *Us* magazine. "With this one, I wanted to wait until we had what I thought was the definitive piece on Barbra at this stage of her career."

Reviews:

"...scenes of her at work on the film make up

the best part of *20/20*. This is because she is a professional, and what professionals do, not what they are, is what makes them interesting. We see Miss Streisand in a studio, for example, supervising the mix, the electronic transcription of a song....[She] seems terribly intent on getting the mix right, and when the result pleases her, she glows; she is beautiful. *20/20* says it took well over a year to put together the program about Miss Streisand, and that Mr. Rivera had to travel 25,000 miles to do it. Better he had just hung around the recording studio and watched Miss Streisand for an hour."

—*The New York Times*

A Film Is Born (BBC)

Written and narrated by Iain Johnstone
Produced by Jake Lush
Executive producer: Barry Brown
Film editor: Les Filby

American version produced by George Suski
Narrated by J.B. Wilson
Edited by Bee Ottinger

Ironically, far more insightful glimpses into the

A special Grammy moment: Barbra & Neil sing "You Don't Bring Me Flowers," 1980.

exhaustive process of making *Yentl*, as well as a more candid, less guarded Streisand, were to be compiled by the foreign media. A BBC film crew headed by Iain Johnstone contributed *A Film Is Born*. (Johnstone had conducted an equally candid interview with Barbra in 1976.) The documentary not only chronicled filming in London and Czechoslovakia, but also managed to capture the filmmaker's state of mind at the time by conducting the interviews while the project was still overwhelming her, before she had a chance to step back from it. The 40-minute special was subsequently abridged to a half-hour format (with new narration) for syndication in the United States.

Canadian television host Brian Linehan taped an in-depth interview with Barbra that succeeded by virtue of his detailed research into her career. In the U.S., *The Today Show*'s Gene Shalit helped to reveal a lighter, more thoughtful side—with the star even speculating on her ideal "last meal." At Academy Awards time, instead of sulking in Hollywood (in view of the Oscar snub), Barbra opted to do an extensive promotional tour for *Yentl* in Europe. She appeared on France's *Champs Elysees* and *A La Une; Coupe der Weijden* in the Netherlands; *Auf Los Gents Los* in Germany; Italy's *Dominica In;* and *Viewpoints* in Israel (where she also did a live interview via satellite with *Good Morning America*).

Taking advantage of the difference in language,

the sly host of *Champs Elysees* (the Parisienne *Tonight Show*) landed a real coupe by maneuvering Barbra into an impromptu performance. "I told you!" a wary Streisand said to Michel Legrand as she finally acquiesced to humming ("Hum? You want me to hum?") a few bars of "What Are You Doing the Rest of Your Life?" With Legrand accompanying her at the piano, she made a valiant effort to remember the lyrics of a song she had mentally filed away years ago, but gave up after the first verse. Although the audience hardly seemed to mind the goof, the pair begged off as soon as they were finished.

"Left in the Dark"
(CBS Music Video Enterprises)

Directed by J.S. Kaplan
Produced by Teri Schwartz
Written by J.S. Kaplan and Teri Schwartz
Executive producer: Robert Abel
Director of photography: Donald Thorin
Edited by Kent Beyda

Running time: 6:07

As to be expected, the videos for the *Yentl* soundtrack ("The Way He Makes Me Feel" and "Papa, Can You Hear Me?") consisted of clips from the motion picture ("Papa" was lifted in its entirety from the film). As the mix on *Emotion* was being

Publicist Lee Solters (center) guides Barbra and Neil Diamond through the backstage pandemonium following their performance at the 1980 Grammy awards. (Photo credit: Bob Scott)

finalized, however, Barbra decided to shoot a conceptual video for the album's first single, Jim Steinman's "Left in the Dark." Working with director Jonathan Kaplan (who directed the feature film *Heart Like a Wheel* and the video of Rod Stewart's "Infatuation") and a creative team from Robert Abel Entertainment, she played an important part in establishing the visual style. "She spent a great deal of time with us, poring over different designs and elaborate storyboards so we knew *exactly* how everything was going to look," said producer Teri Schwartz.

The video was shot the week of September 24, 1984, at Hollywood Center Studios and on location in Los Angeles. Its scenario juxtaposed several different "realities," with Barbra playing the roles of a lounge singer in an Edward Hopper-style nightclub and a character in a '50s film noir drama. Various suggestive realities were explored involving Barbra and Kris Kristofferson (as the bartender/lover). Two brief moments acknowledge the audience as well as display a sly sense of humor: During a short musical interlude, she fans herself, takes a drag from a cigarette and drinks a Coke—all without missing a beat as she begins the next verse. A while later, she lets the vocal track continue as she watches the action in the lounge and takes a very *serious* drag from the cigarette. The final embrace (shot by Donald Thorin, the cinematographer of *Purple Rain* and *An Officer and a Gentleman*) was a nod to Streisand and Kristofferson's *A Star Is Born* association.

The leisurely-paced "Left in the Dark" premiered on *Entertainment Tonight* in October. But, the single's inability to break into the Top 40 and the video's failure to assist the single effectively sealed the fate for both. "Left in the Dark" received an insignificant amount of attention on all fronts.

"Emotion"
(Barwood Films, Ltd.)

A film by Barbra Streisand and Richard Baskin
Produced by Teri Schwartz
Executive producer: Robert Abel
Edited by Kent Beyda

Running time: 5:00

Robert Abel Entertainment also supervised the development of Barbra's second music video (her third single) from *Emotion*. Barbra had a "very general idea" for "Emotion" which director Richard Baskin was able to flesh out; he conceived of the

Closing the ACLU Tribute to Alan & Marilyn Bergman. (Photo credit: Bob Scott)

"Barry...do you feel guilty?" she asked on the 1981 Grammys. "I don't know. I feel like I'm cheating on Neil Diamond!"

video as "a musical dramedy." "We were just having fun with all the different kinds of emotion—or the lack of it," she said. "You have to ask yourself: 'How do you visualize emotion? What does emotion mean to me?' I guess to everybody it's very personal and [she smiled] I've always been drawn to the sensual."

Filming was scheduled to take place in early October at the Jacob Street Studios in London. The English base opened the door for the producers to ask several co-stars who ordinarily might not be available to them to take part in the film. To play Barbra's disinterested husband, Baskin suggested rock star Roger Daltrey. "He'll never do it," Barbra responded. "I mean, why would he want to be in my video?" He did, and he was. "Roger was really fun to work with. He brought a whole new dimension to the character of the husband," she said later. "Although I felt bad for him; he kept wanting to make this into a feature."

Barwood also went after Ringo Starr to play one of the porno barkers, but the former Beatle had a last-minute conflict that prevented him from joining the cast. "And then one night we were having dinner in a Chinese restaurant and in walks Mischa— Mikhail Baryshnikov—and he came over to the table and said, 'Barbra!' I had met him a few times before, and I said, 'Hi! Do you want to be in my video?' That was like the first words out of my mouth to everybody on the street and why should he be any different?...In one's fantasies, Baryshnikov would leap across the stage, sweep you off your feet and sweep you out the door. And that's what he [did]."

The colorful individualism of the youths in London also fascinated Barbra—perhaps reminding her of the avant garde movement in the Greenwich Village of her youth. But, she marveled, "it's not a replay of anything...it's *completely* original." For the mod sequences, she not only cast a cross-section of these styles but also sought to apply some of them to herself. "Our costume designer brought me a picture of a woman who had sprayed her hair white, and it was just so extraordinary to me that I decided to try it," she said. "So we sprayed my hair white, and then even took white make-up and put it on my eyelashes to make white mascara." Her new wave/ punk leather and chains, highlighted by splashes of color in her jewelry and in her hair, was inspired by

112

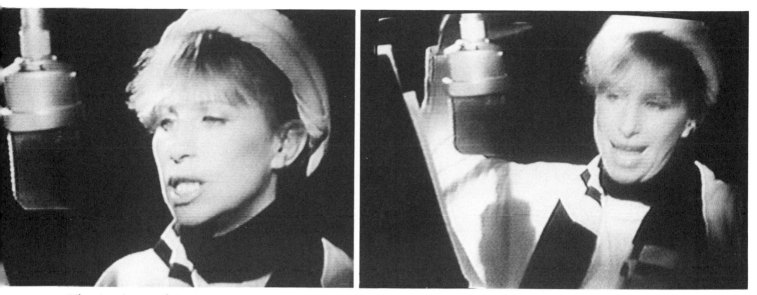

The simplicity of "Memory," 1981.

early pictures of Madonna.

Barbra color-coordinated her fantasies, too. Red in the punk nightclub (impeccably coordinated down to the color of her nailpolish, lipstick, eye shadow, even microphone) and pink in her bedroom; when real life intrudes, all the colors become mismatched. To complete the visuals, Streisand and Baskin designed an homage to Bernardo Bertolucci's *The Conformist* in their recreation of Vittorio Storaro's striking cinematography for Barbra's seduction by a lecherous businessman.

The imaginative background and pacing of "Emotion" broke through the MTV barrier. The video premiered on that cable music network on January 18, 1985. Despite the fact that it quickly became one of their most-requested videos, it was too late to breathe any new life into *Emotion*. A couple of months later, MusicVision released the short film to national movie theaters as a companion piece to a host of new features including the similarly-plotted *Desperately Seeking Susan*.

Reviews:

"Nobody does playfulness better than Streisand, and she turns this video into a much more interesting bit than the song alone would warrant. She's a frustrated wife whose slugabed husband, played by Roger Daltrey, shows no interest in her. So she gussies up to arouse some of that emotion, alternately looking quite ravishing and funny by screwing up her face into one of those mood-breaking looks that says, 'Wait a minute; I'm not supposed to be gorgeous.' Mikhail Baryshnikov has a dance-on at the end."

—*People*

"Somewhere"
(Barwood Films, Ltd.)

Directed by William Friedkin
Produced by Cindy Chvatal and Glenn Goodwin
Executive producer: Barbra Streisand
Director of photography: Andrzej Bartowiak
Edited by Bud Smith

Running time: 4:28

"I think making a video is the answer to filmmakers who haven't found the right films to make," Barbra said as filming wrapped on "Emotion." "Somewhere," her sole video presentation from *The Broadway Album,* would give two errant filmmakers an opportunity to flex their muscles. Packaging the video was actually quite easy once a director was set (Richard Baskin, Michael Apted, Jeffrey Hornaday and Timothy Hutton were also considered). Barbra felt that the *Broadway* video should reflect her theatrical roots, but, respecting the song's theme, she also wanted it to have some social relevance. With director William Friedkin's additional input, "Somewhere" evolved into a romantically photographed performance video which neatly flowed between nostalgia and glimpses into infinity, as the Bergmans stated it.

On October 28, 1985, the production team journeyed to the historic Apollo Theater in Harlem (chosen for its approximation to the plush red velvet seat decor on the cover of *The Broadway Album*) to rehearse and cast the remaining "extra" parts. In

113

"America the Beautiful" was staged exclusively for Norman Lear's "I Love Liberty" special, March 1982.

keeping with the universal theme, the filmmakers envisioned an audience filled with a broad range of ages, races and religions: hopeful immigrants, children, old people, blacks, Orientals, Jews. Filming was acomplished in an all-day shoot the next day.

"Later in the afternoon, after they'd dismissed the extras, Barbra actually sang live to the track," says Peter Afterman. (Afterman is the vice president and general manager of the music division at Guber/Peters Entertainment and he played an important role in coordinating "various business areas" concerning *The Broadway Album.)* "Because she didn't want to sing to a bunch of empty seats, [CBS music video coordinator] Jeanne Mattiussi, myself, [producers] Glenn Goodwin and Cindy Chvatal were treated to what I considered to be a private concert of that one song. We were all seated in the second row and Barbra sang right to us.

"I never grew up as a Barbra Streisand fan, although I certainly know how impressive her voice is and I obviously respect all that. But when I sat in that theater, the first time she started to sing I got chills. My eyes teared up a little bit because I was so blown out.... I was absolutely stunned. The impact of each performance was amazing. I turned to the others and we all exchanged knowing glances. She really, really moved us."

For the first time, Afterman understood why admirers are so exasperated over Barbra's retreat from live performing. "The power was really incredible. She seemed to put so much of herself into the song, there could have been cannons, anything, going off in the middle of the theater and she would never have known it. The concentration was that intense. But I could also see why she says it would be hard to tour, because she'd have to sing the same songs in the same way each night. And to sing with that intensity...I mean, I saw the exact thing on *The Broadway Album.* She didn't just breeze into a studio to lay a few tracks down. She put so much energy and effort into it that *I* was exhausted just watching her." The video shoot wrapped around midnight on the 29th.

Back in Los Angeles, Friedkin supervised the editing, adding space-age graphics to the prelude and an appropriate helicopter shot from his current film, *To Live and Die in L.A.* (Although the overhead shot of the theater skylight is actually the Ritz Theatre in Elizabeth, New Jersey.)

"Somewhere" debuted on VH-1, the Adult Contemporary answer to MTV, on November 15, 1985, and received generous airplay. In a rather ironic but fitting tribute, there was one use of the video neither Streisand or Friedkin could have foreseen. Following the explosion of the space shuttle Challenger, a number of local TV stations used the celestial opening and closing, plus Barbra's "spiritual" vocals (as one writer put it) to accompany footage of the lost astronauts.

Reviews:

"Not since John Landis's *Thriller*—the *Chien Andalou* of concept video—has there been such an achievement....The challenge for Friedkin is clear. He must gild [Streisand's] artistry in an imagistic frame. That he succeeds is less a testament to his genius (or hers) than to their shared *jouissance.*"

—*Village Voice*

Putting It Together: The Making of The Broadway Album (HBO)
Barwood Films in association with CBS Music Video Enterprises

Produced by Joni Rosen
Segments directed by William Friedkin and Jerry Kramer
Production coordinator: Jeanne Mattiussi
Edited by Tom McQuade
Production consultant: Andy Harries
Audio engineers: Ed Greene and Doug Nelson

First airdate: January 11, 1986

"A little bit of hype can be effective
Long as you can keep it in perspective"

Barbara Walters decided to ask Streisand back for her 10th Anniversary Special. Ostensibly, the reason for the interview was to talk about Barbra's life post-*Yentl*—but the focus of the report, telecast on September 13, 1985, turned out to be *The Broadway Album.* To depict "the artist in her environment," as well as document the milestone that the album represented to her, Barwood hired Jerry Kramer & Associates, an independent production company, to make a visual record of the first sessions. These sessions encompassed her work with composer Stephen Sondheim on "Putting It Together" (with director Sydney Pollack, record company president David Geffen and actor Ken Sylk assuming the roles in the Executive Chorus), "If I Loved You" and a preliminary orchestration on "Can't Help Lovin' That Man." Less than a minute of that material wound up in the Walters special.

Home Box Office, in the meantime, continued its on-going discussions with Barbra regarding a special...anything. There were conversations regarding a *Barbra Streisand Theater* (á la Shelly Duvall and Ray Bradbury) which would give her a chance to produce, direct and/or star in any number of the classical roles she'd been talking about over the years.

Pausing for a translation during the Rome television show "Dominica In," March 25, 1984. (Photo credit: R. Emerian)

"Entertainment Tonight" corners her backstage following the 1984 Scopus Awards presentation. (Photo credit: Gary Bornstein)

Geraldo Rivera's "20/20" camera captured Streisand trying to explain to one of the sound editors on Yentl *what was missing from his mix of "The Way He Makes Me Feel." (She played a cassette of the original recording to prove her point.)*

The camera would go backstage and watch her prepare for each role. Similarly, a *Streisand Musical Theater* would be a unique opportunity to essay her favorite musical moments from Broadway to Hollywood.

With the imminent release of *The Broadway Album*, HBO had hoped to convince Barbra to tape a concert on the Great White Way. But, she was more impressed with Cinemax's look at the making of Barry Manilow's, *2 a.m. Paradise Cafe* LP and offered the cable network the Kramer documentary footage instead. Ultimately, HBO was pleased to get "a television version of the album....[Barbra] is an artist who does not do things unless they feel right and this is the first thing [from us] that she's wanted to do," original programming VP Bridget Potter noted. The only trouble was that *The Broadway Album* was now in the mixing stage—and only two sessions plus a conceptual video had been filmed. To fill out the special to a respectable length, an additional interview segment between Streisand and Friedkin was taped during production on the "Somewhere" video.

The added segment was the most heavily criticized element of the show. It is unlikely that so much material would have been used from it if there had been alternate footage, and yet the interview is of interest. Once one gets past a certain pretension (and a surprising sycophantic approach from Friedkin), there is valuable information being imparted here. The special is self-serving inasmuch as any TV program devoted to a film or album currently in release is self-serving. The error was in promoting the documentary—as Barbra preferred to call it—as Streisand's return to creating original programming for television. *Putting It Together* wasn't a full-fledged variety special. It was created by CBS Records for HBO (and would later be released by CBS/Fox as a home video). It was an expensive, elaborate but nonetheless fascinating electronic press kit in which the star looked great, sounded even better *and* was capable of laughing at her own foibles.

Review:

"A must for the diva's devoted fans, the performances here are first-rate and it's often revealing to see how the LP evolved in the studio....Unfortunately, the rhythm of this show is frequently broken by ponderous interviews with Streisand conducted by director William Friedkin. More often than not, these segments just get in the way of the music.... In addition to the Q&A's and studio scenes, there's an opening montage of high points in Streisand's career and a new video of the song, 'Somewhere.' Both the montage and the video clip are skillfully edited, and it's too bad other bits like them weren't included to flesh out the 40-minute special into a full hour."

—*Hollywood Reporter*

POSTSCRIPT

On February 25, 1986, representing NARAS' Board of Govenors, Barbra appeared on the 28th Annual Grammy Awards to present the Trustees Award (posthumously) to George and Ira Gershwin. Her speech, with generous snippets of the Gershwins' lyrics, was a tease of a performance in itself. A month later, her recording of "Putting It Together" served as an appropriate backdrop for her presentation of the Best Director award at the 1986 Academy Awards. (Film clips exhibited during the accompanying montage included several glimpses of Barbra at work as an actress and a director.) Although John Huston was favored to take home an Oscar for *Prizzi's Honor,* Barbra's spontaneous vocal cue, "Mem'ries...," let the audience know *Out of Africa* had continued its sweep—and Sydney Pollack got a big hug from his former leading lady.

In April, Barbra added her presence to an impressive list of specially filmed celebrity cameos for producer Ken Kragen's "Hands Across America" promotional video.

117

"Left in the Dark" (Photographs: Greg Gorman)

With Mikhail Baryshnikov, 1984.

Experimenting with the different looks of emotion.

On the mark for "Somewhere," 1985.

"Oh, Regie, you're so strong!" When the fantasy gets out of control, the remorseful wife runs back to the protective arms of her husband (Roger Daltrey).

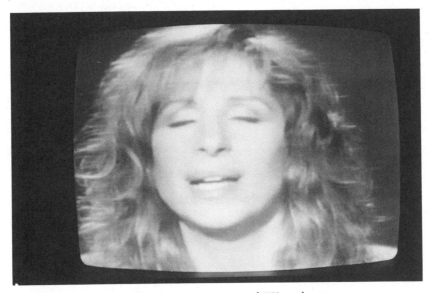

The ending of the video is reminiscent of "I'm the Greatest Star" from Funny Girl. *One reviewer would even call attention to the crucifixion-like imagery of the finale.*

"Putting It Together" with William Friedkin...
...and Peter Matz (L) and Stephen Sondheim (center).

Nearly satisfied that the opening of "Putting It Together" feels right (after the first take had been accidentally erased), Barbra is elated to be ready for "Section B!"

Arriving in London to shoot "Emotion." (Photo credit: AP/Wide World Photos)

A warm hug for 1986's Academy Award-winning Best Director, Sydney Pollack.

Streisand surprised the media by guiding Mrs. Ira Gershwin through each of the press rooms following her presentation at the '86 Grammy Awards.

BBC's "A Film Is Born" followed Barbra throughout her filmmaking journey.

THE MOVIES 1974–1986

Great stardom is often described in terms of the "heat" that is generated. By and large, the response is adulatory, but such an aura can also provoke a dark side, stirring up hostility and controversy in its wake. America, in particular, has had a peculiar love/hate relationship with the very star system it created. Stars are deified, anointed in glowing terms in the press, celebrated for their individuality, and then told, just as quickly, not to take it too seriously. Before they become ingrained in the public consciousness, the press moves on to a new messiah. Most of the time, the public is content to follow; sometimes they are the leaders.

A Star Is Born, for example, is Barbra's most popular film at the box-office; it far outdistances anything else on her list of motion pictures. Interestingly, its release triggered a barrage of unmerciful—and highly personal—criticism. On the other hand, *For Pete's Sake*, without a doubt her least-inspired effort, got a decent cross-section of reviews and few (if any) truly vicious ones. It ranks number 10 on her list—just above *On a Clear Day, Up the Sandbox* and *All Night Long* (all of which received fair to excellent reviews).

Recently, Barbra was declared to be one of the top five female draws of all time. A look at the cinema of the '70s indicates why. As the number of features decreased and budgets escalated, a steady batting average became more and more important. While the presence of Eastwood, Redford, McQueen and Reynolds was enough to dominate theaters across the country, Streisand was the only woman to consistently break into that elite group. From 1973–1975 (when she was ranked by the Quigley Poll at number 6, 4 and 2, respectively), she was the only female star in the Top 10. By the end of the '70s, she was set as the number 3 box office draw of the decade—though she only made eight films during a period when Eastwood and Reynolds were churning out ten to fifteen. The promise of Liza Minnelli and Diana Ross receded with their failing projects and, once again, Barbra was the only woman ranked in the Top 10. Contrast this with Doris Day, Elizabeth Taylor and Julie Andrews all being listed in Quigley's *Top Five* ten years earlier.

Today, the outlook is beginning to change with the emergence of Jane Fonda, Goldie Hawn, Diane Keaton and Sally Field; even so, none has exhibited Streisand's great strength at the box-office. Fonda's best showing was a number 3 and number 4 placement in 1979/80. (With one movie release, *The Main Event,* Barbra was ranked number 5 and number 9 during those years.) The previous year—with no film in release—she was still named 1978's "World Film Favorite." Amazingly, despite a substantial following, our most-acclaimed contemporary actress, Meryl Streep, hasn't even been able to crack the formidable Top 10.

"Anytime there's a war, society concentrates on its masculine qualities," screenwriter Jay Presson Allen theorized in a 1974 *New York Times* interview. "Films have been doing this for the past few years, and I believe that female audiences have been lost because there have been no stars they could identify with in a positive way." Indeed, the '60s and '70s were dismal years for women in cinema. In the roles and prominence accorded them, the '60s began unpromisingly and grew steadily worse throughout the early to mid-'70s. While the great European directors from Bergman to Truffaut allowed women strength, intelligence and wit—as well as their idiosyncrasies—American women had to turn to television to find solid role models in actresses like Mary Tyler Moore, Bea Arthur and Carol Burnett.

Losing the formerly-constant adult female audience meant that films had to address young people more—the final wave of Baby Boomers. Although Barbra sought to retain her core audience, the fact remains that most movie-goers attending *A Star Is Born* and *The Main Event* weren't likely to have much reference for her as a movie star, aside from those films and possibly a *What's Up, Doc?* or *The Way We Were.* They certainly didn't know her from *Funny Girl* or *The Owl and the Pussycat*—unless they saw either picture on television. Not having to struggle with that *Funny Girl* stereotype was an unexpected dividend brought on by this new era in filmmaking. Redefining her image and stardom to reflect the changing times—and a more personal point of view—was the challenge of the Second Decade.

FOR PETE'S SAKE
(Columbia Pictures)

CAST:

Henry................	Barbra Streisand
Pete.................	Michael Sarrazin
Helen...............	Estelle Parsons
Fred................	William Redfield
Mrs. Cherry..........	Molly Picon
Nick................	Louis Zorich
Loretta..............	Vivian Bonnell
Bernie...............	Richard Ward
Judge Hiller..........	Heywood Hale Broun

CREDITS:

Produced by..........	Martin Erlichman
	Stanley Shapiro
Directed by...........	Peter Yates
Screenplay...........	Stanley Shapiro
	Maurice Richlin
Executive producer....	Phil Feldman
Cinematography.......	Laszlo Kovacs
Production design.....	Gene Callahan
Set dresser...........	Jim Berkey
Costume designer......	Frank Thompson
Music................	Artie Butler
"For Pete's Sake (Don't Let Him Down)"	
Composed by.......	Artie Butler
Lyrics by...........	Mark Lindsay
Performed by.......	Barbra Streisand
Film editor...........	Frank P. Keller
Sound...............	Don Parker
Production manager...	Jim Di Gangi
Assistant director......	Harry Caplan
Casting..............	Jennifer Shull

Miss Streisand's hairstyles designed by Jon Peters

Running time: 90 minutes
Rated: PG

A Rastar Production

"I wish some of the film scripts that were written for Bette Davis could be written for me today," Barbra remarked to an English journalist in 1975. Not that she literally wanted to remake *All About Eve* or *The Letter,* but having a studio—which used to have a vested interest in its contract players—develop quality projects on any kind of recurrent basis would have been reassuring. With *Funny Girl, Hello, Dolly!* and *Clear Day* on line, *plus* a four-picture deal with Ray Stark, Barbra predetermined her schedule for several years when she first came to Hollywood. Through the formation of First Artists, she also got an early lead on developing her own projects. By the time she elected to take a break from filming in 1970, she was already firmly entrenched within the system—and aware the next move was pretty much up to her. She had her pick of films—*Cabaret, Klute, The Exorcist, Alice Doesn't Live Here Anymore,* et cetera—but none had the directors who ultimately realized those visions onscreen attached to them.

As screenplays stockpiled on her desk, another problem became evident. "Writers know that if they're going to write something on spec," Paramount Pictures production chief Robert Evans told *The New York Times,* "there are ten male stars and one woman they can put the picture together with." With the competition so fierce over the attention of

128

one female star, promising new writers were naturally inclined to try their luck where the odds were better. It was a classic Catch-22 situation. Fewer scripts for women meant fewer visible female stars; fewer stars meant fewer roles for women. It wasn't, as one movie executive offered, "a short range problem." It would take years to resolve.

Whether she was bankable or not, the trickle-down scenario also stifled Barbra's options. Manager Marty Erlichman didn't wait for things to get worse before seeking a number of tailor-made scripts for his client. People will always go to theaters to hear Barbra laugh or cry or sing—but most of all, Marty wanted to make audiences laugh. One of the projects he acquired for Barwood Productions was *Freaky Friday*, a novel about a mother and daughter switching identities. In May of 1973, Paramount Pictures announced that Marty would be producing *With or Without Roller Skates* for them later in the year. The black comedy revolved around the real-life adventures of a rather unorthodox nurse working in a

veteran's hospital. "Barbra and I met the nurse twice," Erlichman told *The New York Times*. "She is a fascinating woman—hilariously funny, and very realistic about her running battle with hospital authorities over what she considers the rights of her patients." Before he was able to develop a script, however, Barbra told him she couldn't see herself doing the film. After the drama and turmoil of *Up the Sandbox* and *The Way We Were*, she was in the mood for lighter fare.

Undaunted, Marty went to screenwriter Stanley Shapiro with another idea of his, which Shapiro liked. "We pitched it to Barbra and she said, 'If I like the script, I'll do it.' After the script was finished, we took it to her and she said, 'Okay.' The project was a comedy about a young couple struggling to make ends meet in Brooklyn. It was known by the rather unpleasant title of *July Pork Bellies*. 'It's the kind of part I've always wanted,' Barbra joked about her most physical role. "An intelligent, refined, sophisticated woman of the world...a woman who always travels first-class."

In the interest of making the whole package stronger, Erlichman and Shapiro took it to Ray Stark, then producing exclusively for Columbia Pictures. "I felt more secure that everything was being looked after since it was my first picture as the line producer," Marty says. "So Stanley and I co-produced it under Ray's auspices." The elements came together very quickly. Barbra submitted a list of directors she'd like to work with, including Czechoslovakian emigré Milos Forman. "She has a great sense of humor and she can really sell comedy on the screen," Forman says today. But at the time he didn't feel capable of tackling something so intrinsically American. Peter Yates's agent heard about the project and arranged for Yates to meet with Barbra and Marty. Englishman Yates, then capturing industry attention with action pictures like *Bullitt* and *The Hot Rock*, impressed the pair with his ideas.

Three leading men possibilities were tested for the part of Barbra's taxi-driving husband: Michael Landon, James Farentino and Michael Sarrazin. "It's very difficult to cast somebody in a film opposite Barbra," Yates told James Spada, "because unless you have a major star, you're going to have problems of balance. But no major star wanted to play it...It was like playing the girl's part in almost any other film—instead of the girl following two paces behind the guy, it was the other way around. So we had to find somebody who was a strong personality who could act...and get along with Barbra." The lanky Sarrazin won the role.

Originally, the producers planned to shoot most of the film in Brooklyn. But that idea began to

129

The studio set-up for For Pete's Sake's *opening shot.*

A little touch-up before a romantic scene.

With director Peter Yates, 1973.

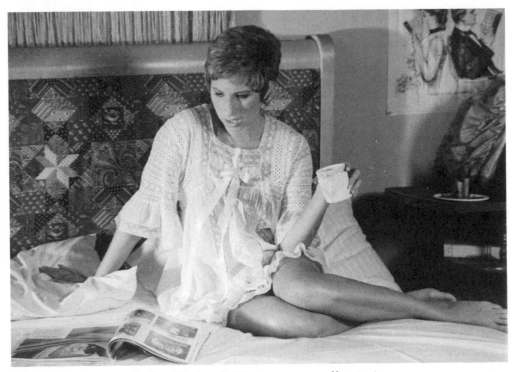

(Photo courtesy of the Richard Giammanco collection)

lose validity as the actual locations were being scouted. Principal photography commenced on September 24, 1973. Sites scheduled for the first two weeks of filming included Prospect Park, the Grand Army Plaza, Borough Hall, the Brooklyn Heights Promenade, the Brooklyn Bridge, the Court and Schermerhorn subway station and assorted side streets. The "atmosphere" was more colorful than anyone had bargained for. Advance publicity had alerted New Yorkers that Barbra was going to be in Brooklyn and camera-toting citizenry lined the streets and sidewalks at every location. "They wanted to see her, they wanted to touch her," assistant director Harry Caplan recalls.

It was difficult enough setting up shots that wouldn't reveal the crowds; dealing with the catcalls was nearly impossible. "You get hoarse asking people not to interrupt a scene," Caplan remarks. But interrupt the scene they did. The most intense situation occurred when Barbra was supposed to climb in and out of a (re-built) manhole in her flight from a law-enforcing canine. "We were right out there on 4th Avenue," notes the assistant director, "and because of the scene, we couldn't be too close to her once we turned the camera on (although there was someone in the manhole with her). The minute she lifted the lid and came out of the sewer and the director said, 'Cut!' the crowd would surge forward. The street was just full; traffic had stopped...It wasn't always

easy to get her back to her trailer. It was a frightening experience for her."

The reaction could be rather comical. "Hey, Barbra! Sing 'On a Clear Day' for us!" one cab driver yelled as he drove by. But when the production stopped long enough to take some publicity photographs, Stu Fleming, the second assistant director on the picture, remembers a couple of people shouting obscenities at Barbra. "I just remember this one crazy girl screaming and Barbra was getting pissed, and I didn't blame her....It was a hassle to film a picture [in Brooklyn]—especially for Barbra." Regarding the shoot at the Court Street Subway station, Fleming paints a memorable picture of Barbra hanging onto a strap inside the car. "I looked at her and she had this far-away look in her eyes. 'Do you remember when you used to take the subway?' I said. 'Yeah,' she said. 'I hated it.'"

Location filming wrapped a week early. *For Pete's Sake*, as it was now called, returned to The Burbank Studios where Brooklyn could be safely re-created on Stage 18, the studio commissary and the backlot. Barbra relaxed considerably, and Caplan, a veteran who had worked with everyone from W.C. Fields to Elvis Presley, delighted in watching her educate herself to everything that was going on on the set. "When she saw something that she didn't understand, she wanted to know what it was [about] to its fullest extent, whether it was part of the camera

132

With Estelle Parsons.

or the special effects," he says. "She liked to know what every technician did, what their function was....She'd go over to Laszlo Kovacs, the cinematographer, and ask to look in the camera. He was very good with her. 'What kind of lens is this? Why are the lights here?' He'd explain what kind of lighting he used on close-ups. She was always gathering information...but, of course, she had a different future lined up for herself...which many of us weren't aware of at the time."

"She does like to ask questions," Yates stated. "I think some of her questions harass people because they are very pertinent. Unfortunately, [for them] she does see things very clearly; she's not befuddled by the bureaucratic detail that sometimes gets in people's way when making movies. Now that she has a much larger knowledge of filmmaking, I think she is, in some ways, easier to work with. On the other hand, she's obviously much more demanding because she would demand that everyone be as quick and imaginative as she is."

Caplan's nickname for her was "Balabosta," the

133

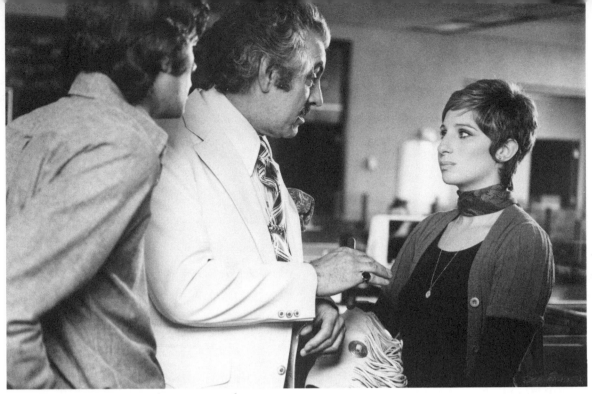

With Michael Sarrazin and Louis Zorich.

Yiddish world for the boss's wife, or "Balaboss," because he did consider her "the boss." The assistant director observed Barbra's outside business concerns to be enormous. "I must say that Barbra was pretty level-headed about the whole thing. She didn't inflict any of her personal life or conditions on people working on the movie set. Nor did she allow it to affect her work. She's a very concentrated gal—once she's on the set, she's there to work." When she wasn't needed on the set, she was on the phone or, on rare occasions, conducting a meeting. But, says Caplan, the only time this caused any tension was when there was a misunderstanding about time and the crew was ready before Barbra was. "That cleared up, *For Pete's Sake* was a fun set to work on," he reiterates. "I loved working with Barbra, I really did. My only regret is that I haven't had an opportunity to work with her since then."

Director Yates, making his first film in Hollywood, found his star to be "far more friendly than her reputation would lead you to believe....She was absolutely delightful. Mind you, we were making a film that was supposed to promote her: a proper Old Hollywood star vehicle. And it's very difficult to quarrel with someone when you're trying to make them look as good as possible." One thing Barbra seemed to appreciate was that Yates wasn't at all intimidated by her. He told her the truth and didn't waste time beating around the bush. "I remember saying to her once after a take, 'That was absolutely terrible!'," he reminisced with Spada. "She collapsed laughing and said, 'No one's ever said that to me

before, thank God!' I think she was really grateful. I mean, that's what a director is for...to be used as a mirror."

Of course, the real news to emerge from *For Pete's Sake* didn't involve revelations about Barbra's star temperament (or lack thereof). More newsworthy was the Beverly Hills hairdresser who designed her closely-cropped wig and stuck around to redesign her personal and professional lives. Their first meeting, carefully negotiated to accommodate two busy schedules, has been well documented. What hasn't is Jon's perception of Barbra prior to that meeting. His first recollection of her was having a girlfriend drag him to the Cocoanut Grove in 1963. "I didn't know who Barbra Streisand was," he says. "But when she came out, I was absolutely, magnetically attracted to her. There was just something that she projected as she sang—I couldn't take my eyes off of her." Peters was 18. As he got involved in establishing his own business, he forgot about Barbra for the time being. Then his second wife, Lesley Anne Warren, took him to see her at the Hollywood Bowl. Warren was not only a Streisand admirer, but she also knew Barbra from New York when she co-starred with Elliott in the short-lived musical, *Drat! The Cat!*. "She often talked about Barbra to me," Jon remembers.

Peters ingeniously turned his revived curiosity about Barbra into a sales tool for his beauty salon: he started telling patrons that *he* cut Barbra's hair (then short and all one length). His business went up 40%. "Many years later, I had opened salons in Beverly Hills and several other locations, I had invested in

134

For Pete's Sake *(1974)*.

real estate…and I decided it was about time to leave the hairstyling business. One of the things I felt I needed to do before I quit was to set the record straight, so to speak. By then, I had met three or four people who had worked with Barbra on different shows and I told them, 'You know, I've always taken credit for cutting this woman's hair; I feel a little guilty. I would really like to meet her and cut her hair for real. Please tell her I'll go anyplace, anywhere, anytime to do her hair—for free.'"

"All he had to say was for free," Barbra joked later, but in reality, such offers are commonplace for celebrities. She never responded. Coincidentally, a year later, Barbra did require Jon Peters' services. She saw a hairdo she thought would be perfect for Henrietta Robbins, also known as "Henry," the mixed-up heroine of *For Pete's Sake*. Upon inquiry she discovered the boyish style was created by Peters and, encouraged by Yates, she tracked the hairstylist down in London, where he was working on another project. The fateful meeting was set upon his return to Los Angeles.

The chemistry between the couple was apparent from the beginning. "She told me she was doing this film *For Pete's Sake* and said she wanted a new style for her hair," Jon recalled. "That was easy because I was good and I could do that for her. Then we started talking about the clothes she'd be wearing in the film. She showed me some pictures of them and I said I didn't think much of them. 'I hate them, too,' she said. 'Okay, then let's go shopping,' I said. 'Great,' she said. Two days later, I picked her up in my car and we went shopping. We bought the clothes together and after that I used to go on the set with her. For four months we worked together. And we became closer and closer. First in a work sense, then in a total way. We started spending the odd night in one or the other of our houses. Then it just seemed to be the natural thing to do—to start being together all the time." By Christmas of 1973, they were. Two months later, they bought a house in Malibu.

Post-production on *For Pete's Sake* was completed in the Spring of 1974. Artie Butler was hired to write a musical score that would reflect the producers' vision of a "yellow and orange film…a madcap, utterly zany frolic." Butler also brought in Mark Lindsay (formerly of Paul Revere and the Raiders) to write the lyrics on a title tune to be

Henry tries to convince her unassuming husband that she's been wearing glasses for awhile.

With son Jason, 7. (Photo courtesy of the Bob Scott collection)

Inspecting the manhole before she makes her comic entrance. The reaction from the crowd nearby was equally comic. "Hey, Barbra! Sing 'On a Clear Day' for us!" one cab driver yelled as he drove past the scene. "Yeah, sure. I'm gonna stop and sing 'On a Clear Day' right here," she replied.

With Molly Picon as Madame Cherry.

performed by Barbra. The composer met with Barbra over at MGM, where she was undergoing rehearsals for the back-breaking musical schedule on *Funny Lady*. "I wanted to write a much more contemporary song for the main title, but the producers needed to have 'For Pete's Sake' in there," he says. "I tried to explain to them that in the old days you made a picture called *Love Is a Many Splendored Thing* and you wrote a song called 'Love Is a Many Splendored Thing.' 'For Pete's Sake' wasn't a contemporary phrase to use in the title song, but they wanted it. I remember specifically playing the song for Barbra and she said to me, 'I know the records you've made, and I know "For Pete's Sake" shouldn't be there. I know it and you know it, right?' I said, 'Right.' She

said, 'But we'll do it, right?' I said, 'Right.' I remember her saying it with a smile...Working with her is many times a challenge and always a thrill."

Barbra's eighth film—intermittently known as *July Pork Bellies, For the Love of Mike, For the Love of Pete* and, finally, *For Pete's Sake*—was set to break nationwide on June 26, 1974. A trailer teasing audiences with comic bits from the movie had been screening with *The Way We Were* since Christmas. Columbia Pictures was intent on making *For Pete's Sake* the comedy hit of the summer. In June, they assembled a massive promotional effort along with an advertising campaign which generously exploited the film as being in the vein of classics such as *The Awful Truth* and *Theodora Goes Wild* and the best of Chaplin, Keaton and the Keystone Kops. "We expect this film will do as well as *What's Up, Doc?*," David Begelman, the studio's new president, announced to exhibitors. With Streisand the sole name above the title, there was no question this one was meant to be

Filming the comic chase through Brooklyn stirred up unpleasant memories for Barbra of riding the IRT as a youth.

her picture all the way. "It's Barbra who gets all the laughs, who initiates the intricacies of the plot and who, ultimately, is responsible for the happy ending," Vincent Canby noted in *The New York Times*. After *The Way We Were*, there was also no question that there was a huge audience waiting for the release of her next film—but how would they respond to it?

Reviews:

"*For Pete's Sake*' a movie put together to honor its star, Barbra Streisand, is an often boisterously funny old-time farce. Its interest is not the truth that is a reflection of reality but an arm-twisting, gag-stuffed exaggeration of it....Without apology, Stanley Shapiro and Maurice Richlin, who wrote the screenplay, and Peter Yates, who directed it, make use of the most ancient devices of farce: outlandish disguises, sudden reversals in fortune, pratfalls, wisecracks. Some of their material is fondly familiar; some is in raucously bad taste. How long has it been since you've seen a movie in which a man has to hide in a closet when a husband comes home early, or in which there's an ill-tempered maid? That is, one who is black? *For Pete's Sake* courts disaster, but most of the time manages to sidestep it."

—*New York Times*

With Michael Sarrazin.

FINAL NOTE: Amply supported by Columbia Pictures, *For Pete's Sake* established itself as a hit summer comedy, though not the blockbuster the studio had hoped for. Peter Yates subsequently found himself in the peculiar position of not being taken seriously for having directed one of Barbra's lesser films. The critical reaction barely affected Streisand. "Not everybody can get up there and interest people the way a true superstar can, even in a bad film," Yates generalized later. Contradicting some of the negative swipes, critic Roger Ebert of the *Chicago Sun Times* actually felt that the trouble with Barbra's performance was that she was *too* good. "A lot of actresses could have played the dizzy dame in *For Pete's Sake* (Stella Stevens comes to mind), but Streisand brings too much reality to the role," he wrote. "We begin to really care about her, because she contributes little quirks of characterization and personality to what's supposed to be in one dimension or it can't exist at all; the minute the people develop depth we find it curious that they'd be chasing cattle through Brooklyn or doing all the other zany things we're supposed to laugh at....Streisand is a rare and original screen personality. Her success wasn't due to formula in the first place, and her future films won't work on that level, either."

Her next movie, however, could also be classified as a formula picture: a Superstar/Blockbuster musical sequel.

140

FUNNY LADY
(Columbia Pictures)

CAST:

Fanny Brice	Barbra Streisand
Billy Rose	James Caan
Nick Arnstein	Omar Sharif
Bobby	Roddy McDowall
Bert Robbins	Ben Vereen
Norma Butler	Carole Wells
Bernard Baruch	Larry Gates
Eleanor Holm	Heidi O'Rourke
Fran	Samantha Huffaker
Buck Bolton	Matt Emery
Ned	Gene Troobnick
Adele	Royce Wallace
Crazy Quilt Director	Byron Webster
Billy's Girl	Colleen Camp
Girl with Nick	Alana Collins

CREDITS:

Produced by	Ray Stark
Directed by	Herbert Ross
Screenplay by	Jay Presson Allen
	Arnold Schulman
Story by	Arnold Schulman
Cinematogrphy	James Wong Howe
Musical numbers directed by	Herbert Ross
Assistant to Mr. Ross	Nora Kaye
Music and lyrics to original songs	John Kander
	Frcd Ebb
Music arranged and conducted by	Peter Matz

A surprise birthday party on the Funny Lady *set yields an unusual gift from Ray Stark: a golden Palomino named Cupid.*

Production design.....	George Jenkins
Set decorator.........	Audrey Blasdel
Costume design.......	Ray Aghayan
	Bob Mackie
Film editor..........	Marion Rothman
Sound...............	Jack Solomon
Unit production manager.................	Howard Pine
Special effects........	Phil Cory
Special photographic effects...............	Albert Whitlock
Music editor..........	William Saracino
Assistant director......	Jack Roe
Second assistant directors.................	Stu Fleming
	Dodie Fawley
Casting.............	Jennifer Shull

Running time: 140 minutes
Rated: PG

A Rastar Production of a Perksy-Bright/Vista Feature

Early in 1974, an advertisement was placed in the Hollywood trade papers:

MOOSE WANTED
(Animal—not lodge member)

For supporting role in *Funny Lady*
Send photo and resume to Jennifer Shull,
    Rastar Productions
    Colgems Square, Burbank CA 91505
    An Equal Opportunity Employer

After years of being in limbo, the sequel to *Funny Girl*, one of Columbia Pictures' all-time box office hits, was due to begin filming in the Spring of 1974. Although not unheard-of, sequels weren't then established as a prerequisite in studio production schedules. As a rule, they weren't even something serious actors wanted to consider—unless pushed up against a wall. Barbra definitely wasn't eager to essay the same role twice so early in her film career. "You can't capitalize on something that's worked before," she told producer Ray Stark early in 1973 when he presented Arnold Shulman's draft of *Funny Lady* to her. "You'll have to drag me into court to do that picture!" (In 1968, he did file suit to get Barbra to honor the balance of her four-picture deal before committing to other projects. That action was dropped when she decided to do *The Owl and the Pussycat*.) Anytime a memorable character is created onscreen, there is the inevitable rush to repackage those elements into a new picture. Producer Stark knew there was a lot of mileage left in the

Fanny Brice saga; he didn't give up on Barbra. "The *Funny Lady* project was going on and off, on and off over many, many years," Marty confirms. " 'Let's do it.' 'Let's not do it.' 'Let's wait to see the script.' And that went back and forth before Barbra finally committed to do it."

There were several reasons why she acquiesced. First, Barbra maintained a relationship with director/choreographer Herbert Ross and his wife, Nora Kaye. *Funny Lady* would not only complete the cycle with him—from *I Can Get It for You Wholesale* in '62 to *The Owl and the Pussycat* in '70 and on —but it would also close the book on her nine-year-old Rastar commitment. A rewrite by Jay Presson Allen, acclaimed for her masterful adaptations of *Cabaret* and *The Prime of Miss Jean Brodie*, delivered "a very bright, literate and humorous" script that touched a spark in Barbra. Peter Matz believes that this was because the essence of the *Funny Lady* scenario predated *Yentl* in its depiction of an independent woman valiantly struggling in a man's world. "For some time, Streisand has been the only bankable female because she alone plays gutsy roles, winners," Jay Presson Allen stated. "Even when she's getting the hell kicked out of her, you know she's going to get up again."

Flush with the success of her best-written role since *Funny Girl*, Barbra looked for a worthy follow-up to *The Way We Were*. A sequel to *Funny Girl*

Fanny tries to explain to her daughter Fran why she married Billy Rose. The scene was cut from the

continued to be a topic of conversation at *The Way We Were*'s premiere in Los Angeles. Irrespective of its origin, the continuation of Fanny Brice's story, culled from an oral history Brice dictated shortly before her death, plus assorted books and tapes, accurately reflected Barbra's personal growth to date. Once again, fiction and reality came together to form an almost spiritual bond between the two women. Not wishing to be slanted towards what Fanny Brice was, Barbra had not read the transcription of conversations between Fanny and Mr. L. that Ray Stark gave her until after *Funny Girl* was behind her. When she did read it, she found a lot about Fanny to identify with: a mutual love of the color white, an appreciation of fine clothes and antiques, a knack for interior decorating…and some belated personal insight. "In the second part of Fanny's life, I feel she starts to discover herself…and finally lets go of her illusions and fantasies about men. She grows up," Barbra said. "[The story] bridges the kind of gap which she feels are negative qualities in her own personality—being open to somebody who is like her, namely Billy Rose, tough and yet gentle. Altogether, it's a most interesting framework for a film."

It seems no idle coincidence, then, that her own life had taken this direction recently. So much about Jon Peters was new—and, yet, not really. He simply re-introduced Barbra to elements of her Brooklyn

general release edition, but did make it into limited release via a special in-flight print for airlines.

persona that she had been tempted to suppress. As the glossy Jewish American Princess faded from view, Barbra seemed to find new excitement in her life and in her work. "He was a good whip for me, because he made me think, made me work harder to keep up with him," Fanny Brice said about shorthand specialist-turned-lyricist-turned-producer-and-entrepreneur Billy Rose, but the same sentiment no doubt applied to the Streisand/Peters union. "In some respects," Jon expressed to English journalist Rosalie Shann, "[Barbra's] a combination of the most difficult and the easiest person I've ever lived with. Because, when I feel like being very male and want her to be subservient to me, it's difficult because she doesn't buy that. She gives what she feels, as opposed to what's demanded of her….But, on the other hand, she can be very loving. And absolutely great as a companion. I think I could say that besides everything else, she's the best friend I've got." Much of *Funny Lady* emphasized that Fanny and Billy were friends who could talk to each other and share experiences long before they became lovers. The angle provided an unconventional twist on the then-popular "buddy" films—one of the buddies was female.

In December 1973, Columbia Pictures officially announced that Streisand, Ross and Stark would reunite for *Funny Lady*. Next on the agenda was casting a suitable male lead. Eleanor Holm, Rose's second wife, told columnist Shirley Eder that she was led to believe Al Pacino would essay the man Fanny Brice called "the Jewish Noel Coward." But it was Robert Blake who actually read for the part. The feisty star of television's "Barretta" went to Barbra's home to talk about the film; she suggested reading a scene together, he insisted on reading the entire script. Two hours later, *People* magazine reported, Blake was offered the role. (Neither Barbra nor Marty recall the conversation progressing that far.) Later in January, Rastar made a surprising selection: the actor who played the explosive Sonny Corleone in *The Godfather*, James Caan. Physically, Caan didn't come close to approximating the man, but he thought he could indeed capture the nervous energy and drive that made the fast-talking Rose a force to contend with in the "tinsel and cheesecloth world" of Broadway. "I'm ready for a musical," he said.

Barbra met Billy Rose at the post-premiere party for *Funny Girl* on stage ("I hear I was married to you once. How was I?" she asked. "Great for the first five years," Rose responded), so she was aware that Stark and Ross were casting against type. But, she added, "It comes down to whom the audience wants me to kiss. Robert Blake, no. James Caan, yes." Omar Sharif was signed for a guest appearance as

Camping it up for the camera during a recreation of Billy Rose's Aquacade.

Nicky Arnstein. Roddy McDowall and Carole Wells would play two of Fanny's friends from the theatre. Tony Award-winner Ben Vereen took a leave of absence from *Pippin* to accept his first featured role in a major motion picture. He would portray Bert Robbins, a composite character suggested by dancers Bert Williams and Bill "Bojangles" Robinson. Once again taking no chances, the production company hired major talent for behind-the-scenes support: new songs by *Cabaret*'s songwriting team of John Kander and Fred Ebb, with Peter Matz composing the underscore; costumes by Ray Aghayan and Bob Mackie; and Vilmos Zsigmond as director of photography. "Ray [Stark] was always good with Barbra," Marty says. "He protected her. And he wasn't penny conscious when it came to putting it on the screen." *Funny Lady*, budgeted at $7.5 million, was to have a fourteen-week production schedule (including time in Atlantic City, Philadelphia and New York City.)

Rehearsals began on Stages 5 and 6 at MGM Studios several weeks in advance of the April 1 start date. Ross and production manager Howard Pine had devised an ingenious schedule whereby fourteen musical numbers (mostly from the *Crazy Quilt* sequence) could be filmed via multiple cameras in sixteen days—representing a cost savings of over $750,000. Cinemographer Zsigmond researched American musical theater of the '30s in order to give audiences an opportunity to experience a realistic theatrical presentation. The final week of rehearsals, Ross brought in the production crew to block and light the major numbers as Barbra and Ben Vereen performed them with the dancers. MGM's unique theater soundstage, complete with proscenium and fly gallery, provided the setting; Zsigmond added to the atmosphere by keeping edges of the stage dark and allowing the audience to be obscured. But, when dailies on the first number, "Great Day," came back, executives were dismayed that the footage was so dark. Over the strenuous objections of the director—and much to Barbra's surprise—Zsigmond was fired.

The next day, according to assistant director Jack Roe, was spent shooting close-ups of Barbra while a suitable replacement was sought. One was found in James Wong Howe, a two-time Academy Award winner whose incredibly diverse work brought more than 120 feature films—including *The Thin Man, The Adventures of Tom Sawyer, Yankee Doodle Dandy, The Rose Tattoo, Picnic* and *Hud*—to life. Howe got a call asking him to meet Stark at Columbia that afternoon. Would he consider coming out of retirement for this one film? "I wasn't sure I wanted to do anything," he told *American Cin-*

A casual pose on the set of Funny Lady.

ematographer shortly before his death. "But they convinced me. I asked, 'When do I start?' They said '7:30 tomorrow morning...' If I hadn't had 57 years of experience in the film industry, I wouldn't have been able to jump into such a big project on 24 hours' notice...and without any preparation. First on the schedule was a big boom shot...I was a bit nervous."

The director of photography passed his "initiation" with flying colors, capturing in his richly-textured and brilliantly-colored work the MGM musical style that often eluded would-be imitators. Other numbers put on film during that three-week period included "So Long, Honey Lamb" (complete), "Blind Date," "I Found a Million Dollar Baby," "Clap Hands, Here Comes Charlie" (two versions), "Am I Blue?" (complete) and "How Lucky Can You Get?" It was an exhausting schedule that, according to Ross, left everyone with "a sort of jet lag from bulldozing ahead." A couple of weeks after their return to The Burbank Studios, Howe took ill and was out of commission for ten days; Ernest Laszlo stepped in to take his place. When Howe re-joined the company, he was back climbing ladders and rigs to check shots. An excellent Chinese cook, the cinematographer endeared himself to Barbra by surprising her with delicacies from his kitchen. He would describe her to *American Cinematographer* as being "a smart gal...very honest and very hep. She came to me one day and said, 'Jimmy, you know they say I'm temperamental. I'm not really temperamental. I just want things to be right for me—and I know what's good for me and what's bad.' Well, I think that's a wonderful trait. She protects herself—and she should."

"When I was setting up to shoot my first close-up of her, I heard a voice say, 'What, no diffusion?' I turned around and said, 'No, Miss Streisand. I'm not using any diffusion, because this is a beautiful lens. It must have cost five or six thousand dollars and it has wonderful resolution. I'm not going to ruin it by putting a $2.50 piece of glass in front of it. I'd rather get the effect with lights.' She didn't say anything else, and from then on we got along great." On a humorous note, Howe noted that one day he decided to use a little diffusion and, after the shot was explained to Barbra, she asked, "Would you make one without [the diffusion], too?" The cinematographer complied, happily.

Streisand and Caan's first scene together was a confrontation at Billy Rose's Backstage Club. Neither star was feeling very hostile, but their acting together did "strike sparks." On the sixth take, *Los Angeles Times* reporter Wayne Warga observed, "everything is going perfectly. Streisand, disdainfully smoking while Caan promotes, is solidly in character and

Chatting with director of photography James Wong Howe, 1974.

remains so as a piece of tobacco gets stuck on the tip of her tongue. She carefully reaches up to pick it off just as Caan, in the passion of promotion, grabs her hand to emphasize his point—and shoves her hand into his mouth. The entire company—several dozen extras in the club, the crew and various supporting people—explodes into laughter and from then on neither Caan nor Streisand can look at one another without giggling. 'I'm sorry, I'm sorry, I'll get it this time,' she says. 'Time is money, time is money and no you won't,' Caan replies."

The opinionated leading man later confessed that "from that day on, I was yelling at her, putting her down and calling her a spoiled rotten thing, and she would call me this or that and we'd carry on and we'd laugh....I just remember giggling quite a bit." Caan reminisced about the scene in which both stars became drenched in talcum powder. "For some reason, it was very important to Herb Ross to get this

146

shot, and here [Barbra] came in this beautiful green-spangled dress and made up just right. She said, 'I don't really think that Jimmy should hit me in the face with this powder. That powder is toxic, you know, and I'll get it in my lungs,' and this and that and I could see that this big argument was going to start, so I kind of winked at Herb and said, 'Stay out of this.' I said, 'Barbra, I think you're right. Maybe I shouldn't hit you with the thing. Maybe you'll hit me and then I'll pick it up and I'll go to hit you with it and then I won't.' She said, 'Oh, that's terrific. That'll be great!' I said, 'Now, mind you—if you blink or back off when I start to raise my hand, I'm gonna whack you with it...'cause it's only the idea that you're ready to accept it that'll stop me.' She said, 'Okay. I won't blink.'

"So we set the scene up and did it. She hit me in the face with the powder. I picked it up and drew my hand back and she just stood there. She did not blink. I hit her right square in the face with it. I'm telling you, I went to the floor laughing. I couldn't stop, and she looked at me...I mean, I really felt bad for a minute because she was so shocked. She called me names. She said, 'You lied to me!' I was hysterical. And then she laughed, too." Barbra: "He had his fingers crossed so God shouldn't strike him dead, and then he let me have it." The first take was the only take.

On location at the Los Angeles Theatre with Herb Ross.

Omar Sharif: "Nicky went on to quite a life after his prison term and Fanny Brice divorced him. He married a very rich woman, took up polo...that sort of thing. He was quite a fellow."

"We looked for a man to compete, on his own terms, with the elegance of Arnstein," Ray Stark said.

"Caan could, not Billy. If Arnstein could be played by an Arab, then Billy Rose didn't have to be short."

Streisand and Caan pose with President Ford and his daughter Susan, 1975. (Caan's hand is bandaged due to a rodeo injury; he postponed corrective surgery in order to participate in the Funny Lady *promotional effort.)*

Another bit had Fanny ordering Billy out of her dressing room. The backstage squabble was based on real life, though not Fanny's. "That scene was based on a fight I had with my producer Ray Stark during the making of *Funny Girl*," Barbra admitted to Dick Cavett. Had the wildly fluctuating producer-star relationship stabilized as both achieved their enormous success? Stark thought it had. "Barbra's changed like good wine," he stated at a New York press conference. "She's gone through those formative years, and she's come out of it magnificently. She's concerned, she's considerate. We fight like hell, but they're all fights about creative opinions on which I can be right or wrong and she can be right or wrong. She's just matured and become a lovely lady instead of a fiery, funny, kooky little girl."

Barbra was not unaware of the tension that can arise when she walks on a movie set, but its existence stymied her. "I really pride myself in professional behavior," she told Barbara Walters in 1975, "even though there have been times when a director has said something to me [that] made me feel very sensitive. Because I'm aware that everybody is listening with such big ears...." She expressed amusement over the stories harkening her "legendary storminess" as a throwback to the stars of Hollywood's golden era. "I don't know whether to laugh or cry," she said, reflecting about such rumors in 1968. "Anyone who knows his craft or is worth his salt and has sensitivity and intelligence doesn't throw tantrums. To have temperament, to be able to get angry and cry, to be vulnerable to emotion is a terrific thing. But negative temperament is childish nonsense."

Studying her lines as she was driven into the studio each morning, Barbra insisted that her lighter attitude was not due to disinterest, but rather to her decision to understate a character who wasn't necessarily as likable as the self-deprecating waif of yore. "Barbra is a canny actress who understands the

149

"Blind Date."

Glove to glove: Barbra with Queen Elizabeth II.

Funny Lady *(1975)*.

essence of her humor and her talent," Ross wrote in 1978. "I don't think she has, in her own mind, what is referred to as a 'set image'—one which shouldn't be tampered with on film. She is anxious to become her part rather than to have it molded to fit the public's image of her—even if it involves altering her physical appearance to better characterize each role she plays."

On *Funny Lady*, however, Ross found himself pushing Barbra more than he ever thought he would need to. After the gratifying experience of *The Owl and the Pussycat*, he was unbridled in his enthusiasm for her talents. "I thought Barbra's possibilities were limitless," he said in 1976, "but *Funny Lady* was a curious experience....It was a movie that was made virtually without her—she simply wasn't there in terms of commitment, and one of her greatest qualities is to make a 1000 percent commitment." The director would later tone down his comments but his disappointment was genuine. Assistant direc-

A tough exterior shields the vulnerable Fanny from further pain. "I don't try to be liked," Barbra said of her performance. "I don't know if she's likeable, this character."

tor Roe explains that "there's no doubt that once Barbra's on the set she gives 100 percent to whatever she's doing: singing, acting...She's obviously an extremely talented lady and she's willing to try anything. But I think by the time she did *Funny Lady* she was fairly wealthy and in love and because she never really wanted to do the sequel, she probably didn't care as much about the film itself."

If Jon was the problem (or "the distraction"), it was because, as second assistant director Stu Fleming points out, getting involved with him was as intense a "project" as any record or movie Barbra chose to make. This relationship demanded a full-time commitment, and it was the first time since she arrived in Hollywood that her major commitment didn't revolve around motion pictures. Looking at the situation with a different perspective, even if the *Funny Lady* crew had to wait fifteen minutes while the star completed a business or personal call, such "imposing behavior" was hardly of the caliber that some top stars have casually assumed to be their privilege without even so much as batting an eye.

And it certainly was nothing compared with the fuss Streisand could have made when the company wrapped shooting within the protective studio environment and went on the road. All of the Eastern

locations were nixed in favor of a variety of Californian ones. First on the schedule was an elaborately choreographed shot of Barbra singing the "Let's Hear It for Me" finale as she took off in a 1937 bi-plane (owned by George Roy Hill). "That was in the script from the beginning," Roe says, "and she said flat out that she wasn't going to do it." Because of her great confidence in Herb Ross and her belief that Nelson Tyler—the aerial photographer who captured "Don't Rain on My Parade" so effectively on film—could get it all in one take, Barbra agreed to one flight. "We made a survey of the Santa Monica airport and had supposedly set everything up so that when the plane took off, as soon as it cleared the shot, they could turn around and land again," the assistant director recalls. "Well…somewhere along the line, that didn't happen, and Barbra had to stay aloft for twenty minutes before they got the clearance to come back down."

Later, she was able to laugh about the experience. "I nearly had a heart attack. I was so scared, but I knew I should do it myself," she said. "We went up and the plane just kept going. The pilot was fiddling with the radio. The first thing I thought was, 'He's kidnapping me.' Then I thought, 'The radio's dead. The guy can't land.'" Circling the coastal city, unable to communicate with the pilot in the open-cockpit plane, all Barbra could think was, "Here I am risking my life for a movie!" Back on the tarmac, the crew panicked as well when they realized the plane wasn't returning to the field. Many anxious minutes later there was an only-in-Hollywood type ending. "The moment they touched down, you could hear Barbra screaming from the end of the runway," says Roe. "She was yelling at Herb. And I don't know how he did it, but he talked her into doing it again!"

The musical bridge of "Let's Hear It for Me" was visualized with Barbra driving Fanny's $85,000 Rolls-Royce in the hills near the Hollywood sign (with second assistant director Fleming teasing her as he hid from view in the front seat). The opening was shot a couple of weeks later at the Beverly Hills Hotel. Later in June, the cast and crew (joined by substitute cinematographer Ernest Laszlo) recreated Billy Rose's Aquacade at the Olympic Swim Stadium adjacent to the USC campus. The outdoor pool was

"This is more of a real acting job for me…a character piece. I was very much true to Fanny Brice—to the lady who called everybody kid because she couldn't remember anyone's name."

Fanny and Billy establish the ground rules of their working relationship.

"I Found a Million Dollar Baby (in a Five-and-Ten- Cent Store)."　　　　"So Long, Honey Lamb."

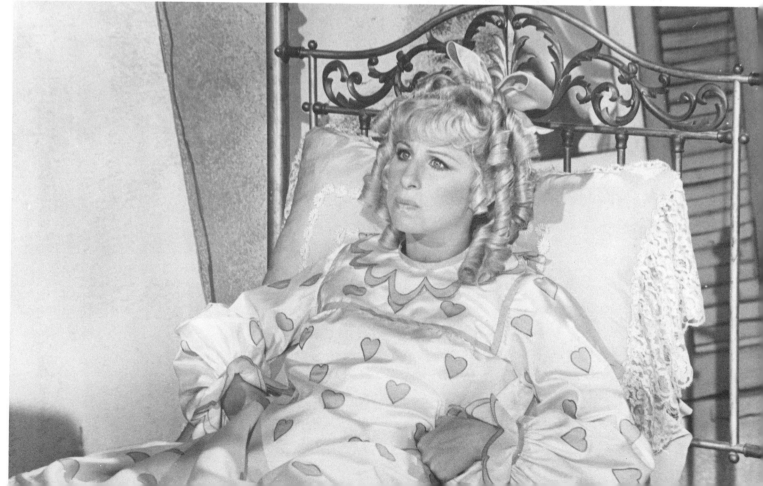

"Am I Blue?"

"How Lucky Can You Get?"

decorated with fountains, flame torches, batteries of colored lights and mirrors (to project the swimmers' shadows twenty feet high), plus "the largest group of aquatic performers ever to appear as an ensemble." Since the sequence was filmed at night, and Barbra would be going in and out of the pool, the star got the producer to agree to heat the pool to a more comfortable 82 degrees. At the end of the night-long shoot, she gamefully tried pulling Ross into the pool, but he succeeded in avoiding her grasp. The troupe left the stadium at dawn.

Other locations on the schedule included the Columbia Pictures ranch, the Beverly Hills courthouse, the Malibu Pier (doubling for Atlantic City), the Pan Pacific auditorium (the exterior was dressed as NBC Radio), the Los Angeles Theatre (an ornate movie palace doubling as a legitimate theatre), an Oakland train station (subbing for Cleveland) and, finally, the polo field at Will Rogers State Park. There, Fanny would encounter the man she could never forget she loved, Nicky Arnstein. Omar Sharif, essaying essentially a cameo role, had not seen Barbra in years. "For the first two or three days, she seemed a little different to me," he stated. "But then I'm sure I appeared somewhat different to her, which is natural. *Funny Girl* was her very first film, and she was married and had led a somewhat sheltered personal life. She has broadened considerably in the intervening years. I think it shows in her performing, as well." In addition, the actor felt that being in a well-made, sumptuous musical "has a magic about it. And, of course, it was great fun to see and work with Barbra again. We played some bridge between scenes. And another thing: now she's almost as enthusiastic about horses as I am. She has her own Quarter Horse and invited me to ride with her and some friends at Malibu."

Principal photography was completed on location at a Bel-Air mansion on July 9, 1974. The wrap party took place that evening. Barbra had spent the better part of the previous evening writing personal notes for each of the gifts she had selected for the cast and crew, taking great care to make sure no one (among two hundred people) was omitted. She gave a sterling silver rodeo buckle (with a personally inscribed message) to James Caan. She found an antique camera for James Wong Howe and had an engraved plaque put on it: "Thank you for your talents, generosity and cha siu bao." For Ray Stark, there was an acknowledgement of their long association. Across an antique mirror she wrote "Paid in Full" in lipstick. The sentiment accompanying the plaque was more endearing: "Even though I sometimes forget to say it, thank you, Ray. Love. Barbra."

Columbia began previewing the film early in

157

Contemplating the highs and lows of her personal and professional success.

1975. Screenings for exhibitors indicated that the filmmakers were as yet unsure of how to end the film and at least two different endings were shown to them. One version ended with Fanny and Billy saying goodbye at a train station. Another was a fictionalized reunion—shot months after principal photography was completed—between the two a year or so before Fanny's death. In February, columnist Joyce Haber reported that Peter Matz's score had been "scrapped" in favor of a lusher one by Marvin Hamlisch. What Hamlisch actually contributed was a couple of "thematic" musical cues linking *Funny Girl* and *Funny Lady*. (The last-minute addition was apparently too late for *Funny Girl*'s composers, Jule Styne and Bob Merrill, to receive their proper attribution in the final credits.)

In the meantime, director Ross was wrestling with the film's two and one-half hour length. Despite comments to the contrary, ultimately the problem with *Funny Lady* would have less to do with the star's performance than with the film's structure. Barbra had filmed several touching scenes detailing Fanny's relationship with her daughter, Fran, and her friends. Again, a chance to define Fanny outside of her romantic attachment was aborted in favor of keeping the names above the title front and center. Another casualty of the editorial process was the Baby Snooks radio show. Few people had known the Fanny Brice of *Funny Girl*, but thousands of radio listeners came to love the Brice they heard in their homes. Snooks was Fanny's most identifiable success—and she got less than a minute in the final cut of *Funny Lady*.

The motion picture premiered on March 9, 1975, at the Kennedy Center for the Performing Arts in Washington, D.C. Two days later, the stars at-

"Until I divorced him, I had a dream that I could change Nick," Fanny Brice said. "I thought if I worked at it long enough, and waited long enough, I could change Nick into what I wanted. And it's a funny thing because everything in my life that I ever wanted, if I tried for it, I can say that I got it. But with men, the harder I tried, the harder I flopped."

Jay Presson Allen: "It was a challenge to make Billy Rose sympathetic. And, at first, I thought James Caan was too attractive for the role. But he was so crude, vulgar and funny. He can really act."

"If I Love Again."   The high-flying finale of "Let's Hear It For Me."

Barbra: "These two films are a set of bookends. My Fanny Brice syndrome 1964—1974 is ending."

saga of Streisand and English royalty.

Funny Lady's opening week in 93 showcase theatres tallied $2.4 million; the Easter holiday box-office pointed to blockbuster status for *Funny Lady*. Competing with Columbia's other scene stealers, *Shampoo* and *Tommy*, its films rentals would, by year's end, total $19.3 million. (Double that figure to determine the actual boxoffice gross.) Liking Streisand, as critic Molly Haskell was to report, seemed to have nothing to do with whether or not people would pay to see her perform; she had become one of the special few to develop a "must-see mystique." She was—and is— a star because she looked and acted the part. But *Funny Lady* was the last film in which admirers were able to truly celebrate that exalted stardom. Other factors, such as one's appreciation of her talent, Barbra's projection of herself and/or her perception of the audience, would play an increasingly important role in future audience support.

Reviews:

"Barbra Streisand, like the picture, extends the characterization she launched so dazzlingly in *Funny Girl*. She sings superbly and with, it seemed to me, more restraint on the remarkable dynamics of her voice, making for more subtlety but also more impact. The Brooklyn brashness just right for *Funny Girl* has been let mellow. It is still there, but it is even easier to see as a defense against rejection—and as an ingredient of the Fanny Brice comedic persona. What I find most impressive and likable about the performance is the softened, bittersweet maturity that Streisand lets us see in Fanny Brice. You sense that Streisand understands the star as well as she understood the impetuous young hopeful."

—*Los Angeles Times*

FINAL NOTE: 1975 wasn't a good year for women in movies. Directors were the stars of the year's most important films: Robert Altman's *Nashville*, Stanley Kubrick's *Barry Lyndon*, Steven Spielberg's *Jaws*...even *One Flew Over the Cuckoo's Nest* was Milos Forman's picture as much as Jack Nicholson's. Early in the year, 1974's Best Actress Ellen Burstyn urged Academy members not to vote for Best Actress in order to protest the dearth of women's roles. Of course, the category was not eliminated; AMPAS knew they could always find five nominees of some distinction. Despite a strong performance in a weak year, 1975's "World Film Favorite" was not to be among them. Isabelle Adjani, Ann-Margaret, Louise Fletcher, Glenda Jackson and Carol Kane were the nominees. *Funny Lady* received four nominations (Cinematographer, Sound, Song and Original Song Score), but took home no awards.

tended another big splash in New York City. Unfortunately, it turned into an unpleasant affair in which the crowd ignited as soon as Barbra arrived with Jon. Photographers and fans alike pushed to get a glimpse, a touch, a photo. A sensation of another kind was caused on March 18 at the Royal Premiere in London. Encouraged by Jon to inquire why women (and not men) must wear gloves when meeting the Queen, Barbra shocked some bystanders by being the one to speak first when presented to Queen Elizabeth II. While a palace spokesman later intimated that Barbra hadn't really broken any rules of protocol, the press had fun with another story in the continuing

A STAR IS BORN
(Warner Bros./First Artists)

CAST:
Esther Hoffman....... Barbra Streisand
John Norman Howard. Kris Kristofferson
Bobby Ritchie........ Gary Busey
Brian Wexler......... Paul Mazursky
Bebe Jesus........... M.G. Kelly
Freddie Lowenstein.... Joanne Linville
Gary Danziger....... Oliver Clark
The Oreos........... Vanetta Fields
Clydie King
Quentin............. Marta Heflin
Nikki............... Sally Kirkland
Mo................. Uncle Rudy

CREDITS:
Executive producer.... Barbra Streisand
Produced by......... Jon Peters
Directed by.......... Frank Pierson
Screenplay by........ John Gregory Dunne
Joan Didion
Frank Pierson
Story by............. William Wellman
and Robert Carson

*The dramatic photography of Francesco Scavullo
enhanced much of* A Star Is Born's *publicity and
promotion.*

Cinematography.......	Robert Surtees
Film editor..........	Peter Zinner
Production design.....	Polly Platt
Art director..........	William Hiney
Set decorator.........	Ruby Levitt
Musical concepts by...	Barbra Streisand
Music supervised by...	Paul Williams
Musical underscore by.	Roger Kellaway
Musical conductor.....	Kenny Ascher
Music and live recordings produced by........	Phil Ramone
Choreography.........	David Winters
Production manager...	Howard Pine
Concert lighting.......	Jules Fisher
Special effects.........	Chuck Gasper
Sound mixer.........	Tom Overton
Assistant director......	Stu Fleming
Casting.............	Dianne Crittenden

Running time: 140 minutes
Rated: R

A Barwood/Jon Peters Production

Rehearsing "Queen Bee" with choreographer David Winters and fellow Oreo Clydie King.

Q: "Do you think your personality has been captured by the press?"
A: "Captured? [Barbra laughs] Slaughtered, barbecued, pickled!"

—1968

On February 1, 1976, Barbra began filming her tenth—and by far most controversial—motion picture. It was a contemporary remake of the quintessential Hollywood story, *A Star Is Born*. The saga of the production's rollercoaster ride from printed page to theater screen has been reported, scrutinized and, occasionally, misrepresented.

The project originated with the screenwriting team of Joan Didion and John Gregory Dunne. Tossing around ideas for a possible film, Dunne suggested "James Taylor and Carly Simon in a rock 'n' roll version of *A Star Is Born*." The concept was simple, visual—and commercial. The story of a star's public fall from grace as his wife finds success in the spotlight worked in 1937 for Fredric March and Janet Gaynor and in 1954 for Judy Garland and James Mason. A properly matched re-telling of that story within the context of contemporary music could mean a licensing goldmine to those responsible. The team pitched the idea to a Warner Brothers executive. The studio not only held the remake rights

With Chuck Norris at a 1975 open casting call for the projected Jon Peters-Martin Erlichman film based on Bruce Lee's life. (Photo courtesy of the Richard Giammanco collection)

At the Sun Devil Stadium concert, Barbra shows the crowd exactly how John Norman's motorcycle will move across the stage and invites them to react accordingly.

on *A Star Is Born*, but was also a sister company to Warner/Elektra/Asylum Records—the home of both Simon and Taylor. Late in August of 1973, the studio announced their intention of making the film, now retitled *Rainbow Road*.

Several months and one different rewrite later, as various actors, directors and singers paraded through the production office, the Dunnes became "thoroughly sick of the project" and expressed a desire to move on to a less exhausting assignment. In addition, Warners had second thoughts about the Simon and Taylor teaming. They feared the film was in danger of becoming a high-budget screen test. And they didn't like the idea of either Warren Beatty or Mike Nichols for director. Agent Sue Mengers passed the script on to Peter Bogdanovich; neither he nor Cybill Shepherd liked the idea much. Didion and Dunne watched in disillusionment as their script was tossed back and forth among creative talent. Early in 1974, producer John Foreman and director Mark Rydell signed on. They set Richard Perry to supervise the musical score.

Misgivings about the project itself continued. The script that Rydell called "frighteningly brilliant... a savage look at the rock world," Perry saw as not really capturing "the contemporary rock-pop milieu. Everything in it was clichéd." Others saw the story as too cold and cynical in an era that seemed to need romance more than ever. That conflict didn't help attract a strong female lead.

As the top female star at the box-office (and certainly the top musical star), Barbra was offered *Rainbow Road* very early in its inception. She turned it down. "I didn't want to do a remake, and that's the truth," she said then. Less than a year later, however, she was reluctantly drawn back into the project thanks to Jon's interest in it. He felt the two of them should produce the film together; she wasn't so sure and challenged him to justify why the story should be retold. He described the film as being about two people "trapped by their money and success. The most important thing to them is communicating... wanting to have children, not the thousands of agents and managers and all that stuff that controls their lives. I just really loved the story."

Peters also thought it was time for Barbra to stop playing older characters. He saw her as "a young, hot, sexy woman—a little ball of fire. None of that had ever been conveyed on film." "People put me

165

into a category; she plays *this* kind of a role, just as the press puts me into a journalistic image they think people will pay to read about," Barbra reiterated. "That whole Brooklyn-girl-makes-good thing is so boring to me, and based on the past. I've contributed to that, in a sense, by the roles I've played. But not anymore."

To prove that he meant business, Peters eliminated his safety net—he sold his chain of salons. In the Fall of 1974, after seriously rethinking what her involvement in such a production might be, Streisand signed to do the picture as part of her Warner Bros./First Artists contract. The film was given a comparatively low budget of $6,000,000; any overages were to be guaranteed by Barwood Productions. A December 1974/January 1975 start date was projected. Once Barbra became committed, Jon says, she really was the heart of moving everything forward. One of the first changes she insisted on was to own up to the movie's origin. Instead of ignoring the previous incarnations of *A Star Is Born* as if *Rainbow Road* were a totally original concept, she invited comparisons so that audiences might contemplate how much times had changed. "I wanted to explore relationships *today*, the role-playing *today*, as opposed to that of the '30s and the '50s," she explained.

A not-so-private conference with Jon on location in Arizona.

Lights, camera, friction.

Jon Peters—*Congratulations on producing one helluva concert in Phoenix. It will be a dynamic part of your production of "A Star is Born", the movie millions will see at Christmastime. Our thanks for your many contributions to a film that has finished on schedule, on budget, on target—a sure winner!*

PRESIDENT FIRST ARTISTS   PRESIDENT WARNER BROS.

A BARWOOD-JON PETERS PRODUCTION

Streisand also visualized *A Star Is Born* as a singular opportunity to express some of her feelings about what it's like to be a celebrity/performer—how frantic and chaotic and unreal that all-too-insular world can be, how hot the spotlight that strips away one's privacy.

As producers, directors, writers and even co-stars were consumed in the deceptive quicksand surrounding the production, the public spotlight focused on the Streisand/Peters relationship. "A lot of what people say is true," Jon stated in 1976. "You know, where there's smoke, there's fire. I *am* riding on the wings of a star. I mean, I've never produced a movie before [and] I never could have produced a movie like this without Barbra.... The theatrics of a hairdresser getting involved with a superstar play right into the Hollywood thing." But Barbra resented the insinuation that she had been hypnotized by this "modern-day Svengali". "I am a professional," she asserted in a 1975 interview with Barbra Walters. "I have integrity as an artist. Do people think that I would risk all that? People get angry at things that have not been done before—it's not that they're wrong, it's just that they're different.... Who's the Svengali? Maybe I'm his."

ButterFly represented Jon's initiation into the creative process. He found it exciting to toss around ideas and then see some of those ideas realized. "I couldn't sleep, it was so exciting. And I think it was fun for Barbra because she had someone she could interact with," he says. "She had a partner. But I didn't know what I was doing. I wasn't a record producer. My instincts were good, but my abilities weren't. Barbra literally had to bail me out.... And then I learned what I could do and what I couldn't do. *A Star Is Born* was what I could do. *A Star Is Born* was something I saw... or rather I saw what it could be. I knew I could be a good movie producer because I knew how to put people together." Once Barbra and Jon became obsessed with the project, the problem became finding people on their wavelength.

Director Rydell left the project to make room for Jerry Schatzberg. Didion and Dunne departed. In their absence, a host of well-known names from Buck Henry to Alvin Sargent and Jay Presson Allen were bandied about in Hollywood, but Jon wanted to hire a relative unknown, Jonathan Axelrod, as the screenwriter. "Peters came in and said that in his and Barbra's view, the screenplay was moving away from being suitable for Barbra," then-Warner Bros. presi-

167

John and Esther discuss marriage over Chinese noodles. Not a part of the original release in 1976, this scene did make it into the broadcast TV version.

A somber moment with director Frank Pierson during the filming of "With One More Look at You"/ "Watch Closely Now."

With Jule Styne at the New York premiere.

dent John Calley stated. "I agreed with them. Forget about whether the screenplay was good or not, the issue was, 'Is it right for Barbra?'...We were most anxious to do the film with Barbra. The worst thing that could happen was that if they took a shot at the screenplay and failed, we'd lose them anyway. But if they succeeded..."

Axelrod suggested switching the male and female leads so that Barbra's role was a self-destructive Janis Joplin-type character. Jon was intrigued with the idea; Schatzberg wasn't. He bowed out, citing the usual artistic differences. Arthur Hiller and Hal Ashby were two of the directors approached at this time. Peters also talked with Richard Perry about co-directing the picture. Finally, word leaked out that Jon had taken the reins himself; this, after an earlier rumor that he planned to co-star in the film.

Although he has never denied that he considered the idea "for about five minutes," Peters now states that he soon realized he had enough on his

The ebullient couple at the Golden Globes, January 30, 1977. "I just want to say it's a helluva way to come into the business," Jon stated. (Photo credit: UPI/Bettmann Newsphotos)

hands as producer. Casting him as her co-star was a desperate joke, Barbra insisted. "It was all just something said in a fleeting moment of panic [when Kris Kristofferson was thought to have exited]. It's now history. Mind you, he would've been quite good—if only he could play guitar." "I think my involvement exacerbated the situation even further," Jon admits. "I was aggressive and loud and had a definite point of view. And I probably irritated people because I spoke my mind and said things that were provocative."

The musical chair-syndrome continued. Richard Perry decided it was time to move on to other projects; executive producer John Foreman was fired. "This movie is going to be the *Myra Breckenridge* of 1975," Jonathan Axelrod stated after becoming the film's latest casualty. That Spring, Streisand and Peters sat down for two hours with Elvis Presley in Las Vegas in a vain attempt to get him to reconsider the role. (His name had surfaced earlier when Warner Bros. hoped to snag other notables such as Cher or Diana Ross.) "He's always been underrated as an actor," Barbra said. "I think this could be a whole rebirth for him." What she didn't know was that the script hit a little too close to home. The King of rock 'n' roll was so enmeshed in his cocoon of protection that it was virtually impossible—if not painful—for him to strip away the layers. "He had always been my hero," Jon says. "Like Barbra, he also had this unbelievable magic onstage. I thought they would be incredible together. But when we went up to see him, we sat on the floor with him and it was real sad. He had this big stomach; he was dying, really. He *was* the character. He *was* John Norman." Not surprisingly, Presley said no.

In April, after Barbra and Jon returned from the London premiere of *Funny Lady*, screenwriters Bob and Laurie Dillon (*French Connection II*) delivered a draft of *A Star Is Born* that insiders were calling "fabulous and very revealing." But, by June, the production team was reported to be leaning more toward the Axelrod draft (which, ironically, did not include the role reversal because, said Barbra, "You get into peculiar problems [with] that one"). Warner Bros. was hopefully pointing toward a September 1975 or January 1976 start date, "depending on the availability of a certain male star." Kris Kristofferson was in Europe making *The Sailor Who Fell from Grace with the Sea*. Rewrites continued with Barbra and Jon contributing to the script, and the team began interviewing directors again. Sidney Lumet, Bob Fosse and Robert Altman were all mentioned in the media, but, according to Barbra, Sydney Pollack was the only director she actually approached.

On August 6, 1975, the *Hollywood Reporter* announced that Frank Pierson had been signed to

"In my wildest dreams, I never, never could ever imagine winning an Academy Award for writing a song. I'm very honored and very excited. Thank you all very much."

adapt the troubled *A Star Is Born* screenplay—and to direct. According to Pierson, he was approached by an executive at Warner Bros. to do "a fast rewrite" of *Star* and, in a moment of "mad ambition," he accepted the assignment on the condition that he direct as well. (Barbra: "But he never told *us* that until after we hired him as a writer.") His job, he was told, was to make sure he didn't get fired. Pierson had some nice writing credits—*Cool Hand Luke, Dog Day Afternoon*—but, with the exception of one low-budget feature film, his directorial creditials were in television. "With all due respect, Barbra really should have directed the film," Jon says. "She ended up directing it anyway. But she was frightened of taking the responsibility."

"All these years I've wanted to direct," she conceded in a 1983 interview, "but I never dared to say it—even to myself."

With the addition of Rupert Holmes to the musical team, work began to progress on the score. Having things back on track gave Barbra a chance to concentrate a little more on her side of the picture. She took music lessons and attended rock concerts.

A Star Is Born *(1976).*

"I'm not that kind of girl," Esther tells John Norman *after an impromptu invitation to watch him perform. "First you have to call me in about a week—and then I think about it."*

A young songwriter's clever feminist statement: "Queen Bee."

Early in '75, she went to The Actors' Studio to observe scenes from *Vanya* directed by her friend, Rick Edelstein. Afterwards, she congratulated one of the actresses, Sally Kirkland (Pony Dunbar in *The Way We Were*), on her performance. "Well, since you thought it was so wonderful," Kirkland responded, "how would you like to do something here?" "I can't," said Barbra. "I'm not a member." But Kirkland assured her that Strasberg would be thrilled with the prospect. "If you ever made connection with him, that's solid enough for him to invite you in. Anyway, if you *could* do something, what would it be?" "Oh, I'd love to do Juliet," Barbra enthused.

The pair talked about doing the scene in which Juliet confronts her nurse regarding the outcome of a meeting with Romeo, "and Barbra got like a little kid. She was so excited." As Kirkland predicted, Strasberg thought it was a great idea. "Don't play for age," he advised them. "Just work on the relationship."

Rehearsals took place at The Actors' Studio, at Barbra's home in Holmby Hills and at Edelstein's home. "The rehearsals were very exciting because of the seriousness with which Barbra worked. She wanted to work long, long hours. She never wanted to stop," Kirkland says. "I remember how utterly amazed I was at how quickly she learned her lines." Also memorable was the mischieviousness with which Barbra attacked her part— "like a thirteen-year-old kid, and Rick encouraged that." One day in Holmby Hills, the two actresses were rehearsing by themselves when Barbra suddenly jumped into the pool. "But she did it so fast I couldn't believe it. It was terribly impulsive. I don't remember whether she jumped in with all of her clothes on or ripped them off, but I do remember her trying to coax me to jump in, too. I said, 'Wait a second, we were just rehearsing. I think I'll just sit here and read my lines, thank you.' So while I was sitting at the poolside doing the nurse, she was in the pool reciting Juliet's lines. Come to think of it, it was a very Juliet thing to do because at that point in the scene she wasn't doing anything the nurse was asking her to do and she was teasing her; Barbra was just acting that out. She purposely forced me to be maternal."

The day of the performance, the tiny Actors'

A glimpse of "Evergreen."

Studio was packed "to the rafters. I've never seen so many people turn out—not for Al Pacino or Paul Newman, not for anyone like they did for Streisand playing Juliet. Members who hadn't shown up at The Studio for ten or fifteen years suddenly showed up that day. The funny thing is I don't know how the word got out because we all made a pact that we wouldn't talk about it."

Backstage, Kirkland ran in place so that she would be out of breath when she made her entrance. Then Barbra, who is shorter and several pounds lighter, grabbed her and physically dragged her across the room. "She did everything but take me by the feet; she treated me like I was a pillow. But it worked! It was so funny—she had the whole audience in hysterics. And, somehow, I managed to talk through it all and she managed to talk through it all, and every single thing she did was so visual, active and kinesthetic that it really was Shakespeare.

"When it came to her private moment in front of the mirror—which was this moment when Juliet was totally alone and discovering herself as a woman—I know she achieved what she had been working toward. The beauty, the love, the tears of joy," Kirkland continues. (In Barbra's frame of reference, this would be the first time she directed herself.) "Lee talked quite a bit about that moment in his critique. He was very gentle with her. Of all the Juliets he had seen, he told her, she brought in this wholly original and creative way to do the role which he never would have thought would have worked, but it did. 'It's a poetic, vulnerable, romantic, classical part of you that deserves to be seen by the world,' he said, and he encouraged both of us to work on the entire play and bring it back in." Although Barbra was to talk about it privately for some time, the business details of *A Star Is Born* eventually took precedence. The next time Sally Kirkland heard from Barbra, it was concerning a possible role in the film.

After toying around with other co-star possibilities (Brando, Jagger), Barbra and Jon agreed that Kris Kristofferson's "gentle craziness" was indeed what they needed for the film. In December, while various members of the production team were scouting locations, rehearsals commenced at The Burbank Studios. "My feelings about doing *A Star Is Born* are real complex," Kristofferson admitted. "If I stop and

173

"Lost Inside of You," the little classical tune Esther hopes will be a sonata "when it grows up."

think about it, it would scare the hell out of me. I'm flattered to even be considered in there [and] I'm really looking forward to working with her—just to see how she reacts to whatever I bring, and whether I can cope with somebody of that [magnitude]. That's a challenge that I kind of enjoy. I could sink. It could be my great white whale."

The role of the once-charismatic rock star who has given up on his audience and himself was not going to be an easy one to bring to life. It would be demanding, emotionally exhausting work. "I remember a discussion that I had with Barbra about this kind of role," music producer Phil Ramone states, "because why would anybody pity a wealthy rock 'n' roller who puts coke up his nose and tells the audience to go screw?...Was this setting realistic? Would that situation be accepted? What would happen in the audience when John Norman goes onstage completely stoned and they realize he's not performing to their idyllic needs? Barbra was adamant about getting that sympathy going so that you felt empathetic towards the man." Kristofferson's casting would add one important element: movie audiences would see an artist tortured by self-doubt, too weary to be truly cynical, too sensitive not to be in pain.

During their initial pre-production meetings, Frank Pierson had distilled the basic *Star Is Born* conflict down to an Oscar Wilde adage: "An actress is a little more than a woman; an actor is a little less than a man." Or, as Pierson discovered viewing the 1937 and 1954 incarnations: "The issue of [Esther's] success and his failure was seen in terms of a competition in which he lost because she won."

The analysis was painfully on target—moreso than the writer/director guessed at the time. He delivered his draft of the script to Barbra and they met. "She doesn't mention anything about [the new pages]," he recorded. "She picks up other drafts and reads scenes from each, one after the other. What does she mean? What does she want? Did she read what I wrote? I sneer at what she reads. Jon takes me aside for a heart-to-heart. I can't understand what he's talking about. I think they've picked the wrong person and suggest they get someone else. *They* don't seem to hear what *I* said. We go on anyway....[Soon] the script takes shape. Cries of delight. And days of picking over dialogue word by word. I get bored." The die had been cast.

After Rupert Holmes left, Paul Williams stepped in as the musical supervisor. Concerned that she would not have enough songs to fill out the broad tapestry of the score, Barbra sought help from outside sources—and she wrote several songs herself. A one-song experiment in composition turned into a joyously prolific period for her. "Night after night she'd sit alone in our living room until one, two, three o'clock in the morning, plucking away on her guitar," Jon recalls.

Gary Busey, the actor/musician chosen to play John Norman's road manager, introduced the couple to Leon Russell. Russell subsequently agreed to contribute something to the *Star Is Born* score. One

A simple love song, simply recorded, renders a tender, magical moment between Esther and John Norman. (Photo courtesy of the Bob Scott collection)

particularly late night as he and Barbra were going over song ideas, Russell watched Barbra fool around with a classical motif that she wrote on the piano. When asked about it, she tried to pass the tune off as nothing special, but Russell disagreed. It could be a terrific beginning for a song, he urged, and he started singing a counter-melody to her accompaniment. The fruit of their collaboration was "Lost Inside of You."

The composition solved another problem for the filmmakers. "We couldn't come up with a way to get the two characters together in their first love scene," Streisand said. "It's always the most difficult thing: How does the love thing happen? How do you all of a sudden start to kiss?" Getting John and Esther to write a song together effectively toppled those walls of anticipation. Transcribing tapes of that evening at Leon Russell's added another dose of realism to the contemporary story.

"Songs begin to emerge," marvelled Pierson. "Barbra reshapes them, attacking the lyrics with a logician's mind. She insists on precision and simplicity—on lyrics meaning exactly what they say and

saying what they mean. It's an education."

Under the pressure of a final, absolute deadline from Warner Bros., the screenwriter seemed to appreciate the lesson more than the musical supervisor. "How can I write when I have to talk with her all the time," Williams complained to Pierson, "and nothing ever gets done because before I finish the damn song she's already asking for changes?" (What's more, he later confessed, most of what he had written was scribbled on cocktail napkins.) Arranger Ian Free-bairn-Smith remembers some tension concerning "Evergreen." "Paul wrote the lyrics and sent them to her, and Barbra sent them back with a note saying, 'That's going to be a wonderful lyric when it's finished.' They're both very strong egos, Paul and Barbra, and it really made Paul angry to have anybody say that to him. He isn't used to having someone tell him his lyric isn't finished when he believes it is. Then they became sort of unreachable to each other for quite awhile. Paul wasn't answering phone calls or telegrams. One day, all of a sudden he found that a nursery had delivered a potted evergreen to his doorstep. It was a peace offering from Barbra and I think it helped to re-open the dialogue between them."

"It was a very difficult time," Williams later

With Paul Mazursky (playing manager Brian Wexler).

The wedding.

told *Billboard* magazine. "The going got pretty tough at times. But I like to have creative control over my projects, so I understood her." Because *A Star Is Born* was his first motion picture project, musical director Kenny Ascher states he didn't know if the pressures were normal or not. "The thing I do remember is that everybody wanted what was good for the movie."

A gifted songwriter, Kristofferson had also been invited to contribute something to the song score, but declined. Unfortunately, neither was he comfortable with the William/Ascher songs assigned to him. He wanted to make changes; Williams did not like them. Furthermore, Barbra and Jon thought Kris's band could use a little more color. The confused messages finally erupted into a much-publicized fallout on the rehearsal stage. "You're trying to dress us like something that was either dead years ago or is dying a slow death in a Vegas lounge," Kris accused Barbra. "I'm not rock 'n' roll, but that look sure as hell ain't...and I'm not trusting my career to the judgment of a Vegas singer and her hairdresser!"

According to Kristofferson, one of his motivations for doing the film was so that his band could be in it. And best intentions often go awry: "Once Barbra decided my band would be fine for the picture, she was rehearsing them day and night. And I needed them. I was very shaky; I needed to work with the music enough to believe when I acted that I *had* written it....Barbra knew I'd worked with my boys forever....She had so much on her mind she just didn't realize that. And it's my fault [because] I never said anything to her."

Pierson: "It's apparent that Kris has been lying about the music. He hates it, and he's frightened of feeling like a fool. He dreams of the moment Dylan sees the movie....Barbra and I seem to be the only ones who recognize the moment when it comes. Go with Kris's changes or find someone else."

By the time production commenced at the Ice House in Pasadena in February of '76, a more serious problem gnawed at the film's delicate equilibrium: the collaboration between producer/star and writer/director was becoming one of constant struggle. Tired and underweight as filming began, Barbra was in danger of spreading herself too thin. She relied on her director/collaborator to follow through on what they agreed on—only to find camera set-ups completely changed around the next morning (and not always coordinated with the production designer, lighting director or cameraman). The dual set of instructions were counter-productive, wearing down a baffled cast and crew. "Truthfully," Jon states, "when I made the deal with Frank...he came to me and said, 'I'll write this if you let me direct.' And when I got back to him I said, 'The only way you can

Her first concert tour.

direct this is if you partner with Barbra—that means a *partnership*. You collaborate, you communicate and the result of that work is what you see on the screen.' But he didn't do that. The minute he got control he was like a child. He became a tyrant. Ultimately, a lot of his stuff was no good. I wanted to fire him [after the second day]—I did, in fact. But everybody, including Warner Bros., felt there had been too much bad publicity and it would kill the movie."

Barbra opted to continue working through Pierson—but with the added insight that she would have to make a special effort to communicate with the cast and crew.

She tried to encourage her collaborator to be more vocal about expressing his opinion, she says, to give the actors some feedback and communicate a sense of their importance in the film. But Pierson seemed to become more and more detached from the process and Barbra found herself becoming even more watchful and attentive on the set. She used video playback to analyze each take after it was shot. "I must say as time went on I looked at it less and less because I began to *feel* [if things were right] without looking at each take. But it was an enormous help in the beginning."

Aware that some members of the crew thought her contributions and attention to detail med-

dlesome, Barbra discussed the situation with Pierson. "One time I was a little sharp with him and I apologized," she revealed to Lawrence Grobel. "I said, 'I have a problem with tact, I only know how to be direct. I'm sorry...' He said, 'That's OK. I agree with you and then behind your back do what I want anyway.'"

The big loser in this tug-of-war was the film itself. Caught in the middle, Kris Kristofferson resigned himself to "tap dancing between two haystacks"—fortified by tequila, beer and plenty of "laughing tobacco." Despite the conflict, Barbra did begin winning support from the crew. "She hung out with them, she spent time with them," Jon says. "I remember many nights when she would sit up until two in the morning with the lighting man designing all the shots and everything for the next day. The director had already gone to bed."

The majority of *A Star Is Born*'s 60-day production schedule was spent on location. Following Pasadena, the crew traveled to the heart of Hollywood, filming at United Western Recorders, the Aquarius Theater and on a quiet residential street not far from the Chinese Theatre. In Beverly Hills, a gorgeous mansion was stripped of its furnishings in order to properly reflect John Norman's devil-may-care lifestyle. The Biltmore Hotel in downtown Los Angeles served as the backdrop for the tumultuous Grammy Awards sequence. In March, the production moved to Arizona; three and a half weeks would be spent in the Phoenix area and another week and a half outside Tucson (where the Warner Bros. production department had constructed John and Esther's $80,000 adobe hideaway). Because of the intense interest in the movie, the studio had convinced Barbra and Jon to allow a three-day press junket revolving around the March 20 concert at Arizona State University's Sun Devil Stadium.

On Friday, 150 members of the press were ushered out to the stadium where they were seated at circular dining tables on the 50-yard line. Drinks flowed freely. Predictably drawn to what they perceived to be a potentially volatile situation, the press was not disappointed. Media scrutiny and the oppressive heat intensified the pressures. Before Streisand, Kristofferson and Pierson joined the press conference, they rehearsed some of the action onstage. "Kris was having some problems with Barbra," notes assistant director Stu Fleming. "Why, I don't know, but I think he was at a point where he didn't know who he was supposed to listen to—Frank or Barbra. Finally, he said one day, 'I'm just passing over,' meaning he was going to listen to whoever gave him instructions."

All of which didn't settle his confused state.

"When you love someone and they make you angry, you'll hate them. It's indifference that has nothing to do with loving."

Frustrated and irritated and primed to be "an emotional charge" for the following day's activities, the actor forsook his tap dancing skills and purposely ignored key directions from Barbra which, ironically enough, both she and Pierson had agreed upon. "Who's the director?" he demanded in exasperation. A volley of sarcastic comments followed, culminated by Jon's offer to slug it out—after the production was completed—and his insistence that Kristofferson apologize to Barbra. The entire argument was picked up by a nearby mike and recorded by a gleeful press. "They were right in front of the mike," Fleming says. "As soon as I realized what was going on, I grabbed

A moment of togetherness at their desert hideaway.

the mike and pulled it away from them."

"I threatened to walk out on the movie so many times," Kris told Geraldo Rivera, "I'm amazed she didn't just tell me to haul my ass home." "It was just bad timing," Barbra added. Pierson: "Now our difficulties have become news events. It heightens the tension and the feeling of being perpetually misunderstood. These clashes happen on all pictures; they become part of the creative process from which the picture emerges. They are unavoidable." Although everyone involved in *A Star Is Born* is quick to point out that what happened during the making of that film wasn't particularly unusual, there is no doubt its executive producer/star was and the press was acutely aware of this. "[Now] the press is uncontrollable and mischievous," Pierson wrote.

Sensitive to jokes about his newly acquired superstar status, Kristofferson explained his point-of-view at the press conference. "In this film, you see, I'm standing up for Janis, Jimi, for every self-destructive artist. If I blow it, I have to answer to that. It's one of the scariest things I've ever done.... The more I get to know [Barbra], the more I respect her. She can divide her attention in a way that is inconceivable to me....Frankly, it's surprised me how authentic and real she is. We may just do something that is an honest portrayal of life in the music business—and if we pull it off, it'll be a first. Compared to the other versions of *A Star Is Born*, in my opinion, it knocks them out of the box."

The concert, coordinated by Jon Peters and Bill Graham, went surprisingly well. "[Graham] told us right from the get-go what the reaction would be from the audience to our filming," Fleming states. "He said, 'You're gonna be able to film for a little while, but then they're gonna get hostile and we're gonna have to give them some music. So you've got to

181

go out there and shoot fast 'cause they'll let you know when they're bored with it.' And they did." In addition to the principal photography, the concert and press conference were covered by a 16mm documentary film crew. Some of this footage would also be incorporated into the motion picture.

Most of the indoor concerts were filmed at Grady Gammage Auditorium in Phoenix. Barwood had taken out ads in the local papers to announce that the theater would be open to the public, and to everyone's amazement, fans showed up from all over the United States and Canada—and stayed all day. Their patience was rewarded with an exceedingly accommodating Streisand who joked with the audience, posed for pictures and capped the day off with performances of "Woman in the Moon," "I Believe in Love" and "With One More Look at You"/"Watch Closely Now." All three numbers had been painstakingly choreographed in front of the cameras. In order to achieve the most effective visual design for each, Barbra worked closely with cinematographer Robert Surtees and lighting director Jules Fisher over several days preceding the event.

The 11,000 seat Tucson Community Center was slated to be the site of the final concert on the *Star Is Born* itinerary (actually John Norman's spectacular introduction). Under budget and ahead of schedule, the production faced a possible delay when Surtees fell ill. Ernest Laszlo was permitted to replace him. John and Esther fled to their isolated desert oasis. With work progressing smoothly, the crew couldn't resist one mischievous prank. Kris: "In one scene Barbra's wearing this white pantsuit and she's supposed to be covered in mud. The prop man smeared it on her and Barbra says to me, 'Come over here. Smell this stuff.' I did. *Whew!* I went over to Frank and said, 'They're putting shit on Barbra.' He says, 'I don't want to hear about it.' Well, the crew *said* it was some preservative they'd put in the mud, but…I know what it was—and so did Barbra! And we both started laughing and Barbra's laughing harder than me!"

Mid-April. Principal photography was completed on location in the San Fernando Valley as Esther proposed to John, and he accepted. Everyone was understandably exhausted at the wrap party, which also doubled as a birthday party for Barbra. Her co-star very nearly didn't make it. "He said he got on the freeway coming in from Malibu," Fleming chuckles, "and he got behind this truck with all these pretty colored lights—and he ended up in San Bernadino."

The nuts and bolts aspect of post-production was accomplished at the Malibu complex where Barbra and Jon converted one of the guest houses into an editing bay. After Pierson delivered his director's cut, Streisand and editor Peter Zinner went to work. Barbra was challenged by the prospect of putting her vision on the line and was more than willing to take the praise or criticism that might result from her efforts. "This is the first time I've gotten so involved in film editing," she told the *Hollywood Reporter*, "and all the aspects of post-production are just as creative as acting." The editorial process became her chance to re-direct the film.

One fight she won concerned the film's sound. Barbra wanted to create a dense, multi-layered soundtrack similar to Robert Altman's innovative *Nashville* where dialogue (and sometimes music) overlapped. During dubbing, she had wanted to record the new lines of dialogue outside so that the audio quality was consistent with the previously-recorded material. "I was told I couldn't do it," she said, but they tried it anyway—and it worked.

By the end of the summer, Peter Zinner and Barbra had assembled a rough three and a half hour cut of the movie. Upon viewing the footage, a Warner Bros. executive would certify the film a hit; there was no more grumbling about "Barbra and Jon's home movie." The next months were spent fine-tuning the picture. Jon worked on its promotion, Barbra labored over the dramatic finale. "When Warner Bros. saw Pierson's cut," Marty says, "they didn't like the ending [an animated rock performance of "With One More Look at You"/"Watch Closely Now"]. As the producer, Barbra now had an opportunity to re-cut the movie, but she only had three weeks in which to do it. When she got to the last scene, she didn't have time to play around with it, so she inserted the master close-ups fully intending to tell Warner Bros., when the screening was over, that she wanted more time to work on it. But they loved her cut, and they especially loved her choice of shots at the end—which was really no choice at all."

Shot as one continuous close-up, the seven-minute medley was an intense, highly intimate portrait of Esther's changing emotional state as seen through her interpretation of John Norman's music. "One thing I remember is that Francis Coppola wanted a year to do *The Godfather*," Barbra told the students at UCLA, "and he still didn't have enough time to finish it. I never understood it until I had to do it."

The Barwood production of *A Star Is Born* was pared down to an economical 140 minutes. In November, the studio began sneaking the picture. Executives were ecstatic over the preview reactions—but hardly overjoyed with Frank Pierson's "tell-all" article, which was published that month in *New York*

A final goodbye.

and *New West* magazines. As with all deceptively clever exposés. "My Battles with Barbra and Jon" contained enough inverted truths to confuse even the most knowledgeable reader. In protecting himself from the potential "embarrassment" of *A Star Is Born*, the author made public the private confidences of many co-workers, in addition to the controversial couple. For the time being, the article was to become the definitive statement on an egomaniacal star and her equally power-hungry lover—instigating a new wave of hostility in the media. "I've always turned the other cheek," Barbra remarked in 1979. "I'm beginning to think it doesn't work."

Historians have duly noted after many a troubled production—from the golden era of *Gone With the Wind*, *The Wizard of Oz* and *Citizen Kane* on through to *Giant, The Misfits* and *Apocalypse Now*—that it is a miracle that most films ever get finished. The miracle of *A Star Is Born* isn't simply that it was completed and succeeded in spite of the conflicts—or in the ingenious ways it circumvented many of them—but that it owes much of its eventual success, on so many different levels, to these very elements. And perhaps most surprisingly, to the negative press they engendered.

Reports that *Star* would be the year's most publicized bomb, "a Barbra Streisand lollipop extravaganza," were counteracted by the early trade reviews. "The new *A Star Is Born* shares with the new *King Kong* the rare distinctions of being a superlative remake," heralded *Daily Variety*. "Barbra Streisand's performance as the rising star is her finest screen work to date, while Kris Kristofferson's magnificent portrayal of her failing benefactor realizes all the promise first shown five years ago in *Cisco Pike*. Jon Peters' production is outstanding, and Frank Pierson's direction is brilliant.... Selznick himself would be proud of this picture." *Hollywood Reporter*, too, predicted a sensational commercial future for this "beautifully photographed and appropriately sad" dramatic love story.

The motion picture had its world premiere at the Village Theatre in Los Angeles on December 18, 1976. In attendance were an assortment of Streisand supporters from William Wyler to Ryan O'Neal. Rita Coolidge, then married to Kristofferson, thought the movie a beautiful love story. "I didn't think [Kris] ought to do it, to tell the truth.... But when I saw [it], I swear I was in tears—and I'm not a crier—from the opening scene on. I caught Kris crying during it, too, and he *never* does. After awhile it wasn't even my husband up there, I got so involved." Frank Pierson

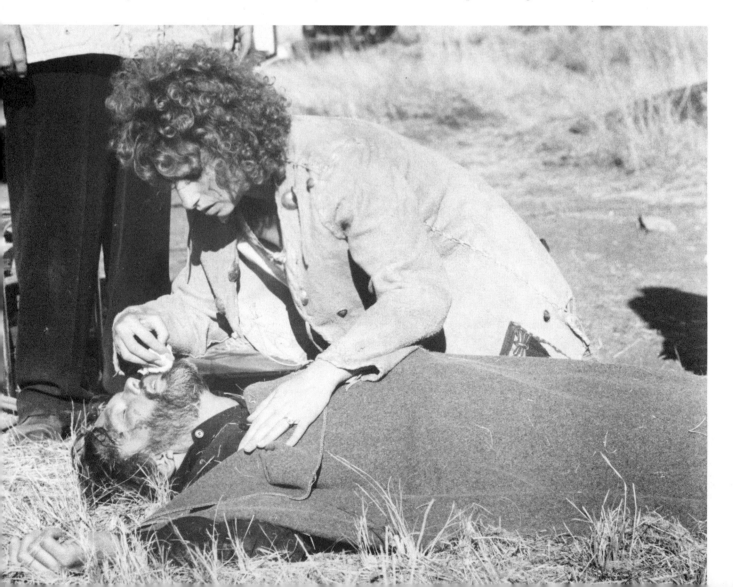

(who did not attend the premiere) declared that he loved the film. "The public statements have gotten out of hand," he stated. "The impression is that Barbra and I differed on everything. It was actually 10-15%. We both cared strongly....I think Barbra is a brilliant editor."

"She made me look better than I've ever looked in a movie, you've got to admit that," Kristofferson told Geraldo Rivera at the New York premiere. "I'm afraid there may be a tendency to knock her—that seems to come with the territory—and then give credit for everything that's good to me or Frank...and I feel terrible about [that] because she's a great filmmaker." Beyond the professional vindication, Kristofferson would have a personal reason for rallying behind the film. "It's the first time I was ever able to look at myself through Rita's eyes," he said. "And I think more than the bad I saw, I think that the good I saw affected me. It gave me enough confidence to think it was worth straightening up the act."

After the largely positive reponse in Los Angeles, Barbra looked forward to the national reviews. She felt she had lost some objectivity toward the end and hoped to learn from the criticism. The financial success of *A Star Is Born* was extremely important to her but she also wanted some validation for putting her personal vision on the line. She was to be brutally awakened. A writer once likened Barbra's appeal to Bruce Springsteen and Sylvester Stallone (as *Rocky*) "in the way she makes every gesture a movement in a battle for self-transcendence. And, like them, she wins her battles more often that she loses." In 1976, she was to lose the war of words but she would win her point.

Reviews:

"I summoned the charity of the holiday season and went to see *A Star Is Born*, knowing it took three years to make and cost $5.5 million, hoping for the best. Now I know the worst. If there's anything worse than the noise and stench that rises from that record album, it's the movie itself. It's an unsalvagable disaster....Every aspect of the classic story has been trashed, along with the dialogue....This is why Hollywood is in the toilet. What the hell does Barbra Streisand know about directing or editing a movie? So many people have disowned this film that I don't even know who to blame. But I do blame a studio for giving $5.5 million to an actress and her boyfriend to finance their own ego trip. Nobody at the studio ever saw any rushes or had any idea what was going on

until the film was finished. Even the director, Frank Pierson, was 'released from duty' after his final cut was rejected. The result is a junk heap of boring ineptitude."

—*New York Daily News*

"The case for or against Barbra Streisand should always be a double one, for the actress without song is never more than half the talent, half the screen presence.... The deepest flaws of the movie run right down its middle like a geological fault.... Streisand knew by instinct what was missing from the other versions of *A Star Is Born*, both in their statements about female suffering and in their emotional architecture. She knew that her film should end in an act of art, not just fortitude.... Yet she knew how to lay a foundation for this only in the music, not the dialogue.... Pitted against the timidities of the script, the musical numbers of *A Star Is Born*, the best of them, still have the nerve and invention of a great film experience. But we have a right as reviewers to ask for more, and Streisand has it in her.... With a script that would finally let her acting sing, there is no telling what wonders her singing might enact."

—*Sight and Sound*

FINAL NOTE:"You have to understand the way [Barbra] saw it," *A Star Is Born* alumnus John Gregory Dunne said a few years later. "It was her life on the line. If the picture went down, she went down with it. She just had to do what she thought was right."

Devastated by the critical response, Barbra nonetheless found tremendous support from the movie-going public. Fans young and old were flocking to theaters in unheard-of numbers. Strangely enough, the movie became a battleground for admirers as well as detractors. Much of this had to do with the schizophrenic way Streisand is perceived by her followers. For some, the gawkish singer who delighted the cult in small bistros and shocked others on TV talk shows was their champion. Her initial success only reinforced what they believed from the beginning—that she was a real find. THEIR find.

As Barbra refined her craft, mass acceptance followed, but many fervently held onto the past: the beehive hairdos, the arms flailing in the air to punctuate off-beat material. *Funny Girl*'s success in Hollywood was fine with them at first, but she wasn't supposed to stay there. And the longer she did—the more she began to appeal to a broader base of fans—the greater the danger of the "specialness" wearing off for those supporters. It was an inevitable separation of ways, but no less disheartening for

those who simply wanted someone to follow in Judy Garland's stead.

Others simply resented what they perceived to be the California-homogenization of their star. That schism was represented most vividly in the declining box-office of her films post-*Funny Lady* in New York. (Even the "ethnic" *Yentl* did better in most midwestern cities than it did in Barbra's hometown.)

Part of the "Streisand mystique" is a genius for exploiting what the public thinks it knows about her. In *A Star Is Born*, the audience tapped into powerful emotions: the pain she might have felt about her star eclipsing Elliott's (when she wanted so much for *him*), her terror of performing in front of a hostile audience, the highs and lows of her fiery relationship with Jon, her delayed anger over the death of her father. As an actress, singer and contributor to the film, she brought an immediacy to the film that was hard to simply write into the script. Audiences could believe what was happening because they knew it had, in all likelihood, happened to her.

Critics were eager to tear apart bits and pieces of *A Star Is Born* for being too much, too little, too stupid, too tame. Its successes were mentioned grudgingly, if at all; few were willing to admit that what they observed to be the film's flaws were incurred by its bravery. And that it was possible for the music, live concerts, the romantic chemistry between Streisand and Kristofferson and the story's contemporary sensibility to combine to create box-office magic. The picture grossed $9.5 million its first nine days of release; exhibitors were ecstatic. What made them even happier was that the film held up eight, ten, twelve weeks after its opening.

A Star Is Born rose above the personal vendettas to become a popular love story at a time when many wondered what had happened to romance in the movies—which may explain why so many people who professed to dislike the film actually saw it more than once. With domestic film rentals of $37.5 million (once again, double that figure for the actual gross), the movie ranks as Barbra's most popular motion picture to date.

At awards time, *Star* took home five Golden Globes (Best Musical, Best Actress, Best Actor, Best Original Score and Best Song). In its predictably superior way, however, the Academy of Motion Pictures Arts and Sciences delegated most of its recognition to nominations in the technical area: Best Cinematography, Sound, Original Song and Original Song Score and/or Its Adaptation. [Robert DeNiro, Peter Finch, Giancarlo Gianinni, William Holden and Sylvester Stallone were nominated for Best Actor; Marie-Christine Barrault, Faye Dunaway, Talia Shire, Sissy Spacek and Liv Ullmann were the Best

Three faces of the dramatic finale.

Actress nominees.]

By then, even the industry snub didn't seem to matter. Aside from the film's success at the box-office, what was important was that the experience woke Barbra up to her own creative potential. "*A Star Is Born* was the beginning of Barbra's examining her own power," Jon says. "It was a discovery period for her. And she started to realize that she could do it, she could take control of her life. I was the tool, in a way. The halfback. I was the one who ran interference for her—because there were a lot of changes she wanted to make, but she couldn't always articulate it....I remember Jane Fonda calling her up after she saw the film and saying, 'Congratulations. Not only for the movie, but you are leading the way for all of us.'...In retrospect, I have to say that the most creative experience I've had in my life to date is *A Star Is Born*. I've never worked with a more compelling, imaginative person."

With The Main Event's *director Howard Zieff (left) and executive producer Howard Rosenman (right).*

THE MAIN EVENT
(Warner Bros./First Artists)

CAST:

Hillary Kramer.......	Barbra Streisand
Eddie "Kid Natural" Scanlon...........	Ryan O'Neal
David...............	Paul Sand
Percy..............	Whitman Mayo
Donna..............	Patti D'Arbanville
Luis................	Chu Chu Malave
Hector Mantilla.......	Richard Lawson
Leo Gough..........	James Gregory

The Main Event *(1979)*.

CREDITS:

Executive producers...	Howard Rosenman
	Renee Missel
Produced by.........	Jon Peters
	Barbra Streisand
Directed by..........	Howard Zieff
Screenplay by........	Gail Parent
	Andrew Smith
Cinematography.......	Mario Tosi
Film editor..........	Edward Warschilka
Production designer....	Charles Rosen
Music supervised by...	Gary LeMel
Music...............	Michael Melvoin
"The Main Event" Written by...........	Paul Jabara
	Bruce Roberts

"Fight"
Written by.............. Paul Jabara
                        Bob Esty
Medley performed by.. Barbra Streisand
Produced by.......... Bob Esty
Music editor.......... William Saracino
Assistant directors..... Gary Daigler
                        Pat Kehoe
Casting.............. Dianne Crittenden
                        Karen Rea

Running time: 112 minutes
Rated: PG

A Barwood Film

"The Main Event was my fault. I pushed Barbra into that. It was time to do a movie and I wanted her to do a comedy. But it was material she really didn't like."
—Jon Peters

Success breeds success; *A Star Is Born* bred contempt. The box-office success of the motion picture was the end of the battle but not the war for Streisand and Peters. Jon didn't suffer the same fate as his *A Star Is Born* predecessor, Judy Garland's producer/husband, Sid Luft. He produced a series of financially—and sometimes even critically—successful films. But the hairdresser jokes didn't stop for years to come, and they were only negated by perseverance and hard work.

Jon planned his filmmaking future, but three years on her last film left Barbra depleted and looking forward to a year's vacation. The discussions about how to follow up *A Star Is Born* didn't stop, however. There was *Loveland*, a contemporary musical to be produced at Universal; a remake of the MGM classic *The Women* (with an updated script by Polly Platt); *Dead: A Love Story*, the true story of

convicted murderess Ruth Snyder; *Fancy Hardware*, a story about "an ERA lady of the '20s" originally developed at First Artists for Steve McQueen and Ali McGraw; and Paramount wanted her back for *Foul Play*. None of the projects were sufficiently developed for Barbra to make a commitment, and after a while she wondered if she ever would. The dilemma she faced, as with most multi-talented artists, was that there was virtually no one to listen to, no one to challenge her on all professional levels. Those providing guidance might give solid advice in some areas, but not others. For Barbra, the only thing that could furnish any kind of mirror for what she must do was the work itself.

Sydney Pollack recalled a series of conversations with Barbra in which she discussed her frustration over her inability to move on to the next project. "What am I doing? Why am I not working?" she asked him, rhetorically. "What am I saving myself for? This is stupid. I should be out there, Sydney. So, every picture won't be great. I mean, I haven't done a picture in so long. I just sit and wait and wait and wait—for what? For Chekhov to come along? For Shakespeare to come along? I'm getting older, and there are a million things I want to do. *What* am I saving myself for? And yet I say to myself, why would I want to go and do something that I'm not really stimulated by? And then I argue with myself. I talked to Truffaut once, who said, 'You do your work and at the end you have a body of work. Some of it is good and some of it is not good, but the stuff that's good will override what isn't good—that's what a body of work is. You can't just sit and wait for the perfect thing to come along.'"

In an era when every producer, director, writer and star wants a film to bear their sole stamp of authorship, Barbra Streisand is someone to be feared. Not for any rational reason other than a struggle over control, which, according to legend, must be deferred to her if she is involved in a project. She wields her power so well, no one can imagine her without it. Barbra's reality was that she was no longer considered simply an actress; she was a conglomerate, and conglomerates must, for the most part, create their own business. She and Jon had hoped to get their next co-production in front of the cameras by the Spring of 1978. Spring came and went without a start date, but Barwood did have at least two projects in development. One was *Yentl, the Yeshiva Boy*. The other was a comedy about the world of boxing written by Gail Parent (best known for her work on "Mary Hartman, Mary Hartman") and Andrew Smith—who once boxed under the name Kid Natural. The project had originated at MGM two years earlier, but rewrites and casting setbacks had forced

"I'm glad there's not a volcano in this town," co-star Paul Sand said when asked about Barbra. *"In other primitive societies, they throw their most talented and beautiful people in volcanos."*

Knockout into a turn-around; MGM dropped it. Producer Renee Missel sent a script to agent Sue Mengers who liked the story enough to suggest it as a possibility for Barbra's next feature. Barwood bought the screenplay. After a succession of writers, Parent and Smith were called back in to re-focus the script.

Ryan O'Neal, who had recently bowed out of MGM's remake of *The Champ* due to a dispute with director Franco Zefferelli, was the only actor considered for the role of the former-boxer-turned-driving-instructor in *The Main Event*. He had been offered the part when it was still attached to MGM, and Goldie Hawn and Diana Ross were looking at the female lead. Not only was O'Neal one of the few stars who could hold his own in the ring as well as onscreen but, in Barbra's words, he possessed "that rare ability to combine romance with comedy. Ryan is really a talented comedian. He does these falls and looks—something Cary Grant was also the master of." Barbra called him in New York and asked him to reconsider the role. "Because, Ryan, if you don't want to do the part, I don't want to make the picture." "If you're in it," the actor responded, "I'll do it." O'Neal was set for the part in April 1978.

The actor hadn't had a solid hit in five years, but didn't really think he was "riding on [Barbra's] coattails." As they matured in the years since *What's*

Up, Doc? so had their friendship. "Barbra said to me once, 'You like the fights? My stepfather liked the fights. I always wanted his approval. He never liked me. He used to sit in his undershirt, drinking beer and watching the fights on television. And, you know, one time I crawled underneath the TV picture when I went by so I wouldn't interfere with his view. He never even noticed. He would *never* see me, he just stared at the fights.'"

"I'll never forget her telling me that. I said, 'Whatever happened to him?' She said, 'I don't know.

Barbra and Ryan 1971 and 1978.

One day he just left and never came back. I thought it was my fault, and so did my mother. Then one day, when I was in *Funny Girl* on Broadway, I scratched the cornea of my eye and my understudy was getting ready to go on in my place. Everyone was telling me not to go on because I might hurt my eye. Then I got this card and a little dish of candy from my stepfather—he was out in front, in the audience.' So she said, 'I'm going on.' The doctors anesthetized her eye so it wouldn't tear, and she went on. She said, 'I never did a show like that. It was the best performance I ever gave.' After the show, she went backstage and waited for him, but he never came back.

Perfume whiz Hillary Kramer is stunned to learn of her bad fortune...

...and hopes to recover some of it at the Main Street gym.

"She never saw him again, but she kept the candy container. That's why I like Barbra—because all of those things in her life have enriched that woman."

Early in 1977, columnist Liz Smith stated that Ray Stark had sent several scripts over to Streisand for her consideration—as a director. After years of observing movie technicians at work and formulating her own ideas about filmmaking—topped off by the experience of producing *A Star Is Born*—directing was certainly something on Barbra's mind. Patrick Kehoe, one of the first assistant directors on *The Main Event*, states that Barbra mentioned to him that the original plan was for her to helm the comedy. Only after she decided that there wasn't enough time to prepare for her directorial debut did she assign another director. "I suppose she felt she couldn't prepare as an actress and also as a director in the time that was available," says Kehoe.

During the time she was making up her list of directors, Barbra saw a modern battle-of-the-sexes comedy entitled *House Calls* and asked to meet the director. So Howard Zieff got the job of director/ collaborator. Motivated by the idea that simply surviving Streisand's first film after the notorious *A Star Is Born* would be "a once-in-a-lifetime set up," Zieff hypothesized that if he could accomplish the task with good humor, his next Hollywood film would be assured. "People look at you in amazement when you say you've just directed Streisand," he explained later. "It gets around. 'Hey, he can handle movie stars and still bring movies in on time and on budget.' That speaks for itself in this town....I went in knowing *[The Main Event]* had to be made and I told myself it might as well be me making it."

Barbra envisioned making a film that was reminiscent of the frantically paced, harder-edged comedies of the late '30s and '40s. As with *What's*

195

The gas crunch added another practical reality to Hillary's predicament (and also provided a little free publicity). This scene did not make it in to the final cut, however.

The battle of the sexes begins.

On location in Los Angeles.

Up, Doc?, she screened many of those cinema classics for the writers. "[Barbra] wanted them to see that we wanted more than just laughs," Jon said. "We wanted it to be funny and real." An important part of establishing that realism was the casting of secondary roles. Jeff Goldblum was going to play David, Hillary's lawyer/ex-husband—but on film he looked too young to have been married to Barbra, so the part went to comedian Paul Sand. "Sanford and Son's" Whitman Mayo signed on as The Kid's trainer, Percy; James Gregory would portray fight promoter Leo Gough; and Patti D'Arbanville won the role of The Kid's girlfriend.

Comfortably budgeted at $7,000,000, *The Main Event* was scheduled to begin production on October 2, 1978. As the start date approached, the screenplay still hadn't been firmed—it was thought that keeping the story open for change might further improve its character and tone. Parent and Smith remained on standby throughout filming, often rewriting entire scenes in marathon sessions at Barbra's house the night before or on the set while the crews prepared the next shot. "Barbra wasn't just lounging around like some old-time movie star saying, 'Write me something clever,'" said Smith. "She was *there* with us, improvising and suggesting lines." Parent especially enjoyed working with Barbra; she got a kick out of the star who "doesn't realize she doesn't have to worry about who is going to take care of lunch. It's as if she were still in New York fifteen years ago."

Filming began on location at the famed Main Street gym in downtown Los Angeles. "There's nothing like setting up the cameras at the actual site, especially when you realize that such boxers as Joe Louis worked out there," said Zieff. From the blood, sweat and tears of Main Street, the crew moved on to an equally physical workout—at Gilda's, a posh exercise salon in Beverly Hills. Zieff and company kept the production out on location as much as possible. A house on the beach at Malibu provided the backdrop for the near fiasco of a fundraising party for The Kid, and a residential neighborhood gained an unusual tenant when the crew constructed the glove-shaped Knockout Driving Academy on one street. There, Hillary and The Kid had an opportunity to act out their aggression/attraction. "Men and women are always fighting, so why not physicalize it?" Barbra contemplated. "But what happens [is that] something that starts out as a joke develops into a kind of passionate exchange. We had to figure out a setup for it, so we figured we'd have them pose for publicity pictures—the two of them in boxing gloves." Demonstrating the punch toward the camera, Barbra would describe the sequence to Zieff as

Ryan: "People have been unfair to Barbra...She's a delicately-made creature, a great lady, and I would never have done The Main Event *without her."*

"a sexual dance...man and woman stalking each other."

"[Barbra] is a special force," Zieff would say years later. "You realize what a big star she is when you go out for a hamburger with her. Fans mob her, like they used to mob Valentino or Garbo. She's that popular." Still, during its ten-week production schedule, *The Main Event* only went into the studio to film a couple of scenes at Hollywood General. The rest of the time, they took advantage of the good weather on a variety of Southern California locations. They took advantage of the unseasonal weather as well. On location for an eight-day shoot at Cedar Lake near Big Bear, an early snowfall forced them to do a quick rewrite on the training camp scenes.

Back in Los Angeles, tensions escalated somewhat as Jon once again had to deal with Barbra's love

Ryan: "I like her energy. It's vibrant and beautiful,
and I think one of the most dynamic aspects of her personality."

scenes with a former beau ["Am I cool about it? Hell, no," he admitted], and Barbra tried to funnel her ideas through a by-now reluctant collaborator. "Howard knew it was a hybridized kind of direction—that Barbra's opinion counted for a great deal and one couldn't dismiss it," assistant director Kehoe says. But in that acknowledgment there may have been a feeling that his position as director had been neutralized. Ryan O'Neal contrasted the experience with his past teaming with Barbra. "In *What's Up, Doc?*, we did what we were told. Peter Bogdanovich ran the show," he told Rex Reed. "This time we tried all kinds of things. [Barbra] played the Bogdanovich role. Howard Zieff was under lots of pressure; I think he held up pretty well." Likening the film to his two-year adventure with Stanley Kubrick on *Barry Lyndon*, O'Neal would tell *Newsday* he worked even harder with Barbra. "She works fifteen and sixteen hours a day," he said admiringly.

Pat Kehoe, who later worked with Steven Spielberg on *The Color Purple*, joined the production at this stage. He feels the mood on the set "wasn't tension so much as a kind of benign exasperation that this was the way it was gonna be. There were a couple of heads operating the body, which happens in film with unfortunate frequency....Barbra, from my brief experience with her, was an extremely professional person. I was pleasantly surprised with her and the way that she conducted herself. She's a perfectionist and has some interesting ideas. She's like Spielberg, in a way. If she has an idea a few minutes before the start of the shot, she'll articulate the idea with maybe a thorough knowledge of what the ramifications of enunciating the idea might be, in terms of what you have to do to make it work. Or maybe a kind of naiveté about it, I don't know [but] I suspect it's the former: that she knows exactly what's gonna happen and what it's gonna take to accomplish it....If she's aggressive, she's aggressive in a very understated kind of way. At least she was on that picture....People ask me that. 'Well, you worked with Barbra Streisand. What was she like?' I say, 'Thoroughly professional.' She was the shining star....one of the glimmering highlights of my brief association with that picture. Because, I'll tell you, the rest of it was pretty ragtag."

With Paul Sand.

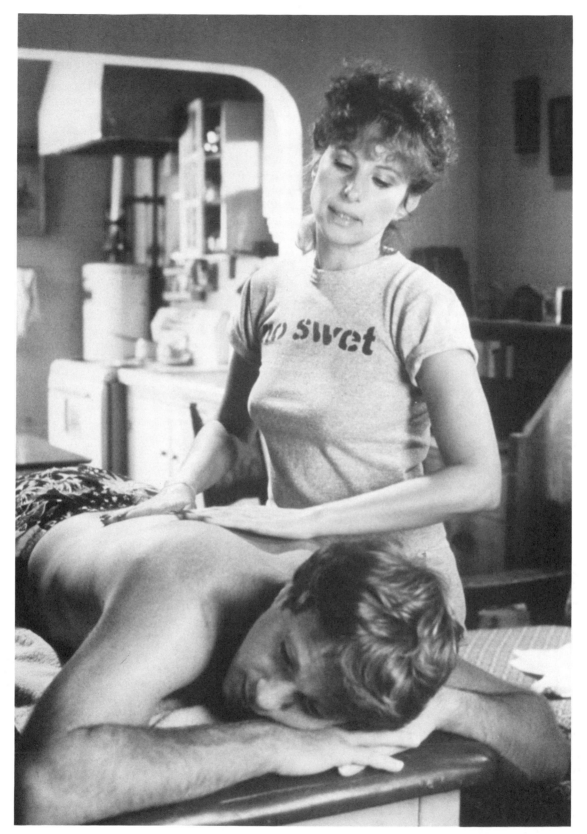

Barbra: "You've got to really hand it to Ryan. I mean, he really took a beating in this role."

The three major fight sequences were shot at the Olympic Auditorium in mid-December 1978. Streisand and O'Neal found working together again to be a special kind of shorthand. "It's so good to have somebody who understands the plot and understands your character as well as her own," Ryan said. "This was not an easy part for me to play." O'Neal had lost approximately forty pounds and boxed over 150 rounds with former champ Jose Torres and O'Neal's own fighter, Hedgemon Lewis, in preparation for this role. "I guess I should know my way around the ring," he told *Hollywood Reporter*. "I started boxing when I was ten. My dad built a ring for us....I fought in YMCA bouts, Golden Gloves, CYO, anything I could." With as many as five cameras going simultaneously to capture the action, O'Neal boxed his way though his final scenes.

...Or so he thought. After principal photography had been completed, Barbra decided there was one scene left to film. Not everyone agreed with her, so she went back and shot it herself. "I just didn't think the relationship had solidified," she explained to television host Mike Walsh. "It didn't culminate in something more tangible than just going to bed with each other the night before—which is a very funny scene, but one has to confront the other person sooner or later. So I thought it would be [a chance] to see where these two people are coming from [and] how different they are emotionally. [A chance] to say something about men and women and the roles they're supposed to play and yet be funny." The morning-after scene was to become an audience favorite.

After the holidays, Zieff commenced work on his cut of the film. "Barbra always has final say on her movies," he said in 1979. "I was optimistic that my final cut would be good enough to prevail. As it turned out, I was right." A year and a half later, however, after the reviews had criticized some of the nonsensical plotting, the director would state that although Streisand was initially "very charming and seductive...she just took over the editing and cut the film to her own purpose." [It is interesting to note that reviews of Zieff's 1981 hit, *Private Benjamin*, would criticize the very same structural problems: inconsistencies in character and a disappointing finale.]

Bob Esty, the producer and arranger of "The Main Event"/"Fight" makes note of the one time he saw something close to "the Streisand I had heard

The relationship warms up at The Kid's training camp. (Also pictured: Whitman Mayo as Percy.)

about....We were at Todd-AO looking at the rough cut of the movie and I said, 'Gee, it's a shame that after all this work it's going to be in mono.' And she said, 'What do you mean mono?' And I said, 'Well, the movie's in mono' and she freaked out. It was explained to her that at the first meetings they had regarding the technical end of the movie it was decided, since it wasn't a musical, they were going to do it in mono because it was cheaper. She was appalled. They said, 'Don't worry, don't worry. It's going to be released as a record and people can play it all they want in stereo. It'll be on the radio in stereo.' And she was appeased, but she learned at the moment that the song had better be stereo if she was going to bother singing it. She was very involved in the scoring aspect and was very particular about what went into the movie."

Supported by an $8,000,000 advertising campaign that exceeded the cost of the film, *The Main Event* hit 1100 theaters nationwide on June 22, 1979. Critically, it was a split decision, but financially the comedy established itself as a champ. With domestic film rentals of $26.4 million, it ranks as Barbra's third most popular film.

Review:

"The secret to Streisand's ability seems to be a rare capacity for intense concentration in a scene, and she seems to fling herself into the roles with such complete abandon that even when she's playing scenes where the script shows some seams and the dialogue falls flat, she's able to bluster and chatter and body-talk her way through by mugging or contorting her limbs. Like the magician's patter calculated to decoy the eye during a slight-of-hand, her expressive eyes and mobile mouth disguise many a flaw in the characterization of Hillary Kramer."

Dallas Times Herald

FINAL NOTE: *The Main Event* completed Barbra's three-picture commitment to First Artists. By 1979, the production company had diversified its interests, establishing a music publishing company, a television production arm, negotiating to buy a hotel in Atlantic City and a casino in London, and purchasing a sportswear company. But while all three original partners expressed an interest in continuing their production affiliation, First Artists had seemingly lost interest in its stars. Steve McQueen

"This is not a pass. This is just thirst."

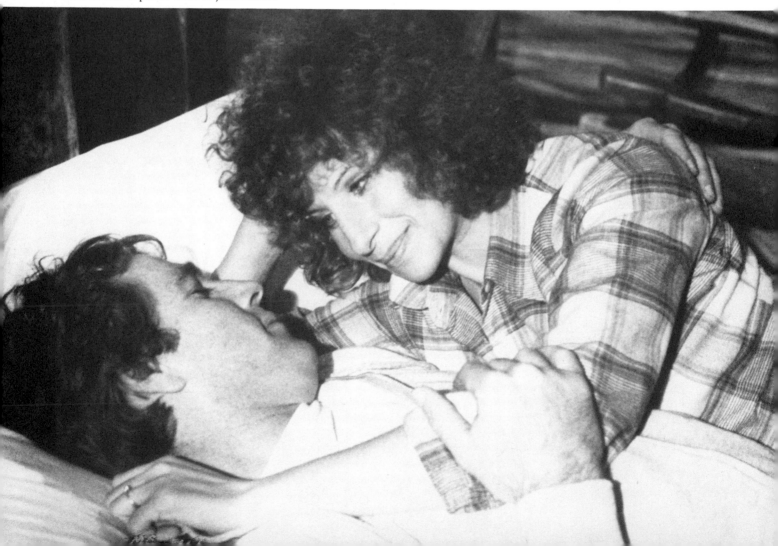

sued the company in 1976 when it failed to give a go-ahead on one of his productions. Dustin Hoffman lost control of both of his films in 1978 and was forced to file suit. Barwood subsequently disassociated itself from First Artists and reassigned several projects then in development to Jon Peters.

"Ryan [plays] a driving instructor from Long Beach. On the surface, not the right match, you know. Not my type."

"People need to know how to drive, Barbra."
"That is true. And I come to realize that by the end of the film. I, too, become a driving instructor!"

ALL NIGHT LONG
(Universal Pictures)

CAST:

George Dupler	Gene Hackman
Cheryl Gibbons	Barbra Streisand
Helen Dupler	Diane Ladd
Freddie Dupler	Dennis Quaid
Bobby Gibbons	Kevin Dobson
Richard H. Copleston . .	William Daniels
Ultra-Sav day manager .	Terry Kiser
Emily	Vernee Watson
Russell Munk	Chris Mulkey

CREDITS:

Produced by	Leonard Goldberg
	Jerry Weintraub
Directed by	Jean-Claude Tramont
Screenplay	W.D. Richter
Associate producers	Terrence A. Donnelly
	Fran Roy
Cinematography	Philip Lathrop
Production designer	Peter Jamison
Set decorator	Linda Spheeris
Costume designer	Albert Wolsky
Film editor	Marion Rothman
Music	Ira Newborn
	Richard Hazard
"Carelessly Tossed"	
Composed by	Alan Lindgren
Lyrics by	W.D. Richter
"Cheryl's Theme"	
Composed by	Dave Grusin
Unit production man-	
agers	Robert L. Brown
	Hap Weyman
Assistant director	Terrence Donnelly
Casting	Anita Dann

Running time: 88 minutes
Rated: R

Any discussion of *The Main Event* and *All Night Long* inevitably becomes interwined with Barbra's pre-production work on *Yentl*. It was during *The Main Event* that her resolve to film the Isaac Bashevis Singer short story was fortified and found realistic dimensions. And, without her eternal commitment to *Yentl*—which obviously threatened a few business associates because it continued to grow in significance (in her mind) from year to year—she, in all likelihood, would not have done *All Night Long*.

Barbra's insecurity about taking full responsibility for directing led to near-catastrophic conclusions on her two last films. She was a producer/ star who had very definite opinions about the way

Cheryl Gibbons

All Night Long *(1981)*.

things should look and feel. Using less talented directors as "middlemen" amounted to hiring them on as "indentured servants"—and resulted in largely unsatisfactory experiences for everyone concerned since both sides could always claim it wasn't their fault. Barbra's strategy to maintain artistic control did not work. "I realized I either wanted to work with very strong directors I could trust or direct a movie myself," she told a friend, writer Joe Morgenstern. "I knew I was taking the chicken way out."

The next step was to do what some people were saying she'd been doing for years: direct. Her passion for *Yentl* made that short story the most logical choice for a directorial debut. Early in 1968, producer Valentine Sherry had delivered a copy of the story to Barbra. He thought it would make a good movie. "I made a commitment to *Yentl* when I read the first four words of the story," Barbra said. They were four highly evocative words for her: "After her father's death..." The story itself was about a young girl in turn-of-the-century Poland who disguises herself as a boy in order to enter a scholarly world forbidden to women. It captivated Streisand. She immediately called her agent to tell him she had just found her next film. Barwood Films subsequently purchased the motion picture rights from Sherry.

As the project evolved, so, too, did Barbra's feelings about her father. Emanuel Streisand died at age 35; passing that age (in 1977) had been a critical step for her. For thirty-six tentative years, she and her brother Sheldon had been led to believe their father died of a cerebral hemorrhage brought on by overwork. The truth, they belatedly found out, was that the cause of death was respiratory failure (probably induced by an injection of morphine used to halt an epileptic seizure). Soon thereafter, Shelly took his sister to see their father's grave in Queens—it was her first visit. Barbra's only picture with her father would be a photograph of her standing near his tombstone. (Later, after the photos were developed, she would notice the name inscribed on the next stone: Anshel.)

Visiting the gravesite was a strange experience, "but that night I had a much stranger experience," she told *People* magazine. Shelly—a very realistic and down-to-earth person, according to his sister—invited a medium to his house. She was "a nice, ordinary-looking Jewish lady," Barbra recalled. "We sat around a table with all the lights on and put our hands on it. And then it began. The table began to spell out letters with its legs. Pounding away. Bang, bang, bang! Very fast, counting out letters. Spelling M-A-N-N-Y, my father's name, and then B-A-R-B-R-A. I got so frightened I ran away. Because I could feel the presence of my father in that room. I ran into the bathroom and locked the door. When I finally came

On location with Gene Hackman in South Pasadena, 1980.

out, the medium asked, 'What message do you have?' and the table spelled out S-O-R-R-Y. Then the medium asked, 'What else do you want to tell her?' And it spelled S-I-N-G and then P-R-O-U-D. It sounds crazy, but I knew it was my father who was telling me to be brave, to have the courage of my convictions, to sing proud! And for that word S-O-R-R-Y to come out...I mean, God! It was his answer to all that deep anger I had felt about his dying."

For years, Streisand's obsession with *Yentl* had been one of Hollywood's inside jokes. An exasperated David Begelman approached his client at a party in 1968. "You've been after us a long time to change your image because you're tired of playing the little Jewish girl from Brooklyn," said the agent. "Now you want to play a Jewish boy?" Barbra was hurt. "It's just a one-liner and it has no bearing on whether or not you should do the film," Marty Erlichman assured her. Jane Fonda told a gathering for the National Organization for Women that many people expected Barbra to be carted off to the funny

farm long before she ever shot a foot of film. "What could she be doing that's taking this long? Re-writing the Talmud?" she reported overhearing at local beauty salons and restaurants. "Why is she doing this? How dare she think she's gonna pull off playing a 16-year-old boy. It's stupid."

All throughout post-production on *The Main Event*, Bob Esty remembers Barbra talking about "this little film she wanted to do. And her explanation of it was really incredible," he says. "I had this vision of *Hester Street*, done very realistically with great attention to detail." But *Hester Street*, a low-budget period film about immigrant life on the Lower East Side, wasn't commercial. Accordingly, Jon tried various means of talking Barbra out of

A hot summer's day in Valencia.

doing the film ever since she first read the story to him. Not only was he convinced the motion picture wouldn't make money, but he thought she'd never be persuasive as a young boy. One evening late in 1978 he came home to find Barbra outfitted to prove her point. "She came out (dressed as a yeshiva boy) with a pipe and a hat and I thought it was a guy robbing the house," he said. "I was going to punch him in the mouth."

Subsequent problems with the script allowed Barbra to procrastinate in making the decision to direct. Czechoslovakian director Ivan Passer had passed on the project in its early stages because he thought she was too old and too famous to essay the role. Maybe Ivan was right, she told herself. "I was so scared that I would talk to everyone about it," she confided to the *Los Angeles Times*' Dale Pollack. "And after awhile I began to really hear myself, hear

this person talking about this dream they had, but being too frightened to go after the dream. There came a point where I just thought, 'My God, life is going by so fast, I have to stand up for what I believe in. I can't be frightened anymore. I don't want to be some old lady saying 'I shoulda made that movie *Yentl*.'"

Even as *The Main Event* was playing in theaters around the country, the talk in Hollywood was that production on "Barbra's Folly" would start the following March. One November 7, 1979, *Daily Variety* carried the announcement that Streisand would indeed direct *Yentl* for Orion Pictures and the Jon Peters Organization. Ted Allan, an Oscar nominee for his script of *Lies My Father Told Me*, would write the screenplay; Joan Marshall Ashby would co-produce. Barbra's on-going research continued as she asked Rusty Lemorande, Jon Peters' executive in charge of creative development, to go with her on a tour of Eastern Europe in late '79. "She wanted to make sure that this place could really exist on screen," he says. A last-minute change in schedule kept her in Los Angeles, but Lemorande went to Europe and took countless photos of authentic locations in Hungary, Austria, Czechoslovakia, Romania, Poland and Yugoslavia that, he adds, had a very positive effect on her by showing her glimpses of that turn-of-the-century world.

But it was just the tip of the iceberg in terms of her research. There were countless museums to go to; rabbis, historians and scholars to consult; books from around the world to read. *Yentl* went into "hiatus" to allow further development. Barbra's advisers became concerned that she not allow herself to remain off movie screens as long as her previous sabbaticals. "You shouldn't be out of the system that long," they warned her. But where in Hollywood does one find a ready-made project for one hardworking, albeit highly idiosyncratic, actress?

"STREISAND REPLACES LISA EICHHORN IN 'NIGHT'; MENGERS IN SHADOWS"

Long before Barbra's involvement, *All Night Long* suffered a series of creative and financial problems. Its checkered past began in 1978 when director Jean-Claude Tramont sold 20th Century-Fox on the idea of doing a film about dissidents—which, in turn, became a story about people who work at night. Tramont turned to W.D. Richter to write the screenplay. Richter delineated a charming, off-beat tale of a middle-aged "man in revolt" who quits his job of twenty years after being demoted to manager of an all-night drug store: he becomes an

Celebrating the dedication of the Emanuel Streisand School at the Pacific Jewish Center in Venice, California, September, 1981.

inventor and has an affair with a younger woman. "What interested me was this man Dupler, going from suburbia to the city to find out what was important to him," Tramont told *Rolling Stone*'s Michael Sragow. "It's as if now, living in the city is seen as living on the fringe." Both the director and writer concurred in their selection of Gene Hackman as George Dupler. A script was forwarded to him via his agent, Sue Mengers—who also happened to be Mrs. Tramont. Anxious to get her #1 client back in front of the cameras, Mengers sent a copy of the screenplay to Barbra. There were two female leads in the cast—neither of which seemed suited to Streisand. Barbra passed.

A few months later, *All Night Long* (then known as *Night People*) went into turn-around at 20th and was eventually picked up by producers Leonard Goldberg and Jerry Weintraub, who had recently aligned themselves with Universal Pictures. The terms of their Daydream Productions contract dictated that they were to determine which films they would do—providing the budget was right. *Night People* was budgeted at $3.5 million. According to William Goldman in *Adventures in the Screen Trade*, "Universal didn't like it, felt they couldn't sell it, didn't want to do it. But for contractual reasons, they were not in a position to pass." Daydream Productions got the okay.

Hackman's casting was announced in December '79. The actor, returning from a self-imposed retirement ["I got tired of doing lousy pictures for the money," he said], loved the script and was more than willing to take a gamble on a small film. He offered to work on the film for less than his usual salary versus a percentage of the gross. Whatever they felt about the film's prospects, MCA/Universal had no intention of giving up its points in the film; they paid Hackman his usual salary. The budget was now approximately $4.5 million. Lisa Eichhorn, the young actress who captured Richard Gere's heart in *Yanks*, was signed to portray Cheryl Gibbons, the shy, picked on "other woman" in George's life. Diana Ladd, Kevin Dobson, Dennis Quaid and William Daniels completed the talented ensemble. French star Annie Giradot consented to a cameo appearance.

Filming began on April 14, 1980. "Three weeks into the production, I parted ways with Tak Fujimoto, whose cinematography in *Melvin and Howard* I admired tremendously," the Belgian-born director revealed the following year. "He had very definite ideas about giving the film a grittier look. Philip Lathrop, a craftsman of the old school…gave me equally 'realistic' images that were still saturated with color. I think of America as saturated with color."

Scarcely a week later, Lisa Eichhorn was to find herself a casualty as well. No official explanation would be forthcoming regarding what prompted her firing. *Daily Variety* reported that "inside sources indicate there was substantial friction between Tramont and Eichhorn." Tramont told journalists in 1981 that the actress simply wasn't working out and since she had just begun shooting her scenes that week, it seemed better to correct the error before more confusion ensued. "The part was too much of a stretch for Lisa," he stated in the *Los Angeles Herald-Examiner*. "It's no reflection on her acting ability."

Voicing the same kind of criticism that Barbra first encountered in Hollywood, the *Los Angeles Times* would uncover one source who insisted, "Lisa was very difficult on the set, objecting to things like camera angles as if she were…a star like Streisand." Another anonymous voice said Eichhorn's role "had

Cheryl confronts George at the Ultra-Sav.

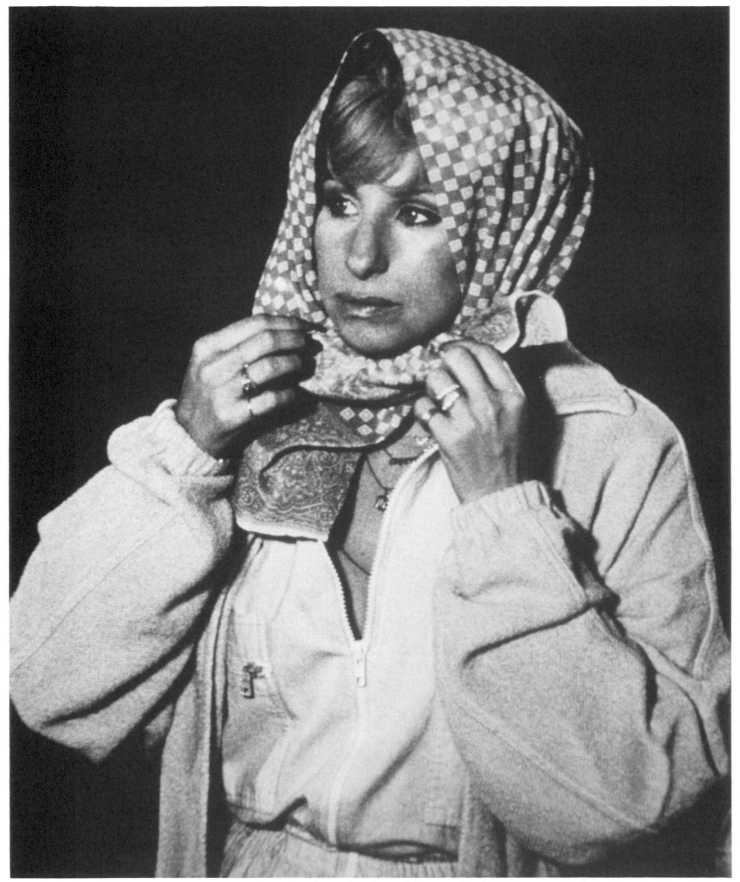

Cheryl does manage a unique twist to her lavendar-draped image: she drives a motorcycle.

an earthiness to it. Lisa is very ethereal; she has metaphysical qualities to her and her part had to be more forthright." Co-star Hackman refused to join the chorus of put-downs. "[Lisa's] got enough problems," he told Marily Beck, "and I've been fired myself [on *The Graduate*]. I know how it hurts."

Eichhorn didn't wait long to tell her side of the story. "What happened to me on *All Night Long* came as such a shock. I'd already done three and a half weeks work on the film when, out of the blue, the director called and said, 'I don't think it's working. You're just not funny. We've got someone else.' I'd never been fired before, so I called my lawyer and agent and asked: Can they do that? They assured me that they could. And then I found out I'd been replaced by Barbra Streisand. I'd been so afraid it would be one of my peers, which would just have devastated me.

"I was in tears. It was so awful. But I did ask to see the dailies—something I hadn't done when we were making the film. They arranged that, and quite honestly I thought it was some of the best work I'd ever done."

Rumors flew fast and furious. Was Streisand, recently named the National Association of Theater Owners' "Star of the Decade" (along with Clint Eastwood), approached before Eichhorn was let go? Did she usurp a role that wasn't even hers—before Eichhorn's release was considered? Was she doing her friends a favor by "saving" an endangered production? Or was the surprise casting the behind-the-scenes work of Mengers, whose agency (ICM) represented Streisand, Hackman *and* Tramont? Writer William Goldman would later speculate that the news of Barbra's renewed interest in the role was simply too important for producer Goldberg to suppress. He had to tell Universal. "Now they love the picture," he wrote. "The sales force loves it, the advertising people are in ecstasy, fabulous." Such a scenario, while not implausible, would be virtually impossible to confirm. In May of 1980, most of the blame was being laid in the departed actress's lap.

"As far as I was concerned, there were no problems on the picture. I loved working with Gene Hackman. And I got on well with Jean-Claude Tramont," Eichhorn stated. "I read somewhere that I was supposed to have walked out because of 'artistic differences.' That's not true. When I got to New York, on my way to Poland, I read in a newspaper that I'd kept walking off the set, and asking about

camera angles. When I got to London I read that I'd been conceited, temperamental and difficult. The further away I went from Los Angeles the worse I seemed to get." She certainly would never forget the weekend of May 10, 1980.

Of equal importance in the entertainment business was the number of precedents *All Night Long* would set in Barbra's career. First, she insisted on second billing for her first supporting role in a motion picture. "It's mostly my film," said Hackman. "She has five or six good scenes and that's it. It would be unfair to audiences to bill her in such a way that suggests this is Barbra's movie. It's about my character, not hers." In addition, Barbra's salary ($4,000,000 plus 15 percent of the gross for 24 day's work) would set a new level for female stars. She'd made more money before, but never for a project she didn't develop herself.

Production on *All Night Long* shut down temporarily to allow the actors and director time to rehearse and work through the new script. Richter's story had already been fleshed out to feature the female role more prominently. The producers anticipated further modification "but nothing substan-

"Night is the new frontier," she tells George. Later, they join forces to bag a would-be thief.

tial." Barbra intended to play Cheryl Gibbons as written. Hackman, who'd known her ever since his lean days in New York with Dustin Hoffman and Robert Duvall, wasn't afraid that Barbra would take over the picture. "My opinion was asked about her joining the cast. I gave my OK and I'm sure everything will be fine," he said. Most of the rewrite focused on the third act where George and Cheryl come to a final realization about themselves, their lives and relationships.

As the screenplay was examined to accommodate the addition of a new actress, Hackman's "financial arrangements" were also re-negotiated. The nice, small film was now catapulted into the $10—12 million range (that figure also included Eichhorn's $250,000 pay-off and the retainer salaries paid to the crew during shut-down).

Principal photography resumed June 9 when Barbra reported for her first day/night of work on location in South Pasadena. Despite the saturation of hurt feelings over the production's initial problems, filming with the revised cast progressed smoothly. Barbra had very quickly—and very completely—acquainted herself with every facet of her character.

Academy Award-winning costume designer Albert Wolsky, who also worked with her on *Up the Sandbox*, remembered her single-minded approach to the role. Accordingly, he designed clothes that Cheryl, and not Barbra Streisand, would wear. "[Cheryl's] a woman with strawberry blond hair that's always too done, fingernails that are always too brightly polished, clothes that are always a little too tight, a little too young," Wolsky described to the *Los Angeles Times*. "The clothes are not expensive, but Barbra doesn't care about that. If she loves it, she doesn't care if it costs $2 or $2,000."

Draped in lavender velour and gold chains, smoking lavender-tinted cigarettes and speaking in a childish whisper, Barbra seemed to enjoy her brief respite as a working actress. Richter's surreal, Marilyn Monroe-styled temptress was just the kind of acting stretch she had been pining for: someone totally different from the stereotypical, self-possessed Streisand character. The outgoing, ever-congenial Cheryl also appeared to have a positive effect on her on-the-set demeanor. Relieved of outside production obligations, she enjoyed remaining on the set (even when she wasn't needed) to visit with friends or

socialize with the crew—while Hackman fought his way through the movie. "As soon as I [returned to Hollywood], I realized why I left," he told the *New York Daily News*. "I like this film, but the waiting around has already driven me crazy."

Dennis Quaid, who played Hackman's affable but somewhat thick-headed son (and Cheryl's paramour), Freddie, admitted he wasn't much of a Streisand fan prior to working with her on *All Night Long*. "I was dreading working with her because I'd heard stories about how difficult she is to work with," he admitted in *Dramalogue*. "I was really surprised because she was helpful on the set." Kevin Dobson, essaying the role of Bobby, Cheryl's errant fireman/husband, likewise told the press that he witnessed "nothing but the utmost professionalism" from Barbra. The actor—who once worked as an extra on *Funny Girl* and *French Connection* (the film that won Hackman his Academy Award)—found his *All Night Long* experience to be very rewarding. "[Barbra's] a doll. She's been really delightful. I've had such rapport with her...to the point where we sit down together and create, talk about the part and how to make it better. Let me tell you, she's all right."

The producer and director had determined that the entire picture was to be shot on location. Most was filmed in a vacant supermarket building which had been realistically converted into a 24-hour Ultra-Sav drug store, replete with $750,000 worth of merchandise. "Fortunately, there was no need to maintain inventory in the back room," set director Linda Spheeris noted. After hours, the filmmakers also took over the Salt Shaker, a family restaurant conveniently located across the street. A remodeled tract home one hour north of Los Angeles in Valencia became Bobby and Cheryl's humble abode. There, the principals struggled to look comfortable in the sweltering 106-degree heat. George's loft was recreated in downtown Los Angeles.

As the final days of principal photography approached in July, there was a great deal of concern that the picture must be finished before the impending actor's strike. The only remaining scenes on Barbra's schedule were set to be shot at a Van Nuys fire station. On July 18, as Hackman discussed his role with Tramont, a bemused Streisand took a tour of the station. The fire pole was of particular interest to her. Firemen supervising the shoot had been very strict about not letting others slide down the pole—but Barbra was being asked to. "Is it safe? How do you do it?" she asked one fireman. Looking down the pole from her second floor perch, she obviously wasn't crazy about the idea. "Uh, uh. Not me. I don't think I could do it," she said. "I have a weak stomach." She got a reprieve.

George is oblivious to the macho antics of Cheryl's husband, Bobby.

At midnight on July 20, negotiations between producers and the Screen Actors Guild broke down and a walk-out was officially declared. "Conspicuously hard hit by the strike is Universal's reported $14 million Barbra Streisand starrer, *All Night Long*," *Daily Variety* reported. The film itself was due to wrap in four days, but Barbra only had one day left. Although small independent productions were signing interim waivers to allow their films to continue shooting, there was no chance of that with *All Night Long* and Daydream Productions completely tied up at one of the major studios. Additionally, since the most heated strike arguments revolved around residuals on the projected increased revenues for home video, cable and pay television,

When George drops in on an in-law's anniversary party, Bobby figures the rest out.

and Universal, as the biggest supplier of television product, was contesting what they perceived to be excessive payments, there wasn't much hope that the matter would be settled quickly. Time, in fact, was on the side of the studios. With sufficient product in their libraries, they could afford to hold out; the actors might not be able to.

Suddenly, all of Barbra's plans were being threatened as well. The delay allowed her to return her attention to finishing the *Yentl* script (which she was now writing), but with her outstanding commitment requiring that she stay in Los Angeles, it put the January/February 1981 start date in serious jeopardy. Goldberg and Weintraub's plans to get the motion picture out in time for Oscar consideration also proved futile, and especially agonizing for Gene Hackman.

Late in October, Barbra slid down the fire pole and out of the film. Unfortunately, neither she nor the producers were able to shake their troubles off with as much ease. At the end of the year, a poorly edited teaser trailer actually drew boos and snickers at local theaters. Scattered previews throughout the country indicated that the movie was too long (100 minutes) and the elements of the comedy needed to be re-focused. "The timing may be wrong for this film," the director bemoaned to Michael Sragow. "These days, American anger is tinged with bitterness. At our sneak previews, the audience I thought would react the strongest to George Dupler's revolt—men over 25—seemed to resent the movie!"

Universal's strategy to compensate for this didn't show much faith in the charming, unpretentious European-style film Tramont & Co. had attempted to make. *All Night Long* was, against everyone's wishes, touted as a zany Streisand comedy; the promotional angle shifted from Hackman to the peripheral, secondary lead. "It didn't fall into any kind of particular category they had any expertise in," Hackman said later. So Universal repackaged it as something they could comfortably exploit. The type of audience that might attend *All Night Long* was never properly addressed. Future advertising of the film would feature Barbra on the fire pole—with her skirt flying à la Marilyn Monroe in *Seven Year Itch*—slyly evading the grasp of Hackman, Dobson and Quaid. "She's got a way with men, and she's getting away with it...All Night Long," read the copy. TV commercials also misled audiences with a glimpse of Cheryl composing "Carelessly Tossed," a goofy country/western song, on the organ.

The movie opened on March 6, 1981—March being a traditionally slow movie-going period. Regardless of the soft competition, the film was advertised, Gene Hackman remembered, in a tiny box in the theatrical section of *The New York Times*. Ironically, just as Barbra was enjoying her greatest recording success with *Guilty*, she was enduring her lowest ebb as an actress. Although the movie appeared to open strongly, a distressing pattern emerged at the box-office: patrons were asking for their money back. "For most pictures, we'll have a full house and maybe one person will ask for his money back," one theater usher explained to *The New York Times*. "For this movie, there will hardly be anyone in the theater and five or six of them will ask." *All Night Long* wasn't failing because of audience indifference, but because deceptive advertising had led them to expect something the film could not deliver. "I don't think the film worked on a lot of different levels," Dennis Quaid said, echoing the feelings of many. "In the timing of it, in the relationships....It seemed long to me—it only ran an hour and a half, but it seemed like two hours and ten minutes."

Barbra bore the brunt of the criticism. "Many critics already dismiss Streisand out of hand as an overachiever whose arrogance is only equalled by the length of her boarding room reach," the *Los Angeles Times*' Patricia Goldstone wrote in 1979. "But that's too easy. She's entitled to more serious consideration because of her power, her phenomenal audience and the flashes of talent evident in even her worst films." Although the journalist was writing about her disappointment in *The Main Event*, her observations are valid for most of Barbra's films. This time, critics complained that the chemistry between Streisand and Hackman was non-existent, that her performance was too subdued. "In most of her pictures, she's criticized for overpowering the screen," Tramont defended. "In *All Night Long* she's criticized for not overpowering the screen." Some questioned the director-star relationship. How did Tramont, a man known for writing one film (*Ash Wednesday*) and directing another (*Focal Point*, which was never released in the US), secure this assignment? Surely, the only reason Barbra did the film was due to her tie with Tramont's wife—and her agent—Sue Mengers. "My wife and I have been together for eleven years," the director stated. "If she had the ability to force Barbra to do a picture with me, I wish she had used it sooner."

But there was plenty of praise, too. Supporters (Pauline Kael, Rex Reed) as well as detractors (Vincent Canby, Michael Sragow) felt Streisand had created a rather touching, vulnerable portrait of a vague, insecure suburban sexpot. Canby gave Barbra a left-handed compliment for playing the role with comparative modesty. "The film is worth seeing if only to witness this ordinarily take-over kid subordinate that overwhelming public personality to the

Dupler steals Cheryl away. But, he says, he's no longer content with sharing her time—he wants a total commitment.

demands of a movie which, unfortunately, isn't worth the sacrifice. (Did I say sacrifice…?)," he wrote in *The New York Times*.

With Universal's failure to capitalize on the art film crowd that might have embraced *All Night Long*, it was hoped that the film might recapture some of its market when it was released abroad. The movie had its European premiere at the 1982 Deauville Film Festival, and response was decidedly mixed. Shortly thereafter, it opened in London—supported by the same disastrous advertising campaign. The movie disappeared within a week. Its worldwide box office was negligible.

Despite all this, if Universal Pictures had it to do over again, they'd probably jump at the chance to have Barbra do a film—any film—for them. They got what they wanted: a Streisand film in their motion picture library.

Reviews:

"When Barbra Streisand and Gene Hackman play their off-beat roles in *All Night Long*—she's supposed to be a wildly sexy suburban wife, and he plays an executive suddenly demoted to drugstore manager—it is impossible to imagine these two are doing anything but acting.

"On the other hand, that artificiality helps make the movie enjoyable. When the housewife character declares ingenuously that she writes music, notably gospel and Hawaiian music, what makes the scene funny is the fact that Streisand is playing it (and playing it straight). In this case, the movie's oddball quality works best when the performers undermine it. And undermine it they do."

—New York Times

FINAL NOTE: "Barbra called me [later] and said, 'you were well out of it, kid,'" Lisa Eichhorn told the *London Sunday Times* a few years later. "I wanted to tell her that with me, it would have been a different film." It is virtually certain, however, it wouldn't have been a more commercial one. "Nobody bats a home run every time," Jon Peters reminds. "Barbra took a gamble and it didn't pay off." But, one shouldn't assume *All Night Long* was a waste of time for anyone. Back in the mainstream once again, Gene Hackman would get several more chances to explore the restless frustration of a man in his prime unable to express the full range of his talents or emotions in films like *Under Fire* and *Twice in a Lifetime*. Barbra's understated work as Cheryl Gibbons reconnected her with her dramatic work in past films such as *Up the Sandbox* and *The Way We Were*. Her keen observations on the set of *All Night Long* made the ensemble acting in *Yentl* that much easier.

It also spelled the end of her thirteen-year professional association with Sue Mengers. While a handful of insiders would speculate that her exit had to do with a dispute over ICM's entitlement to a commission—implying not only that Barbra didn't pay ICM, which she did, but that she did the film strictly as "a favor"—the stronger sentiment indicates a parting of the ways over *Yentl*. By 1981, it was no secret Barbra was absolutely determined to realize that vision, despite concerned advice that it wasn't in her best interest. Those who didn't actively support that decision soon fell by the wayside—albeit temporarily.

With director William Wyler. (Courtesy of the Richard Giammanco collection)

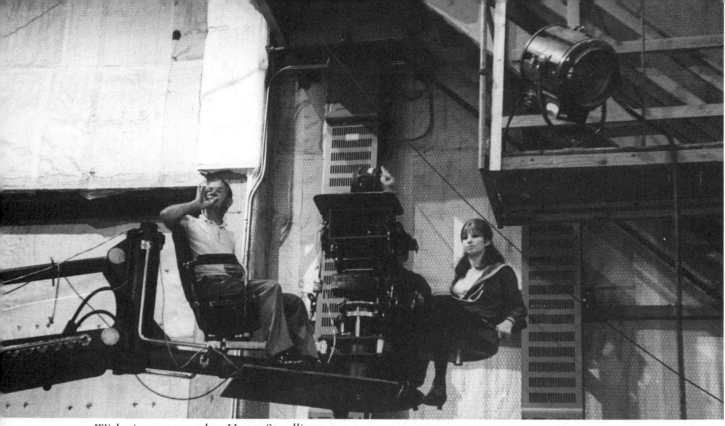

With cinematographer Harry Stradling.

With director Vincente Minnelli (left) and Alan Jay Lerner (leaning on piano).

With choreographer Michael Kidd and Louis Armstrong.

With director Gene Kelly.

With director Herbert Ross.

With director Peter Bogdanovich.

With director Sidney Pollack.

With director Howard Zieff.

With director Irvin Kershner.

With director Frank Pierson.

With Jon Peters.

YENTL
(United Artists)

CAST:
Yentl	Barbra Streisand
Avigdor	Mandy Patinkin
Hadass	Amy Irving
Papa (Reb Mendel)	Nehemiah Persoff
Reb Alter Vishkower	Steven Hill
Shimmele	Allan Corduner
Esther Rachel Vishkower	Ruth Goring
Rabbi Zalman	David DeKeyser

CREDITS:
Produced and directed by	Barbra Streisand
Co-producer	Rusty Lemorande
Screenplay by	Jack Rosenthal Barbra Streisand
Music by	Michel Legrand
Lyrics by	Alan & Marilyn Bergman
Based on "Yentl, the Yeshiva Boy" by	Isaac Bashevis Singer
Executive producer	Larry DeWaay
Cinematography	David Watkin
Film editor	Terry Rawlings
Production design	Roy Walker
Art director	Leslie Tomkins
Set decorator	Tessa Davies
Costume designer	Judy Moorcroft
Music orchestrated and conducted by	Michel Legrand
Wedding dance choreography	Gillian Lynne
Camera operator	Peter MacDonald
Script supervisor	Barrie Melrose
Music editors	Robin Clark George Brand
Sound engineer	Tim Blackham
Location managers	Jim Brennan William Lang
Assistant director	Steve Lanning
Casting	Cis Corman

Running time: 134 minutes
Rated: PG

A Barwood Film

"Yentl wanted to be recognized for what she thought, for what her mind was. She was told she had to stay in a box and never grow; she felt different. I'd always felt different. I'd always been a loner; the men I'm drawn to are loners, outsiders. The story is Yentl's redemption from self-hatred. I found myself

Arriving in London for further pre-production research on Yentl.

evolving as I worked, forgiving my own misunderstandings."

—Barbra Streisand

"Everything Barbra Streisand has done before YENTL has been a rehearsal."

—Amy Irving

Barbra originally planned to produce *Yentl* through her First Artists association. "We submitted our first budget in 1973," says Marty Erlichman. "I remember calling Mel Brooks because he had done *Twelve Chairs* over in Yugoslavia and we wanted to know who his location manager was, etc. Brooks had a funny line. I told him Barbra was thinking of doing a picture (in Eastern Europe) and he said, 'When?' 'I don't know. A couple of years.' 'A couple of years,' he says. 'Jews don't think about "a couple of years."

234

Yentl *(1983)*.

Teaching a Czechoslovakian shammas a few lines of English.

A playful recess.

They take the diamonds, put them in their pockets and walk around. What's this "couple of years"? *Call me in a couple of years.'"

Two years went by...three...four...five. Barbra continued gathering information from a varied assortment of professionals—everyone from Molly Picon to Francis Ford Coppola. With that knowledge came increasing confidence in expressing her vision, not just as producer/star, but as the director and, finally, the writer. Jon Peters vividly recalls the moment when Barbra announced that her decision to diret and star in *Yentl* was irrevocable. It occurred during the location filming for *The Main Event* at Big Bear. "We were standing there in the snow and she said, 'I hate this movie! I'm going to do *Yentl*!' and I said, 'You're not going to do it! You're not going to ruin your life and mine! We're going to do something else together.' I was a little domineering, I guess, and I remember her looking at me and saying, 'Just because you said that, I'm going to do the movie *no matter what!*'" Jon had inadvertently given her the challenge that would carry her through the next five years of planning and executing the production.

"I don't think that anybody (a writer or director) could have satisfied her during that period," Milos Forman states, "because this project was her love affair. It was her pet project; I don't recall that

On the streets of Tabor, 1982.

she was as devoted to any [other] project to the extent she was to *Yentl*. So I think, subconsciously, things didn't happen because deep down she just had her own vision of it and nobody could come even close."

In 1979, Barbra wrote a film treatment outlining *Yentl* as a voice-over musical. "I decided that if I was going to try to direct that I had better put down all the pictures in my head, scene by scene, so I wrote a 42-page outline with an indication of where all the songs would go," she said.

Despite his initial opposition to the project, Peters didn't hesitate in surrounding Barbra with people who shared her enthusiasm for *Yentl*. "Part of working with Jon [at JPO] was to be aware of certain projects Barbra also had in development," Rusty Lemorande explains. "Because I was a great admirer of hers, I took it upon myself to explore more fully the projects that I knew she was passionate about. There were two: *Yentl, the Yeshiva Boy* and *Third Time Lucky*. I responded strongly to both. I thought

they were both well-suited to my particular image of Barbra as a star. And Jon was quite pleased to find that kind of support for her."

Support was also found in Eric Peskow and Mike Medavoy, partners in Orion Pictures, *Yentl*'s home from November 1979 until the end of 1980. After a series of scripts (including drafts by Isaac Singer and playwright Leah Napolin) proved unacceptable to Streisand, Medavoy suggested that she try writing it herself. "You seem to know so well what it is you want," he pointed out. "In all honesty," adds Lemorande, "I don't think Barbra was prepared to recognize herself as a writer. In fact, she didn't put any authorship on the very first drafts that she contributed to. She wrote out of necessity....I got a tremendous lesson in writing by being sort of at the knee of this process—where she and I did a draft and then I would find it being critiqued by the likes of Paddy Chayevsky, Elaine May, Polly Platt, David Rayfield, Bo Goldman....A lot of people were constantly giving her encouragement and opinions when she asked for them; Barbra is certainly a believer in 'Let's hear an idea and *then* decide.' But it goes both

With Warren Beatty and Amy Irving.

ways—they'd ask her [for opinions] as well."

During 1980 she began exploring the musical terrain with Michel Legrand and Alan and Marilyn Bergman. "The four of us were like children playing," Marilyn noted. "We videotaped the first musical performance in our living room. One day, a choreographer visited Barbra at our house just as we were blocking out the wedding scene. We gave her a costume and she instantly became part of the videotape."

Barbra's extraordinary salary for *All Night Long* reaped some charitable benefits as well as monetary ones. The year before, she had endowed the Pacific Jewish Center with enough money to save the struggling young synagogue. As a gesture of gratitude, the school was named after Barbra's father. (Jason received his bar mitzvah there.) In 1980 she gave $500,000 of her *All Night Long* fee to establish the Streisand Chair of Cardiology at UCLA's School of Medicine. Another $50,000 was donated to create

the Streisand Center for Jewish Cultural Arts at the Hillel Center on that university's campus. Rabbi Daniel Lapin of the Pacific Jewish Center and Rabbis Chaim Seidler-Feller and Laura Geller of UCLA were some of the clergy she turned to in order to clarify the theological and spiritual ideas in her film. "I talked to all the rabbis I could talk to," she confirmed, "searching for different points-of-view from the Reform, Conservative and Orthodox."

"There's no doubt Barbra does view this [film] as a contribution to Jewish life," Rabbi Seidler-Feller stated then. "Part of Barbra Streisand is interested in recovering a traditional past. She does want to make some sort of Jewish statement in an industry where there are many Jews reluctant to express their Jewishness, and I find that admirable."

Sandwiched in between *All Night Long* filming dates that year were a series of trips Barbra made with Rusty Lemorande to Eastern Europe. In Czechoslovakia, they shot Super 8mm footage of Barbra in costume as Anshel walking down the streets of Prague. "I always wanted to try everything out and see what the black costume looked like against the

Looking over the various angles of Mandy Patinkin and Amy Irving's final moment onscreen, with cinematographer David Watkin.

color of the walls, against the textures, the cobblestones, the light of Czechoslovakia, the air." The tests would also help to formulate many of Barbra's ideas about art direction and cinematography. On the way back to the United States, she stopped in Amsterdam where Paul Verhoeven took her to see the Rembrandts and Brueghels at Rijak.

Upon his return, Lemorande was asked to prepare three separate budgets for the film: one with Los Angeles as the home base and the villages of Yanev and Bashev being constructed either on the lot or at one of the studio ranches in Malibu Canyon; a second for New York/Lake Placid; and a third for London/Czechoslovakia. "There was tremendous pressure to film *Yentl* in the U.S.," Lemorande acknowledges. "Jon Peters fought very hard to have it shot here because he knew that if it weren't [based in New York or L.A.], he'd have trouble producing the film. Because Barbra would want him over there exclusively. And even though she knew it was right aesthetically, Barbra was hesitant to film abroad. She had to be convinced that there wasn't a reason to do this in Los Angeles—in her own backyard, so to speak."

On November 19, 1980, after endless discussion about location filming, Barwood turned the budget in to Orion; the company had previously indicated a cost ceiling of $13,000,000. That day, Vincent Canby's devastating review of *Heaven's Gate* was published in *The New York Times*. Suddenly, the studios didn't want to hear anything about movies being given budgets over $10,000,000, especially to novice directors operating in a foreign location. Such "unchecked power" did not make good business sense. When Jon Peters pulled out of Orion (to head PolyGram Pictures with partner Peter Guber), *Yentl* followed like an orphan child. It didn't stay there for long. "For personal reasons, we decided not to work together on this film," Barbra confided to Dale Pollock of the *Los Angeles Times*. "It was a time in my life when I needed to really be independent, both personally and professionally. I thought to myself: 'I have to make this picture, and I have to also be the producer.'" At the same time, Rusty Lemorande's status changed from executive producer to Barbra's co-producer.

Streisand gathered up her Super 8mm footage and the audio cassettes of the score and commenced pitching her production to other companies. Studios formerly quite happily associated with Barbra on some of her biggest successes couldn't see past their checkbooks to give her an OK. Warner Bros., despite Barbra's impressive success on that lot, wasn't inter-

Studying the perfectly-matched China at Haddass's family home.

ested; similarly, Columbia felt the project wasn't commercial enough. Paramount Pictures passed. "It's a wonderful shaker-upper," she told the BBC's Iain Johnstone, "a leveller of ego. It really puts you in your place. They say you're a 'bankable star' or whatever—so surely they'll put on something you passionately believe in. Then when it comes time to do it, they say, 'Well…no'—even though I'm singing! I remember having to go into an executive's office to play them my tapes and explain the story. I felt like I was 18 years old again and auditioning for a Broadway show. Would they like it? Would they invest some money? I had to prove myself all over again."

What did she have to do to prove that she was a financially responsible filmmaker and that her motion picture had box-office potential?

In spite of the mounting frustrations and complications, she remained focused on her goal. "The more difficult things became, the more rejections she

encountered in setting up the picture," her co-producer states, "the more tenacious Barbra became." Alan Bergman would note that the feature film's optimistic promotional slogan, " 'Nothing's Impossible,' is also what she believes. Whenever you tell her something's impossible, you're just firing her up."

Late in March '81, industry trades reported that Streisand was meeting with Norbert Auerbach and Steven Bach of United Artists. "She wants me to play her father," production executive Auerbach revealed to *Daily Variety*'s Army Archerd somewhat prematurely. Bach and his staff believed *Yentl* to be risky, but Auerbach was sold on Barbra. "When she went in to play her tapes," say Lemorande, "she would hum over it if she knew that really got you charged. She knew what she was doing; [she was] putting on the disguise of being just a singer in the hopes of getting to be something else."

After visiting her at the Malibu ranch, even Bach was won over by Yentl as impersonated by Barbra Streisand. "Like Auerbach, I fell in love," he wrote in his book, *Final Cut*. "She is intelligent, funny, professional, obsessive-compulsive, a perfec-

After a hasty entrance, publicist Lee Solters brings Barbra back out to greet the press and a gathering of fans at the world premiere of Yentl in Los Angeles.

At the post-premiere party with Steven Spielberg. (Photo credit: Fotos International)

tionist with a soupçon of parsimony, and far more attractive off-screen than on." On March 31 *Daily Variety* announced that a deal was in the offing. Ironically, the studio that spawned *Heaven's Gate*—and ultimately quashed a number of big-budgeted Hollywood pictures—symbolically performed a bit of artistic penance by virtue of its commitment to do *Yentl.* Equally dramatic was the fact that, after a shuffle of studio management, the agents who bought Singer's short story for Barbra (David Begelman and Freddie Fields) were now her compatriots at the MGM/UA Entertainment Co.

That didn't mean, however, that Barbra didn't have to make important concessions to United Artists. Because everyone in Hollywood seemed to know how badly she wanted to do the film, Streisand didn't have much room to negotiate. It was the first time since *Funny Girl* on Broadway that the employer was holding all the cards. "I had to give up everything," she told Dale Pollock. "I didn't get paid for writing, I got paid scale for directing.... I got paid much less as an actress than I did in my last film. And then I had to give back half of my salary if we went over budget." (She had already invested over $500,000 of her own money on the project.) In exchange for a $14.5 million guaranteed budget, she also had to give up "all of my so-called power," including the director's treasured approval of final cut. Admittedly at

the studio's mercy, it appeared that she would retain creative control only under the most perfect of conditions: with the film on schedule, under budget and the director's cut certified as the accepted cut by the studio. But Streisand was poised to put her vision to the test. "Nothing mattered to me except getting this movie made," she reiterated.

An agreement was formally announced on June 22, 1981. The "as-yet-untitled" production was scheduled to be shot entirely on location in Czechoslovakia. Seeking further control on the production reins, UA assigned Stanley O'Toole (he supervised films such as *Sphinx* and *Outland*) to executive produce. Having to endure yet another strike (this time by the Writer's Guild), Barbra turned to England to get a collaborator to help polish the screenplay. One was found in Jack Rosenthal, the writer of *The Bar Mitzvah Boy,* a popular play on London's West End. The balance of 1981 was spent assembling key members of the cast and crew. Avigdor, the romantic male lead, proved to be the most challenging because the choices were so diverse. Richard Gere's name had been introduced as early as December of 1979. Gere agreed to do the picture if Barbra simply acted in it "...or he'd let me direct it if I didn't act." The possibility of adding Gere's raw sexuality to the lusty but brooding role of Avigdor intrigued production executives—but not enough to sweeten the deal by investing more money in the film. Other suggestions included Michael Douglas, Kevin Kline, John Shea and Christopher Walken. In December, Barwood and UA jointly announced that Mandy Patinkin would essay the role.

Barbra saw Patinkin onstage in *Evita* and in Milos Forman's film of *Ragtime.* They met several times throughout 1981 to discuss the script, but Patinkin held back from making a commitment without certain changes. "I thought [the character] wasn't serious enough," he told *USA Today*'s Jack Mathews, "that he didn't have enough weight. We went back and forth, but the bottom line is [Barbra] was absolutely open to whatever feelings I had." The actor would further state that "almost every single thing from that initial meeting that I had any question about was satisfactorily changed by the time we shot it. So I was quite taken with how approachable and how caring she was about the piece, and about the material—about its authenticity, on every level."

Amy Irving's experience with Barbra went back a little farther. "I used to see her (occasionally) when I was living with Steven Spielberg," she said in 1983. "Once, we spent an entire day at her ranch while she was pitching *Yentl* to him." Irritated at the time that Barbra focused most of her attention on Spielberg and couldn't remember his companion's name, Amy soon put the incident out of her mind. "Now I realize that was evidence of Barbra's tunnel vision," she explained. "When she zeroes in on something, she can think of nothing else."

Actually, the actress Streisand and Lemorande originally thought could best project Hadass's wide-eyed innocence was Carol Kane (among other things, the star of *Hester Street*). When sentiment began to lean toward a younger leading lady, Irving was sent a copy of the screenplay. But the actress thought the character was more in line with the type of roles she played almost ten years earlier. "Just another sweet young thing," she thought. "I can do that standing on my head, and it's boring." She declined.

"My agent was astounded," Irving admitted. " 'How dare you turn down a chance to work with Barbra Streisand! At least meet her and let her explain what she's doing.' " A meeting was arranged in which Barbra took the opportunity to describe her own feelings about Hadass. "She took me through the journey that I eventually made in the film," said Irving. "That was more stimulating to me. I just didn't read the script well.... I was also very attracted by Barbra because she was so dedicated to this project. It was obvious she wasn't doing it for fame or fortune. It was something inside of her that she had to realize and when someone asks you to help them realize their dream, you know the focus of the work is going to be something exciting."

Likewise, Nehemiah Persoff was a second choice, and another fortuitous one. (Morris Carnovsky, cast in England, had a heart attack during a reading and passed away some time later.) Persoff, a well-known character actor, had been starring in a one-man show revolving around the tales of Sholem Aleichem. In March of 1981, when the show played Los Angeles, Barbra and her friend, casting director Cis Corman, went backstage to talk with him. By the time they left, the actor knew he was being seriously considered to play the part of Barbra's father in *Yentl*. Persoff would come to believe, as did Steven Hill (Hadass's father) later, that he was being entrusted with passing on the image of the Jew of that period.

He was also entrusted with the responsibility of bringing a rather vague, idealized character to life—a character who only existed in Yentl's memory in the short story. Once in London, Persoff would have a pivotal conversation with Barbra regarding his role. "She was very bright and very smart about it because she didn't make me feel that I was being directed (or told what to do). She really told me about herself and about her relationship with her father, about her years of growing up and her frustrations. She wanted to find her father on a personal level, and she wanted a person she could relate to as a daughter."

Meeting with the Hollywood Foreign Press, November 1983. (Photo credit: Frank Edwards/Fotos International)

The names behind the camera began to fall into place. Larry DeWaay, a production associate of director Norman Jewison's, replaced Stanley O'Toole as executive producer. Director of photography David Watkin and editor Terry Rawlings (both Academy Award winners for their work on *Chariots of Fire*), production designer Roy Walker (another Academy Award winner) and costumer Judy Moorcroft joined the talented ensemble. One brief disappointment for Barbra was her inability to secure Italian cinematographer Vittorio Storaro (*Reds*)—complex union entanglements determined that his participation would be too costly.

The exhaustive research conducted on behalf of the film went far beyond the needs of a single film,

Having lost the Best Actress in a Comedy or Musical award to Julie Walters, Barbra nearly fell out of her chair when her name was announced as Best Direc- *tor—over* Terms of Endearment's *James Brooks—at the 1984 Golden Globes. (Photo credit: UPI/Bettmann Newsphotos)*

but in many ways it assured Barbra that every question she might have had been answered. "To get the feel of the music, movement and crowds, and also because of the wedding scene in the film," historical consultant Jeanette Kupferman illustrates, "Barbra would try to attend as many Chasidic weddings as she could possibly find. 'Can you find me a wedding?' became a familiar request. At one wedding at the Wembley Town Hall, all seemed to be going well as I introduced her as a friend, Mrs. Peters, and she sampled cherry brandy and advocaat (for the first time, it seems) and waxed eloquent over the fish balls. But there's always one *maven* who has seen *Funny Girl* twenty times.... Needless to say, Barbra was a great hit with all the gorgeously attired

Chasidic matrons at our table, who were greatly flattered by her interest (professional, of course) in them. Barbra, in fact, left them fairly breathless with her questions: 'Is that really a sheitel?' she would inquire, sticking one finger under the elastic of a magnificent upswept coiffure. 'You must give me your wig-maker's name,' or 'Say, could you tell me about Havdala candles?'"

Barbra also expected the other members of the cast and crew to do research in their respective areas. "She was almost like the professor who got annoyed if the students didn't do their research," says Lemorande. "She expected it. She judged people by the amount of research that they did." Just prior to filming, Barbra gifted Mandy Patinkin with a seven-volume set entitled *The Legends of the Jews*. Amy Irving received books about how to make a kosher kitchen, how to prepare fish, how to bake bread. Individually, Persoff and Patinkin continued their search by attending local yeshivas.

Authentic costuming was another important detail. For the wedding sequence, Barbra had selected embroidered petticoats made in central Europe for the folk dancers. UA thought it was an extravagance. Finally, Jeanette Kupferman found some comparable wares in London. "I'm trying to learn the difference between settling for less aesthetically, which is an idea I hate," Barbra stated, "and when enough is enough. It was harder to give up the petticoats than the limousines. But I did."

After the year-end holidays, most of the *Yentl* principals journeyed to London to complete the final phase of pre-production. That first step, Lemorande ventures, is what constituted the real act of courage for everyone. "The giving up of family life and isolating yourself in a foreign culture—whether it was London or Prague, it wasn't New York or Beverly Hills." For Barbra, it also meant putting in long hours while trying to provide continuing support for her 16-year-old son. One relationship that didn't make it through the transition was her romantic involvement with Jon Peters. "By the time we had been together for eight years," Barbra told *People*

"Where is it written what it is I'm meant to be?"

magazine's Brad Darrach, "our relationship had reached a turning point. We were butting horns because I was passionately involved in *Yentl*, and neglecting him. We had also been too dependent on each other. And you come to resent dependency. We needed to be apart."

"I don't think Barbra chose between me and the film," Jon says. "I think she chose the film, and I think it was time for us to separate."

Another relationship that had to make an adjustment was the mother/daughter one. Diana Kind was very skeptical about her eldest daughter filming in a Communist-bloc country. "She was like a typical mother crying on the phone," Barbra told Canadian TV host Brian Linehan. "'You can't make a movie in Czechoslovakia. There's a war in Poland and they haven't got fresh vegetables there. It's so far away from home, how can you go away like this?' She didn't want me to go; she was scared."

Two weeks prior to principal photography, the cast reported to Lee International Studios outside London for rehearsals. Lensing began April 14, 1982. The production schedule called for four weeks at Lee International, ten to twelve weeks on location in Czechoslovakia and then a return to London. Having gotten to know their producer/director/writer/star over the past few months of preparation, the *Yentl* cast and crew rallied behind Barbra. By then, everyone recognized the enormity of the undertaking. "I'm getting paid for all the times I thought I knew the answers," she told author Chaim Potok. In a gesture

With Nehemiah Persoff.

After her father's death, Yentl contemplates her future in Yanev; she decides that masquerading as a boy is the only way to maintain her independence. Cutting her hair announces that decision. "I had a crack made in the mirror," Barbra said, "that would divide my face in half. Male and female."

of support, on the first day of filming, the cast and crew gave her a custom-made, personalized director's chair. "I never had a present presented to me at the start of a movie before," Streisand exclaimed.

"When I arrived on the set that first day, this prop man shook my hand with a sweaty palm. I said, 'Are you nervous?' and he said, 'A little,' and I said, 'Well, feel my hand. No one's more nervous than I am. If you make a mistake, it's fine, because I'll be the one making most of the mistakes.'...I had dreaded that first day. But when the time actually came for the first shot, I suddenly realized, 'Oh, I know how to do this. I just have to trust my instincts.'"

Since the average European shooting day begins around 10:00 a.m. and extends without an official break until 7:00 p.m.—no overtime—Barbra had been anxious about shooting abroad. She was concerned that the crew might pack up and leave before she had concluded the day's work. But they never did. "I found the experience very humbling," Barbra said. "I was very moved by it. That power is very humbling. And I found myself being very soft-spoken, feeling even more feminine than I have ever felt. More motherly, more nurturing, more loving. I had patience I never dreamed I would have. I never wanted people to feel that I was so powerful....As the director and producer, I could set the stage for the atmosphere that I wanted on the movie set, and that was that anyone could come up to me and give me a suggestion. Because if they can make it better,

then I'm gonna use anything they can offer me."

Barbra felt wearing all four hats to be beneficial because one person made most of the decisions. And there no longer was the urge to please the "Daddy" director—she only needed to please herself. As the producer, she was to find taking charge of the purse strings, as well as the artistic integrity of the film, to be quite uplifting. "Art is disciplined. Art has boundaries. Art has limits, you know? You have to create this scene but you have X amount of time. That's life. Life is a compromise. Life is imperfection. So my so-called perfectionism is quite realistic....And one wouldn't want everything perfect because it is too sterile, too inhuman. It's the striving for perfection that interests me."

Understandably, the transition between roles was sometimes puzzling for the other actors, but they found it no less intriguing. "I found myself dealing with [Barbra] in different ways," Mandy Patinkin explained. "If I needed something from the producer, I would talk to her in a different way than I would with the director about a scene. Sometimes I'd be talking to the director, but I'd really be talking to the actress. But I didn't want to talk to the actress, I wanted to talk to the director, and I certainly didn't want the *producer* to hear. Then I'd want the writer in on the discussion, and wait—the writer is here. It was wild.

"When the energy was high, she really flew. We

shot one whole section in no time. If another actor had something going, she would sacrifice her own part to get what he had to offer. Then she'd do her own scenes later."

Streisand's dedication, concentration and stamina endeared her to the crew. But some aspects of it also worried them. With her typical day beginning at 6:00 a.m. and ending at 2:00 a.m. the next morning, many expressed concern that she would run out of energy. "Yet she never flagged and [she] looks wonderful in the film," Patinkin added. "Some mysterious power sustained her."

"I don't know how I survived it but I'm proud I survived it. I didn't think I would at certain points," she admitted to Iain Johnstone. "It was so overwhelming, you know, I was sick every morning on the way to work. Just sick. Then I kept remembering a friend of mine, Irvin Kershner, said, 'One day at a time.' And Rusty would remind me, 'Remember what Kersh said, one day at a time…'" The *Yentl* set attracted many outside visitors, including Steven Spielberg (then shooting *Indiana Jones* on the lot), George Lucas, Warren Beatty and screenwriter Alvin Sargent.

In order to dispel the usual trouble-on-the-set rumors, the crew sent a letter to the London *Times* and several other publications describing how easy they found Barbra to work with. "She has captivated us all with her dedicated professionalism," they wrote. The letter took her by surprise and touched her deeply. "[It] is one of my most treasured possessions," she said.

Streisand and Irving seemed to have had a particularly trusting, responsive director/star relationship. Recognizing that Amy was one of the few actresses to be featured in a prominent role opposite her, the director took special care to make the leading lady look as good as possible. "She'd fix my hair ribbons, brush an eyelash off my cheek, paint my lips to match the color of the fruit on the table. I was like her little doll that she could dress up. For the scenes where I had to laugh, she'd stand behind the camera pulling the strings of an imaginary Hadass doll, making it burp and cry until I'd completely crack up." She would get an equal charge out of filming one of the movie's most famous scenes, Hadass's seduction of Anshel: "In rehearsal," Irving stated, "we never actually kissed. When it came time to shoot the scene, she said, 'Well, we'll do some takes with the kiss and some without it.'" After the first take with the kiss, it was obvious there was no need to shoot an alternate. "I had asked [Amy] to be very maidenly before that scene, and she did it

With Mandy Patinkin as Avigdor.

beautifully," Barbra agreed. "But then in the bedroom, when she comes on erotically, I asked her to let all her sexiness out, and wow! did she let it out."

In July, *Yentl* moved behind the Iron Curtain to the tiny village of Roztyly, about two and a half hours outside Prague. Location filming had been delayed several weeks due to unseasonably heavy rains. In spite of the unexpected weather conditions, however, Roy Walker had magically created the entire village of Yanev out of an area that had formerly contained a few wooden houses on a pig farm. The British crew was joined during those weeks by a Czech unit under the supervision of Karel Skop of the Barrandon Film Studios. Most of the Czech crew had never worked on a western film before, and they worked hard to keep pace with the more sophisticated techniques used by the English crew.

Nehemiah Persoff found filming in Czechoslovakia to be very interesting. "It started being interesting, actually, when we were received at the airport by the Czech movie people and some government officials. We were shown into a small room that had a table with food and beverages on it and we sat there (waiting for customs to clear us). And it was fascinating to see Barbra in that light. At first she made a very strong attempt at small talk, and there were questions to be asked: How's this going? How's that going? Did you do this?...As soon as all the questions were answered, I suddenly saw her just sitting there I imagine hoping it would soon be over because it all had become very heavy. There was nothing else to say. It was an interesting sidelight to see her discomfort at just wasting time at a time when she was most anxious to get on with the work."

She was a new director in a strange new environment, and yet, on the outside, Barbra hardly seemed to be fazed by it. When Jon visited the distant location, he was immediatley struck by the smell of sewage and urine pervading the area. "Barbra never noticed," he commented. "There were flies in that village as big as beetles but they never bothered her. She just swatted them." Lemorande: "The chameleon-like nature of an actress provided Barbra with the adaptability she needed. She was an American woman directing her first film in a European and Eastern European film culture, yet she was able to react as the situation required. My respect for Barbra grew enormously." A favorite hang-out of the local residents acting as extras in the opening scenes was the buffet table which Barbra made sure was stocked with fresh vegetables and other provisions she thought might not be available in Czechoslovakia.

From Roztyly, the company moved on to the old Jewish quarter of Zatec, which was used for the exterior of Bashev, the town where Avigdor and Anshel study. Next, they moved back to Prague. Among the locations chosen there by Streisand and Walker was the famous Charles Bridge, the oldest standing bridge in that capital city. Normally it was restricted to foot traffic, but Barwood got permission to close it for a couple of days and bring on a few carts and horses. While shooting in Prague, Barbra also met up with Milos Forman, who was then scouting locations for his next film, *Amadeus*. They exchanged notes about different members of the crew.

William Wyler had died a year earlier, but Barbra felt him to be a continuing source of inspiration, thanks to a letter she received from Wyler's widow. "Talli sent me a beautiful card that I kept with me during the making of the film," Barbra told Gene Shalit of *The Today Show*. " 'You never got a chance to talk to Willie (about *Yentl*),' she said, 'but I know there were things he would have liked to have told you. So when you're on the set and there's a moment [when] you don't know what to do—just be very quiet and maybe you'll hear Willie whispering in your ear.'"

For Barbra, the experience of shooting in Czechoslovakia was physically gruelling, but exhilarating—directing, acting, singing, watching the budget, maintaining a happy set, learning lines, having wardrobe fittings at 11:00 p.m. when everyone else had finished for the day. Lacking the extra time to spend on her vanity reaped wonders in terms of her understated characterization of the young boy, Anshel. "*Yentl* was a stretch for her because there was no way she could fall back on past mannerisms," Marty Erlichman says. "Barbra the director was smart enough to know that Barbra the actress couldn't do that."

By September 1982, the production team was ready to return to its Lee International Studios base. With all of the dialogue scenes and material involving other actors out of the way, all that remained for Barbra to do was Yentl's first soliloquy under her new guise, "Papa, Can You Hear Me?", shot on a soundstage, and the dynamic finale, "Piece of Sky." The latter was shot outside Liverpool. After returning to London, the filmmakers discovered the footage had been damaged, so they had to re-shoot it.

Production officially wrapped in late October. For the next nine months, Barbra continued commuting back and forth between London and the States in order to oversee other production details. She followed the film through every single facet of post-production. "How far is too far?" Marilyn Bergman asked. "Until they tell you this is it, this is the deadline, you don't have one more minute to work on that piece...Isn't it your obligation to make

it as good as you can make it?"

Barbra's most poignant battle to protect her vision did not involve the film's editing or scoring, however. It involved a completion bond agreement that had been foisted upon her a day before commencement of principal photography. Although it was not part of her contract with UA, the studio nonetheless insisted that she take out a policy protecting them against any cost overages. Barbra had no choice but to acquiesce, and the $700,000 premium was deducted from *Yentl*'s budget. Scarcely 11 percent over budget (an acceptable figure for movies shot on location) when she brought the film in, the Completion Bond Company demanded Barbra finish dubbing the film in six weeks—even though it wasn't due to be released for a year. "It was all about money," she clarified. "I did anything to get it done so that they couldn't take it away from me."

Unfortunately, the ultimatum started rumors in Hollywood that Streisand had lost control of her dream project. "I want to make it clear that Ms. Streisand is, has been, and will always be the credited producer of the film, retaining full artistic control," MGM/UA vice chairman Frank Yablans stated. "I've never dealt with a person more responsible in terms of cost than Barbra was on this film. Every dime ultimately ended up on the screen."

Next phase: promotion. Although *Yentl* was longer in the works, two films about male/female role-playing managed to precede it to the screen in 1982: *Tootsie* and *Victor/Victoria*. Barbra wanted to sell her film simply as "a film with music." All jokes about *Tootsie on the Roof* aside, the studio once considered changing the title. One executive wanted to call it *A Secret Dream*. Early in its inception, Barbra thought about re-naming her characters Leah and Leon in order to allow a simpler title, *Leah*. "But surveys showed people wanted to see me in a film and it didn't matter what the title was," she told the Associated Press's Bob Thomas, "so I stayed with *Yentl*." United Artists took advantage of its extra lead time and did additional testing on the film. The results showed young women to be the biggest audience for the film. "They accept the way I look," Barbra observed. "Younger boys and older men have some trouble believing (in the fantasy)."

As the days drew anxiously near *Yentl*'s November 16, 1983, world premiere at the Cinerama Dome in Hollywood, Barbra also became extremely anxious. For one thing, she worried about Isaac Bashevis Singer's reaction. The Nobel Prize-winning author had never accepted that she might be capable of handling multiple production responsibilities on *Yentl*. Believing it to be an ill-fated project, he resisted most of her efforts to embrace him as a contributor. "It's not really my child," he said. "First, I'll see the killing, then I'll perform the autopsy."

"Don't worry that even if you fall flat on your face with *Yentl*—and I have every faith that you won't—don't ever think that people will start to reconsider the brilliance of *Funny Girl*, *What's Up, Doc?* or *The Way We Were*," co-producer Rusty Lemorande tried to impress upon her. "Nothing will ever tarnish those films; your stock is safe."

Steven Spielberg's response following a screening of the film was even more encouraging. Dubbing her work one of the most dynamic directorial debuts since Orson Welles and *Citizen Kane*, the director

would tell the *Los Angeles Herald-Examiner* that he was struck by the generosity of her direction. "I think she tried to put everyone ahead of her in her list of priorities. It's selfless directing....I have a feeling that all this comes from her experience not as an actress being directed and watching other directors work, but from her autonomy as a musician and a vocalist. If you listen to her songs, they're impeccable on every level. That's Barbra directing herself."

Much would be made of the movie's dedication "To my father—and to all our fathers." Jon Peters' perspective is that *Yentl* represented Barbra's chance "to say kaddish for her own father. She created him on film so she could love him and say goodbye to him. She buried her father in the movie." Respecting everything that Barbra's commitment to the picture had come to represent, Jon ended up doing "everything within my power to help her get that movie out. I was one of her biggest opponents, but once she committed to do it, I got behind her 100 percent....And she did it. I cried when I saw the movie. I sobbed, actually. I wish I had produced it."

Two days after the highly-successful Dome premiere (where the overflow was such that a second screening had to be held concurrently at the Director's Guild), Barbra was in Westwood overseeing the final details for the actual release. Even with the near-rapturous trade reaction, she was still nervous. "I ran out and bought all the chocolate-covered marzipan and walnut cookies I could carry and sat there and stuffed myself. That's how scared I was." The nerves would be for naught. The "small, esoteric Jewish film" did find an audience.

Reviews:

"To put it succinctly and at once, Barbra Streisand's *Yentl* is a triumph—a personal one for Streisand as producer, director, co-author and star, but also a triumphant piece of filmmaking....At long last, with backing from United Artists, she has realized her dream. Magnificently. One finds, not surprisingly, traces of other directors she has worked with; but the concept, particularly the integration of the Alan and Marilyn Bergman lyrics into the progression of the story line, is uniquely her own. And she makes it work seamlessly, effortlessly. Streisand is the only character who sings in the movie; and the songs become a projection of her inner feelings....The device itself, like the soliloquies in Shakespeare's plays, is so perfectly attuned to the psychological needs of the character that it becomes not only acceptable but fascinating in its own right....Streisand's performance alone could carry the picture, a star vehicle if there ever was one. Happily, she is too great an artist to let it go at that.

As director, she has elicited outstanding performances from her entire cast....Every role, right down to the momentary glimpse of the fish seller in the shtetl marketplace, has been not only astutely cast but completely realized."

—*Hollywood Reporter*

"This is by no means a playing-it-safe movie. It's a movie about restrictive social conventions and about internal conflicts—about emotions and how they snarl you up. There are no chases, no fistfights or fights of any other kind. The picture is closer to the sensibility of Ernst Lubitsch musical comedies than it is to films such as *The Turning Point* or *Rich and Famous*. And even when the character's sex roles are blurred—when they're lost in a multitude of roles—Streisand as director keeps them all clear. Her vision is sustained....*Yentl* is never static or stagy; the images move lyrically. The same intuitions that have guided Streisand in producing her records and her own TV specials have guided her here."

—*The New Yorker*

FINAL NOTE: "Usually when a new director starts directing," Sydney Pollack said, "you can see the wheels turning, so to speak. You see the ideas at work, and usually the ideas are not quite within the grasp of execution of the director. Oftentimes you are giving something credit for being well-executed but not particularly polished in its execution. *Yentl* was seamless. It would be polished for a 20th film, but particularly so for a first film. I was terribly impressed with it."

On November 18, 1983, *Yentl* opened in thirteen showcase theaters across the nation; the exclusive engagements produced excellent word-of-mouth. Two weeks before Christmas, the motion picture received its general release. It was to become the number 3 performer at the box-office that season (below *Sudden Impact* and *Terms of Endearment*). With film rentals of $19,630,000, it ranks number 6 on Barbra's all-time list.

Since both Barbra and her film had been highly visible in the print and broadcast media, and there were uniformly excellent reviews for the film, it was assumed *Yentl* would be a prime contender for awards recognition. At year's end, the National Board of Review and *Time* magazine placed *Yentl* on their Top 10 lists. In January, the movie tallied six Golden Globe nominations (Best Picture, Director, Actor, Actress, Song and Score). Proof of the industry's suppressed resentment regarding Barbra's work on *Yentl* surfaced on January 31 when the Directors' Guild nominations were announced—with no citation for Streisand in sight. That evening Barbra won two Golden Globes for her movie: Best Picture (Musical or Comedy) and Best Director.

"I feel very grateful to have had the opportunity to make this film, and that to me is its own reward," Barbra said in her speech as she accepted the award for Best Musical. Up against James Brooks and Ingmar Bergman in the Best Director category, even she did not expect to be making a second journey to the stage. An extremely vocal reception greeted her when the assemblage discovered she was indeed the first female filmmaker to take home the Best Director Golden Globe. "Gosh. This is really, really thrilling! Because I *really* didn't expect this, believe me.... Gosh." She started to speak and then stopped to hug the award. "Directing for me was a total experience. It calls upon everything you've ever seen or felt or known or heard. It was really the highlight of my life. My professional life. This award is very very meaningful to me and I'm very proud because it also represents, I hope, new opportunities for so many talented women to try to make their dreams realities, as I did."

"It's funny," Barbra told Lawrence Grobel in 1977, "I never thought about the women's movement while I was moving as a woman. I didn't even realize that I was fighting this battle all the time. I just took it personally; I didn't even separate it from the fact that I was a woman having a hard time in a male society." Two weeks later, the Academy nominations were released and, this time, even the major technical nods were to be sorely missing. No acknowledgment for cinematography, costume design, sound, editing. No nomination that could potentially add to *Yentl*'s box-office strength. Paradoxically, two of the most "criticized" elements of the film—the music and Amy Irving's sweetly modulated performance—were to account for four out of five nominations (the fifth was for art direction).

Streisand's first reaction to the shut-out was that people simply didn't like the film; they didn't believe. Then she began hearing from her peers, people who previously had shrugged off the idea of any kind of "conspiracy." "One needn't be a rabid fan of *Yentl* or a Streisand fanatic to accuse the Academy of a serious sin of omission in banning *Yentl* from all important awards categories," Gregg Kilday wrote in the *Herald-Examiner*. "No best picture nomination. No best director. Not even a best actress consideration was alloted to Streisand. Instead, as if it were telling Streisand to stay in her place, the Academy awarded a token nomination for best supporting actress to Amy Irving, who, tellingly, played a conventional Jewish woman in the movie."

"When the achievement is measured against the challenge and the obstacles, I think Barbra Streisand was severly shortchanged by the [Academy] voters," Charles Champlin wrote in the *Los Angeles Times*. "Not nominating her was unconscionable," producer Martin Bregman protested to a *People* magazine reporter.

Barbra called Amy Irving to congratulate her, but Irving could tell she was hurting. "Personally, I just hope she doesn't let this take away from the gratitude she should have for making a film of such excellence," Irving stated. "I believe in the film, and I am so proud to be in it." The actress would tell another journalist that she'd never seen "a cooler director on the set. And you wouldn't believe how much her crew loved her and supported her. She was even-tempered and helpful and she gave more direction than I've ever gotten in any film. I thought she deserved to be nominated for an Academy Award in some areas. I thought the excellence of her work was there."

The public outrage over the obvious snub inspired a group called Principles, Equality and Professionalism in Film to organize a demonstration outside the Dorothy Chandler Pavilion, the site of the Academy Awards presentation, to protest the lack of recognition for *Yentl*. "Oscar at 56—Is he still a closet chauvinist?" read one placard. Another counted "The score from 1927—present, Best Director nominees: Men 273, Women 1."

"I would rather not theorize negatively about the reasons [for the omission]," Barbra told "Good Morning America's" David Hartman. "I leave that to journalists, to you, to anyone who wants to take a guess because...my reward has come from the people's support and from my peers." Indeed, co-producer Lemorande feels that the most intriguing aspect of *Yentl*, "apart from how one observes the film, is how the task affected the taskmaster. Without any one of us realizing it at the time. Now she can look back and laugh at the fact that the Academy didn't nominate it and not really judge it."

With the movie due to open in Europe in the Spring of 1984, Barbra decided to do some in-person promotion abroad. She would follow the film from the Royal Premiere in London to an international press conference in Hamburg to Paris (where she received the country's highest artistic honor and met with director Roman Polanski) to Rome (where she lunched with Lina Wertmuller, Michelangelo Antonioni and Federico Fellini) and, finally, Jerusalem. In Israel she would dedicate a building at the Hebrew University in her father's name.

Barbra and MGM/UA were thrilled with the international reception. *Yentl* was a hit in Taiwan; it broke records in Finland and Norway. Accepting an award from Women in Film, the writer/director noted with pride that her film was doing better box-office in Texas than in Brooklyn. Big business was also recorded in a diverse array of cultures from Denmark to Panama, from Greece to Chile, Portugal, Austria, the Netherlands, Australia and Argentina.

On June 6, the National Organization for Women held a dinner in Beverly Hills celebrating Barbra as a "Woman of Courage." Mistress of ceremonies Jane Fonda entertained the audience with early recollections of Barbra: "And I'm here to tell you that I never would have dreamt back then that we would be here tonight. When I think back to those days, and who we thought we were...and how we related to each other...When I think back to those times, this evening seems so special to me that I could just explode!...Yentl speaks to us about faith and passion, about being a woman, about having the courage to not accept less than what we deserve as human beings....It is a treasured example of how a personal quest and the creative process [can] become fused."

The second miracle is how, in time, even some of the cynics would come around. "Yentl sits up there on the screen screaming its head off much of the time, singing one long, dreadful song," Vincent Canby complained in The New York Times in 1983. Three years later, while reviewing two failed feminist comedies, he would venture a more enlightened opinion: "Though the limited vision of Just Between Friends and Wildcats is depressing, it has one unexpected side effect. It makes one marvel, after the fact, at Barbra Streisand's great leap into the unknown—when she set out not only to produce and star in Yentl, but also to write and direct it. We could use a little more of that kind of audacity today."

THE FUTURE

The experience of making Yentl left Barbra "wiped out for the next two years." At the same time, it instigated a new wave of activity in terms of the projects she hoped to proceed with—and which studios were now more than willing to take on with her as producer, director and/or star. "Steven Spielberg asked me if I'd like to direct a film he wants to produce," she told one journalist. "Not to be in it, just direct. Hearing the word put me into a traumatic state."

At United Artists, there was talk of an adaptation of Colette's autobiographical novel La Vagabonde, screenplay by Arthur Laurents and musical score by Stephen Sondheim. The studio also considered a film biography of Sarah Bernhardt, an actress for whom Barbra has always expressed great admiration. "I am the most misaligned woman in Europe,"

the controversial French star once told the press. Either role represented a challenging acting assignment. "I always thought Streisand was capable of far more than playing the pussycat or the little Brooklyn Jewish girl," director John Huston stated recently. "She could have played Cleopatra better than Liz Taylor. With her enormous power and the subtlety of her singing, she is one of the great actresses, and she hasn't been well used."

In August of 1985 it was leaked to industry trades that Barbra was talking to her friend Mark Rydell about his film, Nuts. The story was originally produced as a play and concerns an accused murderess who must fight for her right to a fair trial. Most of the action takes place at a sanity hearing in which her parents, seeking to avoid the scandal of a public trial, hope to have their daughter declared insane. Barbra's interest in the project gave it new life at Warner Bros. In March of 1986, after countless discussions about "opening up" the play (and the budget) as opposed to shooting it entirely at The Burbank Studios, producer/director/writer Rydell exited. "It is with absolutely no animosity to any of the parties concerned that I take leave of this project," he told the Hollywood Reporter. "If I have any regrets, it is that I will not be able to work with Barbra Streisand, an immense talent with whom I have enjoyed an excellent working relationship."

Any discussion as to whether or not she would take over the reins as director, Barbra hastened to add, "is totally premature." Two weeks later, following a heart-to-heart conversation with Rydell, Martin Ritt indicated an interest in directing the film. (Ritt's credits include Hud, Sounder and Norma Rae.) After several respected names, including Darryl Ponicsan and Alvin Sargent, had been called in to look at the screenplay (but to no avail), Barbra began to fashion a draft of her own. With her involvement in the writing phase, the difficult-to-translate story took a 180-degree turn, Dustin Hoffman reported, and became something exciting and cinematic. (Hoffman was briefly mentioned as a co-star possibility when Richard Dreyfuss left to honor another film commitment; Dreyfuss is now back with the project.) Filming will commence this November.

Barbra will also produce The Normal Heart, another explosive theatrical property. The story revolves around a gay journalist who tries to break "the conspiracy of silence" surrounding the AIDS epidemic. The only female role is an effective supporting bit concerning a paraplegic doctor who fights for "every person's right to love." At this time, it is not known if Barbra will direct or star in the picture.

Warner Bros., the new home for Barwood Films, has also signed Linda Yellen to write a screenplay about photojournalist Margaret Bourke-White. The Bergmans are working on a translation of the French comedy, *And Now My Love*. The production would also include a new (background) musical score.

One of the disappointments of the '70s has to be Hollywood's failure to get behind a Streisand-Ingmar Bergman teaming on his adaptation of *The Merry Widow*. "It was a marvelous screenplay," Arthur Laurents recalled. Another mystery is the disappearance of *Third Time Lucky*, the story of a troubled actress and the young admirer who guides her back into the real world—only to slip over the brink himself. "Mark my word, the film will be made one day and it will be an incredible piece of filmmaking," assures Rusty Lemorande. "It will have the kind of guts that a film like *Who's Afraid of Virginia Woolf?* had, the kind of honesty that a film like *Terms of Endearment* had and a star at a time when there will be even fewer stars than there are today."

In *Yentl*, Nehemiah Persoff observes, "Barbra came up with a piece of work that I hope she can match. I think she will. I think she's brilliant; I'm sure she's got something cooking. She has tremendous drive and tenacity and sense of purpose."

Phil Ramone sees Barbra still agonizing over details. "At 90, she will still be standing there and saying, 'Why is this like this, why do you want to do this and what are you doing with that?' The curiosity will never stop. She's never changed," he says. "She's always been the same Barbra to me."

"Yesterday's achievements are just photos on a wall. They have a very lifeless quality. Today is the 'now' moment," Lemorande continues, "today is the test. It was important the first day she stepped on the stage at the Bon Soir for Barbra to prove she was something special. And it will be important the first day she steps on the set of *Nuts*, I promise you. Those same feelings will be going through her: 'I am going to prove that I am a gifted actress.'"

"There is no one truth. Everyone has their own, and the art of living is to know your own reality and respect that of others. What a great thing to learn! My own truth."